CW00516603

Adam Smith

Classic Thinkers series

Richard T. W. Arthur, *Leibniz*
Terrell Carver, *Marx*
Daniel E. Flage, *Berkeley*
J. M. Fritzman, *Hegel*
Bernard Gert, *Hobbes*
Thomas Kemple, *Simmel*
Dale E. Miller, *J. S. Mill*
Joanne Paul, *Thomas More*
A. J. Pyle, *Locke*
James T. Schleifer, *Tocqueville*
Craig Smith, *Adam Smith*
Céline Spector, *Rousseau*
Andrew Ward, *Kant*

Adam Smith

Craig Smith

polity

Copyright © Craig Smith 2020

The right of Craig Smith to be identified as Author of this Work has been asserted in accordance with the UK Copyright, Designs and Patents Act 1988.

First published in 2020 by Polity Press

Polity Press
65 Bridge Street
Cambridge CB2 1UR, UK

Polity Press
101 Station Landing
Suite 300
Medford, MA 02155, USA

All rights reserved. Except for the quotation of short passages for the purpose of criticism and review, no part of this publication may be reproduced, stored in a retrieval system or transmitted, in any form or by any means, electronic, mechanical, photocopying, recording or otherwise, without the prior permission of the publisher.

ISBN-13: 978-1-5095-1822-7
ISBN-13: 978-1-5095-1823-4 (pb)

A catalogue record for this book is available from the British Library.

Library of Congress Cataloging-in-Publication Data
Names: Smith, Craig, 1977- author.
Title: Adam Smith / Craig Smith.
Description: Cambridge, UK ; Medford, MA : Polity, 2020. | Series: Classic thinkers series | Includes bibliographical references and index. | Summary: "Craig Smith's new crystal-clear introduction reveals a far more complex and nuanced figure whose rich legacy remains highly relevant today"-- Provided by publisher.
Identifiers: LCCN 2019033302 (print) | LCCN 2019033303 (ebook) | ISBN 9781509518227 | ISBN 9781509518234 (pb) | ISBN 9781509518265 (epub)
Subjects: LCSH: Smith, Adam, 1723-1790. | Economists--Great Britain--Biography.
Classification: LCC HB103.S6 E36 2020 (print) | LCC HB103.S6 (ebook) | DDC 330.15/3092 [B]--dc23
LC record available at https://lccn.loc.gov/2019033302
LC ebook record available at https://lccn.loc.gov/2019033303

Typeset in 10.5 on 12pt Palatino
by Fakenham Prepress Solutions, Fakenham, Norfolk NR21 8NL
Printed and bound in Great Britain by CPI Group (UK) Ltd, Croydon

The publisher has used its best endeavours to ensure that the URLs for external websites referred to in this book are correct and active at the time of going to press. However, the publisher has no responsibility for the websites and can make no guarantee that a site will remain live or that the content is or will remain appropriate.

Every effort has been made to trace all copyright holders, but if any have been overlooked the publisher will be pleased to include any necessary credits in any subsequent reprint or edition.

For further information on Polity, visit our website: politybooks.com

Contents

Acknowledgements   vi
Abbreviations for Smith's Works   vii

1   Smith and the Scottish Enlightenment   1

2   Science and System   20

3   Morality and Sympathy   40

4   Justice and Virtue   67

5   Jurisprudence   88

6   The Nature of Wealth   108

7   Government and the Market   128

8   Legacy and Influence   155

Notes   179
Bibliography   192
Index   200

Acknowledgements

When I was first approached to contribute a volume on Adam
Smith to the Polity Classic Thinkers series, I decided that I would
attempt to produce a work that both introduced readers to the
whole of Smith's body of thought and, at the same time, made
the case for reading that body of thought as a consistent and
coherent intellectual project. In writing the book, I have received
much valued support and guidance from the editorial team at
Polity, particularly George Owers and Julia Davies, and from the
comments of three anonymous readers. Christopher J. Berry, Maria
Pia Paganelli, and Kate Spence kindly agreed to read the draft
manuscript and offered helpful constructive criticism. The book is
a result of fifteen years teaching Adam Smith to undergraduate and
postgraduate students. My position as Adam Smith Senior Lecturer
at the University of Glasgow has allowed me to teach Smith to an
interdisciplinary group of students drawn from Politics, Sociology,
History, and Philosophy. Many of the formulations and examples
included here first sprang from that classroom experience. As a
result, this book is dedicated to the students of my courses on the
Scottish Enlightenment and the Wealth of Nations at the University
of Glasgow.

Abbreviations for Smith's Works

All references to Smith's works will be to the standard scholarly edition, the Glasgow Edition published by Oxford University Press, and will refer to the volume by title and page. Other notes will direct the reader to helpful secondary material listed in the bibliography that further explores the issues at hand.

Ancient Physics: 'The Principles which Lead and Direct Philosophical Enquiries; Illustrated by the History of the Ancient Physics', in *Essays on Philosophical Subjects*, ed. W. P. D. Wightman. Oxford: Oxford University Press, 1980 [1795], pp. 106–17.

Astronomy: 'The Principles which Lead and Direct Philosophical Enquiries; Illustrated by the History of Astronomy', in *Essays on Philosophical Subjects*, ed. W. P. D. Wightman. Oxford: Oxford University Press, 1980 [1795], pp. 31–105.

Correspondence: *Correspondence of Adam Smith*, eds Ernest Campbell Mossner & Ian Simpson Ross, rev. edn, Oxford: Oxford University Press, 1987.

Imitative Arts: 'Of the Nature of that Imitation which Takes Place in What Are Called the Imitative Arts', in *Essays on Philosophical Subjects*, ed. W. P. D. Wightman, Oxford: Oxford University Press, 1980 [1795], pp. 176–213.

Jurisprudence*: Lectures on Jurisprudence*, eds R. L. Meek, D. D. Raphael, & P. G. Stein. Oxford: Oxford University Press, 1980.

Moral Sentiments*: The Theory of Moral Sentiments*, eds D. D. Raphael & A. L. Macfie. Oxford: Oxford University Press, 1976 [1759].

Rhetoric*: Lectures on Rhetoric and Belles Lettres*, ed. J. C. Bryce. Oxford: Oxford University Press, 1983.

Wealth of Nations*: An Inquiry into the Nature and Causes of the Wealth of Nations*, 2 vols, eds R. H. Campbell & A. S. Skinner. Oxford: Oxford University Press, 1976 [1776].

1

Smith and the Scottish Enlightenment

Adam Smith (1723–90) is unusual among philosophers from over two hundred years ago. He is unusual because his work is still widely read and discussed today. But more significant than this, his name is still widely known by the general public. Smith has become one of the few world historical figures who have entered into the common intellectual landscape of our culture. Unfortunately the 'Adam Smith' that exists in the popular imagination is somewhat different from the Adam Smith who lived and wrote in eighteenth-century Scotland.

Smith and his thought have become the focus of increasing interest among scholars since the publication of a critical edition of his writings in the late 1970s. Part of the aim of this scholarship has been to dispel the mythology and correct the caricature that has arisen around Smith. Adam Smith the first economist, the father of capitalism, the defender of laissez-faire economics, the advocate of selfishness, and the prophet of the invisible hand of the market has been seized upon by both advocates of free market economics and critics of capitalism. Smith has been set up as both the hero of the libertarian right and the villain of neo-liberalism. This caricature is something that Smith scholars have sought to correct by careful study of what he actually wrote. While such views are commonplace among the general public, those who read Smith's two great books, *The Theory of Moral Sentiments* and the *Wealth of Nations*, quickly see that there is much more to the man and his thought. That said, many of those who do this are then struck by the apparent tension between the discussion of sympathy in the former and the analysis of self-interest in the latter. This seeming contrast between a description of humans as benevolent in one book and selfish in the other led some of Smith's nineteenth-century German readers to regard his thought as self-contradictory. As we will see, the so-called 'Adam Smith Problem' has been dismissed by Smith scholars, but its residue lingers on in the popular imagination.

The present volume is intended to be a contribution to these tasks of dispelling a caricature and dismissing an accusation of inconsistency. Its aim is to present a reading of the whole of Smith's work, to indicate the systematic and interconnected nature of his writings on topics as diverse as economics, moral philosophy, science, and literature. In so doing, it will present a reading of Smith that is unified by his consistent application of a particular methodology, a way of doing philosophy or science, which acts as a powerful tool when applied across a range of what are now distinct academic disciplines. In addition to providing an argument that focuses on Smith's texts, we will trace his intellectual context and explain why he was interested in the particular ideas and subjects that he discussed.

Understanding where Smith came from, how he was educated, whom he interacted with, and what he hoped to achieve, will illuminate his thought. Showing that Smith was a man of his time helps to dispel the contemporary caricature, but it will also show the reader that he remains an enduringly relevant thinker, one who should not be confined to history. The basis of this argument will be two-fold: it will stress the relevance of Smith's understanding of the nature of what we now call the social sciences, and drawing on that it will emphasize the centrality of his attempts to explain the unintended consequences of human action. Taken together, these two aspects of his thinking open up a Smithian way of understanding the world that lies at the heart of this book.

Life

Adam Smith was born in the small Scottish port town of Kirkcaldy in the county of Fife in 1723. His family, whose background lay in a mixture of minor gentry and farming, was connected by patronage to many of the powerful families of eighteenth-century Scotland. His father, also Adam Smith, died before he was born. Smith senior was a comptroller of customs at Kirkcaldy and a writer to the signet (solicitor) who was attached to the Whig and Presbyterian cause that formed the backbone of the new Scottish establishment that arose after the Union of Parliaments between Scotland and England in 1707 and the Hanoverian succession to the throne after the death of Queen Anne. Smith's father served a number of influential politicians, including the Earl of Loudon, who were supporters of the Union. Smith senior played an active role in opposing the first Jacobite rising, an attempt to restore the Stuart family to the British throne in 1715, and his reward for this was a steady advancement through the patronage network of government positions that dominated life in Scotland.

Smith's mother, Margaret Smith, née Douglas, was related to several of the most prominent families in Fife, so the young Adam was born into a very particular set of social and political connections. The death of his father left him in his mother's care, and this seems to have built a particularly strong bond between them that lasted until Margaret's death a mere six years before his own.

Kirkcaldy had developed as a port which traded with the Baltic States and the Low Countries. In addition to fishing, it depended on coal and salt production. Both of these had begun to decline by the time Smith was born, and there was a significant level of smuggling along the Fife coast – an activity that Smith's father was expected to help to police. Smith was born into a respectable, but by no means wealthy, family and received a first-rate education at the Burgh school in Kirkcaldy. Here the forward-thinking school master, David Miller, taught the young Smith the usual mixture of Latin, arithmetic, geometry, and rhetoric that passed for the standard Scottish curriculum, but he did so in a manner that stressed the practical value of the often abstract knowledge. One of Miller's key innovations was his stress on polite learning and public speaking. Pupils like Smith were required to read a passage, often from *The Spectator* (a popular collection of 'polite' essays by Joseph Addison and Richard Steele), and then present its content in their own words. The exercise was designed to aid both comprehension and rhetorical skill. Smith was a gifted student and he seems to have thrived in an environment that sought to produce confident and articulate young men able to occupy the leading places in society.

With the support of his father's political and family connections, Smith was accepted into the University of Glasgow in 1737 at the age of 14. Glasgow was just beginning its spectacular growth into one of the industrial powerhouses of Britain. At this time it was small, relatively quiet in political terms, and had a reputation of being a safe, Protestant, and Hanoverian city. But more than that, it was beginning to develop a reputation as one of the most innovative centres of learning in Europe. Glasgow had recently reformed its teaching practices to abandon the regenting system, where students were taught all subjects by one generalist tutor, in favour of a system of specialist professors. Among these were Francis Hutcheson (1694–1746), Smith's beloved teacher of moral philosophy, who was central in encouraging the practice of teaching in English rather than Latin, and in introducing modern philosophical texts to the classroom. Another was Robert Simson (1687–1768), whose classes on mathematics and geometry quickly became a favourite of Smith's.[1]

Smith's early education had provided him with a level of skill in Latin that allowed him to bypass the remedial first year and move directly into the higher-level classes in Latin, Greek, Natural Philosophy, Logic, and Moral Philosophy. He spent the next three years proving himself to be a brilliant student and was able to secure a Snell Exhibition to fund further study at Balliol College, Oxford. We know very little about how Smith spent his six years at Oxford, but we do know that he found the unreformed nature of the colleges and the lack of attention to teaching to be a sore disappointment after the rigour of his early training at Glasgow. Most accounts suggest that he spent his time in private reading and research and continued to develop a broad range of interests across the arts and sciences. It was also likely that this period saw Smith first come across the work of the man who would later be his closest intellectual friend, David Hume (1711–76). Indeed, Smith's poor health at this time, which he attributed to excessive study, paralleled the experience of his friend Hume in the composition of his *Treatise of Human Nature* (1739/40): a book whose arguments clearly shaped much of Smith's thinking from this time onwards.

Smith was safely, if (given anti-Scottish prejudice) uneasily, ensconced at Oxford during the political upheavals of 1745–6, which saw the final attempt to restore the Stuart family, led by Charles Edward Stuart (Bonnie Prince Charlie) at the head of a force largely drawn from the clans of Highland Scotland. The defeat of this uprising at Culloden in 1746 marked the end of the Stuart cause as a serious threat to the political stability of the new Great Britain, but it also reinforced the fragility of the political institutions with which Smith and his family identified themselves. If the city of Edinburgh itself could fall to a poorly armed clan uprising, then nothing was certain. Smith returned to Scotland, and his mother's home in Kirkcaldy, in 1746. As the political situation stabilized, he began to cast about for a suitable career. The Snell Exhibition had originally been intended for those training to become priests in the Episcopalian Church, but this condition had lapsed by Smith's time and it seems that he never seriously entertained an ecclesiastical career.

In 1748, Smith began his professional career as an academic. Henry Home, Lord Kames (1696–1782), the acerbic doyen of Edinburgh society, arranged for him to give a series of freelance lectures in Edinburgh. The lectures proved to be highly successful and he repeated them in the following two years. Kames hoped that Smith's erudition and eloquence, honed during his time at Glasgow and Oxford, would find a ready audience among the emergent public intellectuals of polite Edinburgh society. Smith took as his topics rhetoric and jurisprudence and delivered his lectures in competition to those of the University of Edinburgh. That said, the material that he covered and the way in which he covered it meant that it was unlike anything then taught at the University. His theories of rhetoric and law, which we will cover later in this volume, have their genesis at this time.

The popularity of the lectures led to Smith being appointed to the Chair of Logic at the University of Glasgow in 1751. His inaugural address, *De Origine Idearum* (On the Origin of Ideas), does not survive, but the title is intriguing as it points us towards the theory of ideas, which would become central to his conceptions of how the human mind operates. On arriving at Glasgow, Smith revised the curriculum to make it more to his own taste. The old medieval logic syllabus was discarded in favour of one that centred on rhetoric, or, to be more accurate, argument and speech in modern English. The focus on plain ordinary language is a key feature of Smith's thinking.

In 1752, soon after his employment at Glasgow, Smith was faced with something of a professional and personal dilemma. The death of the Professor of Moral Philosophy prompted him to move from the Chair of Logic to that newly vacant post, and the idea was mooted that David Hume should be considered for the Logic Chair. This proved too controversial an appointment for many, as Hume's supposedly radical anti-religious views did not sit well with the rest of the faculty. Smith was forced to admit that, though he would have loved to have Hume as a colleague, his appointment would have been too contentious and may have harmed the institution. Smith's earliest publications, including a letter to the short-lived *Edinburgh Review* of 1755–6, appear at this period.

Smith was a popular professor who took his educational role very seriously. Many of the personal reminiscences that his contemporaries have about him suggest that he approached the stereotype of the absent-minded professor: talking to himself, wandering out of doors in his nightgown, accidentally trying to make tea from rolled-up pieces of bread. While these images are endearing, they sit in more than a little tension with the reality of Smith as a gifted and professional teacher and a skilled university administrator whose roles included complicated tasks involving the finances of the University and the development of the library. In addition to his university duties, Smith was able to publish his first great book, *The Theory of Moral Sentiments*, in 1759.

As his reputation grew, Smith was able to attract students from as far afield as Russia, Geneva, and the American colonies. Among those who attended Smith's classes were the future biographer James Boswell (1740–95) and the gifted legal scholar John Millar (1735–1801), who would himself become a Glasgow Professor and later educate Smith's heir David Douglas (1769–1819). Smith's reputation attracted the attention of the politician and future Chancellor of the Exchequer Charles Townshend (1725–67). Townshend was the stepfather to the young Henry Scott, the 3rd Duke of Buccleuch (1746–1812), one of the wealthiest landowners in Scotland. Townshend persuaded Smith to resign his position at Glasgow after 13 years and become a travelling tutor to the young Duke. Though initially reluctant to leave his professorship at Glasgow, Smith was persuaded by the fact that the position would not only allow him to travel to the Continent, but would also come with a lifetime pension that would allow him to devote himself to study and writing.

Smith spent the years 1764–6 chiefly in France, basing himself in Toulouse and then Paris. He met many of the leading figures of the French Enlightenment, the so-called *'philosophes'*. Among these were Voltaire (1694–1778), Anne-Robert-Jacques Turgot (1727–81), François Quesnay (1694–1774), and several of the French economic thinkers known as the Physiocrats. Smith's time in France was cut short by the tragic death of the Duke's younger brother, and he returned to London with his pupil. Smith remained in London in 1766 and 1767 and used the time to produce a revised third edition of *The Theory of Moral Sentiments*. He would remain close to Buccleuch throughout his life and acted as an adviser on the Duke's financial matters and on his improvements to his vast estates.

Returning to Scotland in 1768, Smith retired to Kirkcaldy and began work on what was to become his most famous book, the *Wealth of Nations*. His friend Hume complained of his infrequent visits to Edinburgh during this period, but Smith assured him that he was making progress with his studies away from the distractions of the city. Smith travelled to London in 1773 and remained there until 1776, when the *Wealth of Nations* was published to great acclaim, and was soon followed by a second edition in 1778 and a third, significantly revised edition in 1784. The London of the 1770s was dominated by the dispute with the American colonies, and this context surely shaped Smith's thinking on international trade (as we will see below). But 1776 also brought a personal blow with the death of Hume. Smith penned a memorial to his friend that was published along with Hume's own autobiographical essay. He was later to observe that this memorial caused more personal attacks on him than the far more, as he saw it, controversial economic arguments of the *Wealth of Nations*. There is a certain irony in this as Smith had informed Hume that he was uncomfortable in acting as his literary executor as it would involve publishing the highly controversial, and now classic, *Dialogues concerning Natural Religion* (1779). The *Dialogues* is a sustained attack on many of the most popular philosophical arguments for belief in God, and Smith clearly feared this would attract the ire of the religious. In the end, Hume's essay was published, but to little abuse, while Smith's memorial produced sustained criticism.

In 1778, Smith's influential political contacts secured him a position as one of Commissioners of Customs for Scotland and he moved his mother and cousin, Janet Douglas, to Edinburgh and his new residence at Panmure House in the Canongate. By all accounts, Smith was as assiduous in his customs office duties as he had been in his professorial duties. One anecdote from the time tells how he read the list of smuggled goods, realized that he owned many of them himself, and promptly burned these to avoid any accusation of impropriety. He soon became a well-known figure walking up the High Street of Edinburgh from his home to the Customs House opposite St Giles' Cathedral. One of the very few images we have of Smith is a sketch by the artist John Kay (1742–1826) of him walking up the street holding a posy of flowers to his nose to block out the stench of eighteenth-century Edinburgh. Smith also became an integral part of the Edinburgh social scene and was a leading light in the Oyster Club, a group that met for intellectual debate in a tavern in the Grassmarket. In addition, he hosted Sunday evening dinners for close friends and visitors to the city.

88   *Smith and the Scottish Enlightenment*

Smith was troubled by poor health in his later years and shaken by the death of his mother in 1784 and by that of his cousin and housekeeper Janet Douglas in 1788. He had never married, and we have almost no evidence of him having any kind of romantic engagement. So his household was gradually reduced to a few loyal servants and the son of his cousin, the young David Douglas, whose education Smith was directing and who would become his heir.

Smith's late career as a civil servant was complemented by his growing reputation as a policy adviser to government. The success of the *Wealth of Nations* meant that his ideas were taken seriously at the highest levels. His opinion was sought on the American crisis, on free trade with Ireland, and on the changes to banking regulations. During a trip to London in 1787, many of the leading figures of the government, including the Prime Minister, William Pitt the Younger (1759–1806), attended a dinner in his honour where Smith's influence on economic policy and free trade was acknowledged. Also in 1787, Smith was elected Rector of Glasgow University. He was particularly delighted by the honour as it reflected the good opinion in which the students at his old university held him. He travelled to Glasgow with his friend the Irish philosopher Edmund Burke (1729–97) for the installation ceremony and gave a talk on the Imitative Arts which he intimated elsewhere was part of an unfinished new book.

By 1790, ill health had set in while Smith was working to produce a final revised edition of *The Theory of Moral Sentiments*. Although he managed this task, he did not manage to complete unfinished books on jurisprudence and on the arts and asked his executors, the scientist Joseph Black (1728–99) and the geologist James Hutton (1726–97), to help him destroy his papers. On his death, the bulk of Smith's estate passed to David Douglas, later Lord Reston, an influential judge. Smith left small bequests to his friends and gave significant amounts to charitable causes. All of the evidence we have of his character is that he was a modest and unassuming man who was a loyal friend. Beyond that he seems to have been a very private man who sought to avoid public controversy. Indeed, the care with which he revised his two great books suggests that he wanted them, rather than any details of his personal life, to stand as his reputation to posterity.[2]

The Scottish Enlightenment

While the details of Smith's life give us some insight into the connection between his biography and the content of his ideas, we are limited in what we can build upon this as he was a poor correspondent and ultimately a very private man. We actually gain considerably more insight by examining the intellectual climate in which he lived, the so-called 'Scottish Enlightenment'.[3]

The Scottish Enlightenment was an outpouring of intellectual achievement that occurred during the middle years of the eighteenth century (roughly 1740–90). It forms a subset of the wider phenomenon of the European Enlightenment. The 'Century of Light' or 'Age of Reason' was a time when many of the features of the modern world came into focus. Ideas of science, academic freedom, progress, and civil liberty became increasingly popular amongst a newly emerging class of public intellectuals. The idea that the darkness of superstition was being replaced by science and reason as part of a movement of cosmopolitan intellectuals, 'daring to know', as the philosopher Immanuel Kant (1724–1804) would later describe it, and refusing to accept truths set down by authority, has become central to understanding the intellectual history of the eighteenth century. This idea of thinking for oneself as enlightenment takes a very particular form in Scotland.

At first glance, eighteenth-century Scotland might seem a surprising place for a world-changing flood of science and philosophy. At the time, many considered the country to be a poor, isolated, and war-ridden backwater, more notable for its warring clans, religious fanatics, and wild landscapes than for intellectual achievement. But a combination of historical circumstances, together with a generation of remarkably talented men (and they were all men – it is worth observing that the Scottish Enlightenment, unlike the French Enlightenment, was a remarkably masculine movement), put Scotland at the forefront of the Enlightenment. Some have conjectured that it was precisely a sense of shame at the country's supposed backwardness that proved to be the spur for this group to pursue Enlightenment in its particular Scottish form.

The history of the time also gives us good reason to understand why the emerging Scottish middle class were so attracted to the idea of Enlightenment. Seventeenth-century Scotland had been torn apart by a series of civil and religious wars. The Church of Scotland (the Kirk) had developed a particularly rigorous form of

Presbyterian Calvinism that stressed strict discipline and punished heresy with excommunication and even, in the infamous case of the student Thomas Aikenhead in 1697, with execution. Beyond the religious and political situation, things were not much better. A series of famines had ravaged the country in the 1690s and the failed attempt to found a colony in Central America had virtually bankrupted Scotland's leading families by 1702. In this setting, the fraught negotiations for the Union of Parliaments in the early years of the century, in which Smith's father played a minor supporting role, represent the emergence of a social grouping who saw themselves as forward thinking and modernizing.

As we noted above, the Union of Parliaments with England in 1707 and the defeat of the final Jacobite rebellion in 1745–6, ushered in a long period of relative civil and political security as part of the new Great Britain. This stability came with access to new markets in England and its American colonies and this led in turn to unprecedented economic growth in the second half of the century. Scotland became a place of development and growth. Industries such as linen, glass, and tobacco boomed. Glasgow became the centre of the global tobacco trade as the short journey times to Virginia gave it a comparative edge over other British ports. Tobacco 'Lords' such as William Cunninghame (1731–99), Alexander Spiers (1714–82), and John Glassford (1715–83) began to diversify and develop other industries in the city. The growth of Glasgow's economy at this time saw the beginnings of industrialization and the concomitant development of a particularly advanced banking system to encourage the circulation of capital for investment in new industries. The small city that Smith knew as a student was subject to growing urbanization, with its population growing from 13,000 in 1707 to 77,000 in 1801, to over 200,000 by the end of the nineteenth century.

Stable government and economic growth allowed the already fertile soil of native Scottish institutions to thrive. This was particularly true of the school and university systems. Scotland had one of the most developed education systems of its time. During the Reformation, the spread of Calvinism, with its focus on reading the Bible, encouraged a desire for literacy and led to the creation of an extensive network of Burgh schools. Scotland was also well served for higher education, with its five universities outnumbering England's two. This meant that the structures were in place for a group of young men to take advantage of this education system and launch themselves on professional careers in the universities, the law, and the church. And that, indeed, is precisely what did happen. A new class of public intellectuals, a gentleman class, arose and transformed the nature of Scottish society over the course of the century.

Smith was at the centre of this milieu. He saw the changes in Scotland, and had a first-hand view of the investment and development in Glasgow. He socialized with many of the merchants and was able to draw on this experience in his economic thinking. The changes that he saw at this time were generally regarded as a good thing: as an example of that most central of Scottish Enlightenment concerns, 'improvement'. In many respects, this was a self-conscious movement. The Enlightenment belief in science and progress took on a very practical and applied meaning in Scotland. The lessons of science were to be heeded and deliberately applied to improve the state of the country. Some of these, such as the development of scientific agriculture and the reform of landholding, were uncontroversial, while others had a darker side, including the suppression of Highland dress and language.

The upheaval of the Jacobite rebellions convinced the new establishment of the need to civilize Scotland's northern fringe. The military suppression of the clans was followed by attempts to encourage development in the Highlands through agricultural reform and by opening up the area with new roads and the imposition of a uniform system of justice. The proceeds of the estates confiscated from the Jacobite leaders were used to fund these investments and to encourage a series of planned villages which sought to offer employment to the Highlanders. Towns such as Ullapool and villages like Luss provided modern homes and the promise of employment. The old clan chiefs lost their civil and political power and the century saw movements of people from the Highlands to the towns and cities and to the colonies.

Scotland saw enormous social change in the eighteenth century, and in the circumstances of a rapidly changing country it is little surprise that its intellectual class, the so-called 'literati', became preoccupied with an attempt to understand social and historical change. The thinkers of the Scottish Enlightenment gathered in the cities could see the beginnings of urban commercial society and modern agriculture in the Lowlands, but they could also look north to the Highlands and see a much older form of clan-based subsistence economy. The difference fascinated them and posed the question of how the Highlands might be 'improved'. If we look at Smith's writings, the *Wealth of Nations* in particular is filled with Scottish examples. It is no surprise that Smith was interested in society and in economics because he had around about him a living laboratory of rapid social development. But like his fellow literati, his interests were not parochial: he believed that the attempt to generalize from the experience of a particular country would allow for the understanding of universal features of human social life.

Smith's friends, his fellow literati, were a close-knit group of people from remarkably similar backgrounds. None came from particularly ancient or wealthy families: they were the sons of church ministers, minor landowners, and lawyers and they were making their way in Hanoverian Britain as members of a newly emerging middle class. What they shared in common was a similar educational background and a desire to improve their country. Many of these thinkers became leading figures in their respective disciplines. For example, Smith's teacher the Irish-born Francis Hutcheson, sometimes referred to as the 'father' of the Scottish Enlightenment, developed the style of philosophical education that became the backbone of the Scottish universities during this period. Hutcheson's success as a lecturer popularized the reconstructed version of the moral philosophy curriculum that became the shared basis of education in the Scottish universities. All students had to take moral philosophy, and the subject, which covered what we now think of as ethics, jurisprudence, aesthetics, politics, sociology, and philosophy of religion, formed a shared background to the thinking of the time. Hutcheson's desire was to provide a system of moral philosophy that contributed to our knowledge of social life, through a natural jurisprudence and a theory of a moral sense (the innate sense in the human mind that allows us to identify the right thing to do). But more than anything, Hutcheson saw his primary role as the education of virtuous citizens and good Christians. Enlightened education had a social as well as an intellectual function, and this notion deeply influenced Adam Smith's under-standing of what was expected of him in his role at the University of Glasgow.

Hutcheson's role as a father figure to the Scottish Enlightenment in Glasgow is paralleled by the role of Henry Home, Lord Kames, in Edinburgh. As we saw above, Kames was a senior judge, but he was also a philosopher and legal theorist who produced works of literary criticism and history. Kames sat at the centre of Edinburgh intellectual life, and his reputation as a sarcastic and combative thinker does not detract from his energy in promoting the careers of the younger members of the literati. Kames also acquired a significant estate through marriage and set out to apply the latest scientific knowledge to agricultural improvement, with his book *The Gentleman Farmer* (1776) intended to be a practical guide to improving land by the introduction of crop rotation and new crops such as the potato.

Another figure who applied himself to amateur scientific agriculture was Adam Ferguson (1723–1816). The long-serving Professor of Moral Philosophy at the University of Edinburgh, who was the only member of the group born in the Highlands, kept a farm at Hallyards in Lothian, where he would experiment with the latest agricultural methods. Ferguson's fame was built on *An Essay on the History of Civil Society* (1767), which has earned him the reputation as one of the founders of sociology. Ferguson's book was intended to trace the development of human social life through history, and it is a clear example of what we will see as the Scottish Enlightenment's fascination with social change. Ferguson was interested in the details of the descriptions of different types of society that were being collected by explorers. These suggested that the divergence between the Highlands and Lowlands of Scotland was merely a particular case of a more general division between savage, barbarian, and civilized societies. The interest in types of society became the characteristic feature of Scottish thinking about society and history. Like his fellow literati, Ferguson attempted to explain how a universal human nature adapted to different circumstances to produce diverse social institutions. Ferguson's history of civilization was accompanied by his *History of the Progress and Termination of the Roman Republic* (1783), which sought to trace the social changes that led Rome to move from republic to empire. Ferguson, like Hutcheson, was keen to draw a moral lesson from his work, and both the *Essay* and the *History* are characterized by an interest in the dangers of moral corruption that face commercial societies.

Thomas Reid (1710–96), who succeeded Smith at Glasgow when he left for the tour with the Duke of Buccleuch, was the founder of the 'common sense' school of philosophy and a critic of some aspects of the work of Hume and Smith. Reid, like Ferguson, was also a Minister of the Kirk and shows the intimate relationships that existed between the various institutions of Scotland at the time. Another prime example of this is Hugh Blair (1718–1800), who was Minister of the High Kirk of St Giles in Edinburgh, and perhaps the most famous pulpit orator of his generation, while also holding the post of Professor of Rhetoric and Belles Lettres at Edinburgh University, a position which is often regarded as the first university chair in English

Literature. Before his appointment to Edinburgh, Blair succeeded Smith in giving the public lectures on rhetoric in the city and closely followed Smith's model for a modern rhetorical education.

William Robertson (1721–93) also maintained a parallel career as Kirk Minister and Edinburgh Professor. He was a Professor and later the Principal of Edinburgh University, the leader of the Moderate faction in the General Assembly of the Church of Scotland, Moderator of the Kirk, and Historiographer Royal for Scotland. The Moderate faction within the Kirk was the main political manifestation of the Scottish Enlightenment. Under Robertson's leadership, the literati were able to advance their Enlightenment project in the face of opposition from the evangelical traditionalists of the Popular faction. The Moderates were active in protecting thinkers like Hume and Kames from prosecution for heresy. They were also able to place sympathetic Ministers in the most influential parishes and to promote a form of religion that was far milder than the rigid Calvinism of the traditional Kirk. The decline in the enforcement of social conformity through the Kirk was accompanied by a shift in focus from strict adherence to the literal word of the Bible to a form of teaching that stressed conscience and good moral behaviour. In a period of less than fifty years, Scotland had moved from a near theocracy where heresy was punishable by death to a more liberal society where David Hume's heterodox views on religion were met with social disapproval rather than prosecution.

Another interesting feature of this group was their tendency to move around the Scottish universities. For example, Smith's friend and executor Joseph Black was a Professor at Glasgow and then Edinburgh. Black's fame rests on isolating carbon dioxide and conducting ground-breaking experiments on latent heat. The other executor of Smith's estate, James Hutton, studied chemistry and made a fortune by perfecting the production of ammonium chloride. Hutton's true interest was geology and he travelled around Scotland observing rock formations, eventually producing his *Theory of the Earth* in 1795, the first modern account of geology. Black was also a physician and acted as doctor to several of the leading members of the Scottish Enlightenment. Scotland became famous for producing some of the leading medical men of the century. John Gregory (1724–73), William Cullen (1710–90), and the brothers John (1728–93) and William Hunter (1718–83) were pioneers of modern medicine. They built the reputation of the Scottish universities as the most advanced centres of medical training in the world.

True to the interest in applying scientific knowledge, the Scottish Enlightenment also produced some of the most successful engineers of the century. James Watt (1736–1819) worked as instrument maker at the University of Glasgow while Smith was a professor there. He went on to develop the separate condenser for the Newcomen steam engine, an innovation that paved the way for the Industrial Revolution. Thomas Telford (1757–1834) was a gifted civil engineer whose work on the Caledonian Canal helped to open the Highlands to commerce and, together with the Forth and Clyde Canal, facilitated water transport in the Scottish mainland.

Smith's childhood friends from Kirkcaldy included the architect Robert Adam (1728–92), whose Palladian style and neo-classicism dominated architecture at the time and helped to shape the most obvious physical symbol of the Scottish Enlightenment, the New Town of Edinburgh, whose Georgian elegance stands in contrast to the medieval old town. The building of the new town also involved the significant engineering feat of the draining of the Nor Loch and its replacement with Princes Street Gardens.

Adam was among the leading figures in the arts who emerged from Scotland at this time. Others include the portraitists Sir Henry Raeburn (1756–1823) and Allan Ramsay (1713–84), who painted many of the central figures of the period, the historical landscape artist Gavin Hamilton (1723–98), and the cartoonist and caricaturist John Kay, who provided amusing sketches of Edinburgh life. Two great pioneers of the English-language novel, Tobias Smollett (1721–71) and Henry MacKenzie (1745–1831), are also of note, as is a tradition of poets, including Robert Fergusson (1750–74) and Robert Burns (1759–96), who sought to preserve the Scots language and traditional songs from a fashion for Anglicization. The century also saw the foundations of fine art schools and printing presses, notably by the Foulis brothers in Glasgow.

These individuals formed a tight-knit group who met in the clubs of Edinburgh, Glasgow, and Aberdeen: clubs like the Select Society, the Poker Club, the Oyster Club, the Aberdeen Wise Club, the Glasgow Literary Society, and the Political Economy Club, where they heard papers and discussed the latest publications in philosophy and science. Many of these clubs, like the Edinburgh Society for Encouraging Arts, Sciences, Manufactures, and Agriculture, which later became the Royal Society of Edinburgh, were set up to apply scientific knowledge to practical improvement.

The latest ideas from England and Europe were absorbed and debated along with the latest Scottish ideas. The Scots corresponded with and met the leading thinkers of the time as part of a cosmo-politan intellectual environment. Enlightened visitors to Scotland such as Ireland's Edmund Burke and America's Benjamin Franklin (1706–90) were welcomed into a ferment of intellectual debate. Indeed, Tobias Smollett described the Scotland of this time as a hotbed of genius. Thinking about Adam Smith as moving in this context is helpful to us, as we can see the thinkers whose ideas influenced the development of his thought and those with whom he interacted in the discussion clubs of Enlightenment Scotland. Understanding Smith as a man of the Enlightenment, and particu-larly as a man of the Scottish Enlightenment, helps us to grasp a number of centrally important themes in his work: the most important of these being his commitment to science.

Newton

Perhaps the greatest inspiration for the Enlightenment was Sir Isaac Newton (1642–1727). Newton's towering achievements in the natural sciences made him the template for the successful public intellectual. Voltaire heaped praise on him as supplanting the thought of René Descartes (1596–1650), and his fame became such that he was even lauded in poetry by Alexander Pope (1688–1744). Newton's heroic status rested on his refinement of the scientific method first mooted by Francis Bacon (1561–1626). The method was grounded on the importance of observation and the generation of simple general rules of cause and effect based on the regularities observed in nature. This method avoided the error of Descartes, whose search for first principles led him to theorize beyond what the evidence supported.

Newton's *Principia Mathematica* (1687) popularized a new under-standing of what science was and what we could expect from it. The Newtonian, or experimental, method also had a further decisive advantage over its rivals: it provided testable predictions. French expeditions to Peru in 1735 and to Lapland in 1736 appeared to confirm Newton's description of the shape of the earth, while the reappearance of Halley's Comet in 1758 again demonstrated the success of his ideas. Colin Maclaurin (1698–1746) popularized Newton's work in the Scottish universities, ensuring that the young Scots whom he taught had the opportunity to experience cutting-edge science. By the time Smith was a student, the spirit of Newtonianism had become deeply embedded in the curriculum.[4]

Another major contributor to the modern science that Smith absorbed was John Locke (1632–1704). Locke's writings on education and on the theory of knowledge became a staple part of the understanding of psychology during the Enlightenment. Locke argued that all knowledge was based on experience and observation. He rejected the idea that human minds came stocked with innate ideas. Instead humans arrive with a *tabula rasa* or clean slate, and then proceed to build the content of their minds through experience of the world. All of our ideas arise from sense perceptions or as the result of reflection on sense perceptions and come to form increasingly complex thought processes. In terms of education, this led Locke to stress the importance of socialization and the need to state ideas in as plain and straightforward a fashion as possible.

Hume

The ideas of Newton and Locke form the backdrop to the thinking of the man who is the single most important influence on Adam Smith's thinking: David Hume. Hume came from a very similar background to Smith and, being around a decade older, had already passed through the Scottish university system and written his first great work, the *Treatise of Human Nature*, by the time Smith was at Oxford in the 1740s. In Hume's hands, the logic of the experimental method and the Lockean theory of ideas were pressed inexorably to their sceptical conclusions: the idea ultimately being reached that we must accept that all human knowledge is based on conditional probabilities acquired from experience by induction. In other words, there could never be any definitive 'proof' or truth outside systems of human concepts such as mathematics.

Hume begins the *Treatise* by noting that science is plagued by excessive abstraction and dedication to systems of thought. The only response to disputes between the adherents of these different systems of thought is recourse to empirical evidence. For Hume, all science is based on human understanding, and so all science must be based on a secure understanding of how human beings understand: on what he called the science of man. In turn, the only secure basis for such a science of man is experience and observation. Like natural scientists, we must conduct experiments and generalize from them. But experiments in the science of man cannot be the same as experiments in the natural sciences: we cannot manipulate people in the same way we mix chemicals. For Hume, we must instead have recourse to the observation of human life as it is and as it has been lived by actual people. If we look for examples and then compare them, we will gradually be able to build a picture of what is universal in human experience. The evidence that this provides us with will give insight into what motivates human behaviour and how humans think. Crucially for the development of the ideas of Smith and the Scottish Enlightenment, this led to the view that history was the data for a science of society.

The most controversial part of Hume's *Treatise* is his deconstruction of how humans come to make connections between the ideas that they draw from experience. Perhaps the easiest way to understand his position is to trace his basic understanding of the core scientific idea of cause and effect. Hume sets out to understand how humans make connections between phenomena. His answer is to say that we attribute the relationship between two phenomena to be one of causation – that one thing causes another. Hume then breaks down the steps in how we form that sort of belief. He argues that we draw on our experience of the world to observe that the two phenomena are closely connected, that one of them precedes the other, and that they have always been found this way. In the classic example, one billiard ball strikes another and so 'causes' the movement of the second ball. Hume says that this leads us to form a belief that there is a 'necessary connexion' between the two. So far this is similar to Locke's theory, but it is where Hume goes next that built his reputation as a sceptic. Hume argues that this form of knowledge is based on habit rather than reason.

Hume wants to understand why we think like this. The first thing to note is that we come to believe that the two events are connected because there have been repeated cases in our experience where they have been. The evidence of our senses is corroborated by multiple examples. But then Hume raises the question of why we assume that future cases will always be like past cases. His answer is that we believe this because we form beliefs based on custom and habit rather than demonstrative reason. Knowledge and expectations are based on induction from past experience. Humans believe that the world will continue as it has always done, that there is a 'necessary connexion' between two phenomena that are always found together; but the key point is that we cannot prove this through detached philosophical reasoning.

Hume's point is that constant conjunction from past experience can allow us to believe that the sun will rise tomorrow as it rose today, but we cannot provide any definitive proof that this will be the case. If our knowledge of nature is based on generalization from past experience, we can never reach absolutely certain knowledge about the future. Instead we can develop increasingly sophisticated descriptions of past behaviour that we assume will allow us to understand the future, but such beliefs rest on probability rather than demonstration. For Hume, human reason is limited and conditional in what it can hope to achieve, but this is not a counsel of despair. Instead, for him, it is a call to modesty, a realization that beyond generalization from evidence we have no reliable source of knowledge. Hume thought that metaphysics was a waste of time. All we can do is refine generalizations from experience and come to increasingly accurate descriptions of the general forces that drive the natural world. The human mind is an increasingly sophisticated system of generalization from experience, and the scientific method is merely the deliberate formulation of this process into a method of inquiry. Once we realize this, we recognize that the experimental approach, the generation of evidence from observation, is the only reliable guide to the uniform operation of nature. Hume summed up his position by noting that: 'A true sceptic will be diffident of his philosophical doubts, as well as of his philosophical convictions; and will never refuse any innocent satisfaction, which offers itself, on account of them.'[5]

The power of Hume's philosophical exploration of the basis of human knowledge made a deep impression on Adam Smith. Nicholas Phillipson has described Smith as the 'perfect Humean',[6] and while this may be taking things too far, it is nonetheless clear that Hume deeply influenced his thinking on the nature of philosophy and science, the topic of the next chapter.

2

Science and System

Adam Smith is most famous as the author of the *Wealth of Nations*, but as the current volume aims to show by introducing the reader to his complete body of thought, this sits within a wider systematic body of work. In this chapter we will examine the outline of Smith's system and then proceed to look at his views on science and system. This will set the scene for the following chapters, where we will look in some detail at his moral, political, and economic writings.

Smith published two books during his lifetime: *The Theory of Moral Sentiments* in 1759 and *An Inquiry into the Nature and Causes of the Wealth of Nations* in 1776. Both books went through several editions before he died and he made significant revisions to them, particularly to the *Moral Sentiments*. We can draw a number of conclusions from this about Smith's attitude to his work. The fact that he significantly revised the *Moral Sentiments* for the 1761 second edition shows that he was willing to respond to the critics of the first version of the book (including his friend David Hume). Second, the fact that he returned to the *Moral Sentiments* and prepared a final edition with significant further additions in 1790, just before he died, shows us that he remained committed to the arguments of the book and to presenting them in the most convincing fashion possible. Moreover, the fact that he revised the *Moral Sentiments* after he wrote the *Wealth of Nations* suggests that he saw no necessary contradiction between the content of the two books – a point that escaped some of his nineteenth-century German readers. who saw a contradiction between the arguments of the two and sought to explore this under the heading of the

'Adam Smith Problem'. The Germans were puzzled by what they saw as a contradiction between the focus on sympathy in the *Moral Sentiments* and the emphasis on self-interest in the *Wealth of Nations*, a point we will address as we move through the book and to which we will return in the final chapter on Smith's legacy.[1]

In addition to these two books, we have the posthumous collection of unfinished essays, the *Essays on Philosophical Subjects*, published in 1795. We will cover the more important of these essays in the section below on science, but the volume also included some reflections on the role of imitation in the arts, an essay on poetry, and another on sense perception. The modern edition of this collection, part of the Glasgow edition of Smith's works, also includes a series of minor letters and reviews.

In his correspondence, Smith mentions two other projected volumes: one on the history of the arts, literature, and sciences and another on justice and politics. Neither of these came to fruition. However, we have been fortunate enough to discover student notes covering his Glasgow University *Lectures on Jurisprudence* and *Lectures on Rhetoric and Belles Lettres*. These are reasonably complete and have allowed us to reconstruct both his teaching and the main themes that he sought to convey to his students. They also show that Smith was developing many of the ideas that would later appear in the *Wealth of Nations* while he was a Professor at Glasgow in the 1750s and 1760s.

Overall, Smith is a remarkably consistent thinker. The various elements of his system seem to fit together reasonably neatly. As we will see in a moment, this is largely due to his adoption of a single underlying method of inquiry that unites his views in such apparently diverse areas as rhetoric and economics. Smith, like many of his fellow Enlightenment thinkers, was a man of polymathic interests, a voracious reader, and a regular attendee at discussion clubs and salons. But he was also a careful and systematic thinker. His books are skilfully constructed and he makes no wild or unsupported claims. This care is matched by his attention to detail in providing evidence for his claims. And all of this is an expression of his belief that his philosophy was part of the new science of man, an empirically grounded attempt to achieve in the human sciences what was being achieved in the natural sciences. Smith clearly understood himself as deploying a particular version of the scientific method. One of his books is a 'Theory' and the other an 'Inquiry', and this signals to the reader that these are not occasional or unsystematic pieces, like an 'Essay'. They are supposed to be an addition to human knowledge that will surpass previous attempts in the field as the result of the innovative methodology being developed.

Smith develops this method because he is dissatisfied with how a lot of philosophy had been undertaken in the past. He is generally dismissive of the view that philosophy can helpfully be pursued in seclusion from everyday experience of the world. Excessive abstraction can lead philosophers to produce elegant theories and beautiful arguments that crumble as soon as they come into contact with experience of the real world. Smith is absolutely committed to providing evidence for his claims and to avoiding the danger that 'wrong systems' that are a 'refinement of philosophy'[2] can take root and mislead us. Smith, in line with the mainstream of the Scottish Enlightenment, demands that theorizing must be supported by actual data gained from observation of life as it is, or as it has been lived.

Science

To start to understand Smith's methodology and the version of the science of man that he developed in response to his reading of Newton and Hume, we should turn to his final, posthumous, publication, the *Essays on Philosophical Subjects*. The *Essays* were published in 1795, five years after Smith's death, and represent the only unpublished papers that he thought worth saving. The rest of his papers were burned shortly before he died. His executors, the scientists Joseph Black and James Hutton, prepared the essays for publication and added a biographical essay by the Edinburgh philosopher Dugald Stewart. It may seem odd to look to Smith's posthumous writing to start a consideration of his philosophical method, but this becomes less surprising if we understand that the most interesting essays in the volume were written early in Smith's career and revised through his life. The three historical essays on *Astronomy*, *Ancient Physics*, and *Ancient Logics and Metaphysics* form part of Smith's projected, but uncompleted, book on the history of art, science, and literature.[3]

The full title of the longest of these essays is 'The Principles which Lead and Direct Philosophical Enquiries Illustrated by the History of Astronomy'. This reveals that Smith's true interest is not the details of the development of astronomy, but rather the exploration of the nature of philosophy (including what we would now call science). His main contention is that the formal practice of science is a deliberate version of the underlying way in which the human mind operates. Smith follows Hume's views on the association of ideas through repeated experience as the source of the habitual mental patterns that form human understanding. As we saw above, Hume's reputation as a sceptic arose from his view, first laid out in the *Treatise of Human Nature*, that the power of philosophy to provide absolute certainty for our beliefs was radically limited.

For both Hume and Smith, humans form their beliefs about the world from experience. We form expectations drawn from repeated past experience of links between phenomena and these suggest to us that a similar relationship will hold in the future. As a result, our knowledge is always a probability rather than absolutely certain. Our minds flow from one idea to another through a set of habitual expectations and associations of ideas. We think that the sun will rise tomorrow because it always has done in our past experience, that fire is hot because it has always been found to be so; but we cannot be absolutely certain that these generalizations will continue to hold. This observation colours Hume's and Smith's understanding of what we can expect from philosophy and leads to a sort of epistemic modesty that is characteristic of the latter's entire career.

That said, both Hume and Smith were clear that such knowledge was reliable and that nature did provide us with universally applicable laws that could be explored through observation and theorization. The point, as Hume had observed at the start of the *Treatise*, was that experience and observation were the only truly reliable basis for belief. Smith seeks to explore how it is that human beings understand the world by understanding how the mind creates these regularities from its experience of the world.

Wonder, Surprise, and Admiration

At the heart of his argument is the idea that we are prompted to science not by reason, but by our emotions. Smith believed that we do not originally pursue science for the utilitarian reasons that Francis Bacon had suggested. Instead our scientific method is an extension of an emotionally driven need to understand the world. Science has its origins in our emotions; more specifically it arises from three particular emotions: 'Wonder, Surprise, and Admiration'.[4] When we come across something that we have never encountered before, we try to situate it in relation to our past experience, and when we cannot do this, it makes us uneasy.

Smith thought that this was precisely because our knowledge of the world comes in the form of habitual generalizations drawn from experience. Our understanding of things is a pattern of connections that exist in the imagination and which help to orientate us. The 'natural career of the imagination'[5] flows smoothly and allows us to make sense of the world until it comes across something that does not fit with our established mental patterns. The emotion of wonder is produced when we come across something we have never encountered before; we are surprised by the new or by the familiar appearing in an unexpected context; and we admire an explanation that is able to fit the wondrous and surprising into a coherent account of nature. Smith's point here is that our pursuit of understanding of the world comes from a natural curiosity that is driven by our emotions.

Surprises are unsettling, they upset the smooth operation of our minds, and this uneasiness, this anxiety, is what drives us to science. Smith thinks that our first inclination is to try to account for a surprising event by fitting it into our established patterns of knowledge. If we can do this, our uneasiness dissipates. Indeed we become content and admire the way in which we have been able to place the phenomenon within a system of understanding. Smith regards this experience as both emotional (anxiety dissipating) and aesthetic (in the sense that we admire the beauty of the systematic explanation). Once someone has provided us with an explanation, we are no longer puzzled. Like someone who has seen behind the stage curtain, the special effects of the opera no longer strike us with awe – instead we admire them for the manner in which they are systematically arranged to produce the desired result. However, if we are unable to do this, we remain anxious to make sense of the phenomenon.

It is at this point that we develop more sophisticated systems of understanding. Here Smith makes a startling claim: that the first attempts to respond to the wondrous were religious. Smith provides us with an account of the development of polytheistic religion as a natural attempt to make sense of things that do not fit with established experience. Floods, lightning, famine, are made explicable by seeing them as the deliberate actions of a deity.[6] The anger of a superhuman entity might seem an odd source of consolation, but it is better than something that is totally inexplicable. The psychologically unsettling impact of the inexplicable is far worse than that which is supernaturally explicable. This provides a degree of calmness to the mind as we now have some sort of explanation. Such superstitions arise from exactly the same emotional needs as science. The difference for Smith is that science becomes more successful at banishing unease than superstitious religions.

It's important to understand why science comes to displace superstition and how Smith thought that this had happened in particular societies. First of all, he thought that certain social conditions had to be in place before a scientific method could be developed. Science is only possible when 'order and security'[7] have been secured and people have been freed from absolute want. It is only when we develop some leisure time to pursue our curiosity that we are able to recognize the order that exists in nature and to develop a conscious system of scientific inquiry to understand it. Poverty and superstition go together because the struggle to secure subsistence occupies all of our attention and leaves us ignorant. Science is also facilitated by the division of labour. A separate class of professional philosophers emerges who set their mind to observing nature and seeking its patterns. As this develops, the branches of knowledge divide and specialists develop.

Once the scientific method arises, it begins to supplant superstition precisely because it is more systematic and coherent in its ability to explain the world. In order to understand Smith's view here and his entire understanding of the task of philosophy, it's vital to grasp that he sees the task of religious explanations and science as the same. They try to make sense of the world and to calm the mind by banishing anxiety. The test of all such explanations is that they are able to account for what is experienced. A theory or a system of thinking must be subject to a 'reality check'. If it fails adequately to lead our minds through the order of nature in a smooth fashion, then it will be supplanted by another account that is able to achieve this.

Philosophy is the 'science of the connecting principles of nature'.[8] Its success depends on its ability to render things 'familiar to the imagination'.[9] Smith sums up his view in the following terms:

> Philosophy, by representing the invisible chains which bind together all these disjointed objects, endeavours to introduce order into this chaos of jarring and discordant appearances, to allay this tumult of the imagination, and to restore it, when it surveys the great revolutions of the universe, to that tone of tranquillity and composure, which is both most agreeable in itself, and most suitable to its nature.[10]

Smith's account of the development of science is undertaken through an account of the move from one system of thought to another. For Smith, a system is an 'imaginary machine invented to connect together in the fancy those different movements and effects which are already in reality performed'.[11] A system for Smith suggests a coherent body of explanation, a theory that accounts for more than one observed phenomenon. Recognizing that there are regularities in nature is what leads humanity from the belief in a multiplicity of gods acting on their own whims to a monotheistic conception of God acting in accordance with rules of nature. One principle that explains a great many things is better at relieving our 'anxious curiosity'[12] and leading our imagination in a smooth fashion. Once we begin the self-conscious exploration of the world through observation, we begin the attempt to organize our ideas into a single coherent system, making sense of the world by ordering our thoughts and calming our minds.[13]

Systems

Smith then provides us with an account of the gradual evolution of astronomy as a science. The point of this, as we noted above, is to illustrate the more general point about how we come to understand the world. Smith's account tells us how one system of astronomy is replaced by another, and it is in the detail of this process that we learn why it is that the scientific method has become such an effective means of satisfying our curiosity. Smith's account relies upon two basic principles that lead us to prefer one system of thought to another and which provide increasingly intellectually and emotionally satisfactory explanations. The first of these is that if our imagination is to be led smoothly, then there must be as few 'gaps'[14] as possible in a theory. If a theory fails to account for part of the observed phenomenon, then we will notice the gap and the lingering anxiety will remain. The system with the fewest such gaps at any one time is the one most likely to be favoured. New theories arise in response to dissatisfaction at the gaps in existing accounts, and in order to succeed they must not only account for the gap, but also account for all that the preceding theory had explained. A new theory must be 'more completely coherent'[15] than its predecessors.

Smith's second basic principle is the Newtonian preference for identifying a few simple generalizations that explain a multiplicity of phenomena. Explanatory simplicity – elegance, you might say

– not only makes it easier for the mind to follow the theory, but it also avoids the danger of a convoluted account that fails to dispel our anxiety. If the system of ideas necessary to explain a complex phenomenon is as complex as the phenomenon itself, then it will fail to relieve the 'embarrassment'[16] in which we find ourselves. This is itself a product of the desire for systematic knowledge. Our desire for a coherent explanation means that we tend to run too quickly into the belief that our system can account for everything: over-ambition leads to over-complexity and eventually to unease that we are over-reaching.

This is a particular problem in the 'infancy of science', when 'the curiosity of mankind, grasping at an account of all things before it had got full satisfaction with regard to any one, hurried on to build, in imagination, the immense fabric of the universe'.[17] Smith's argument in this respect shows the influence of his teacher Francis Hutcheson. In Hutcheson's *An Inquiry into the Original of our Ideas of Beauty and Virtue* (1725), there is a chapter on the beauty of theorems. In it, Hutcheson argues that the human reaction to a coherent intellectual system is an appreciation of its beauty and that this beauty comes from the uniformity that the principles of the theorem provide. For Hutcheson, this has some potentially dangerous side-effects. As he puts it, referring to Samuel Pufendorf (1632–94), of whom he otherwise approves:

> How awkwardly does Pufendorf deduce the several duties of men to God, themselves, and their neighbours, from his single fundamental principle of sociableness to the whole race of mankind? The observation is a strong proof, that men perceive the beauty of uniformity in the sciences, since they are led into unnatural deductions by pursuing it too far.[18]

The beauty, the emotionally and intellectually satisfying nature, of a theory comes from its ability to explain the phenomena at hand in a coherent, gapless fashion which is parsimonious in its core explanatory principles. The ability of a theory to banish anxiety and secure our admiration depends on its ability to explain the observed phenomena and connect them together in the most satisfying fashion possible. We will move from one theory to another when we begin to perceive that it has gaps that it cannot explain, or when in its attempt to plug the gaps it becomes convoluted and overly complex. Smith leads us through the main systems of astronomy showing how each was supplanted by a successor that plugged a gap or provided a more theoretically simple account of nature. For example, the advance made by Copernicus over Ptolemy allowed him to explain astronomy in 'a more simple as well as a more accurate manner'.[19] Similarly, Kepler's increasingly complex use of analogy led to a theory that was 'of too intricate a nature to facilitate very much the effort of the imagination in conceiving it'.[20]

In between these shifts between philosophical systems, the scientists operating within a given system spend their time following through on its implications and refining its account to smooth over any gaps that arise.[21] Smith ends his survey with a brief description of Newton's position that dwells on its success in refining the method of science as well as his ability to supplant the system of Descartes.[22] In an interesting observation, Smith explains to us how the adherents of a system of thought commit themselves to a particular way of thinking on an emotional level. This means that they are generally hostile to those who propose a new system and seek to preserve the existing way of thinking. This devotion to systems of thought fascinated him, but it also troubled him because he recognized that it was a barrier to the advance of knowledge. Smith himself, as we noted above, believed that a 'reality check' would allow the pragmatic scientist to accept that his system did indeed have a gap that needed explaining. Moreover, in the case of superstitious religions, the preservation of the system in the face of evidence to the contrary becomes a very serious matter indeed. The political side of disputes between the adherents of systems in the advance of knowledge is an area where Smith recognizes the power of vested interests – something that is a running theme throughout his work.[23]

In the other two essays, on *Ancient Physics* and *Ancient Logics and Metaphysics*, he does much the same, though they are far less developed than the *Astronomy*. One interesting development in the *Ancient Physics* is the exploration of the observation that we attempt to explain the new by bringing together elements that are familiar to us. Creating a chain of familiar ideas and connecting them together in a new way allows our mind to move more smoothly through the systematic account that is being offered. This also underlines another feature of Smith's epistemology. Like most of his fellow enlightened Scots, he regards the human mind as a system of classification that is constantly being refined. This means that science has two tasks: the discovery of new elements of experience from observation; and the subsequent systematic arrangement of these through a system of connecting principles. Both of these are vital to its success.

This idea clearly struck a chord with Smith because he makes it central to his explanatory outlook throughout his career.[24] When he comes to write his own great books, we see him adopt a methodology that is clearly based on the account developed here. The aim is to work from observation of the phenomenon (morality or the economy) to provide a gapless and coherent system that accounts for what is observed in as simple and smoothly connected a fashion as possible. Moreover, he also draws on the idea of arranging the analysis as the exploration of a single simple principle which provides great explanatory reach demonstrated through a series of illustrations. This allows him to provide a systematic and methodical examination of his subject. As we will see, the *Moral Sentiments* uses sympathy as its master principle while the *Wealth of Nations* uses the division of labour.[25] Smith's modern biographer Nicholas Phillipson describes this method as mathematical and drawn from the geometry that was one of his favourite subjects while a student at Glasgow.[26] The point is that Smith was committed to the twin ideas of empirical observation and systematic and methodical explanation. The test of his own theories would be whether they could account for all of the elements of the observed phenomenon and do so in a more straightforward and persuasive fashion than his rivals.

Rhetoric

The influence of this attitude towards explanation can also be seen in Smith's thinking on the style of writing best suited to conveying one's argument. The discovery of a set of student notes from Smith's *Lectures on Rhetoric and Belles Lettres*, together with the posthumously published essay 'Of the Nature of that Imitation which Takes Place in What Are Called the Imitative Arts', has given us insight into his views on literary criticism and aesthetics.[27] The theory developed there dwells on the sentimental nature of the aesthetic experience, the need for a sense of the style appropriate to the social context, and the need for literature to convey ideas in as clear a fashion as possible.

In his essay on the *Imitative Arts*, Smith's idea that we admire the beauty of a system is deployed in the field of aesthetics.[28] He grounds his observation on the idea that our admiration of an imitative art is not based on the exactness of the copy, but rather on the invocation of the original in another medium. Our admiration of a fine portrait of ourselves is something distinct from the exact image we see reflected in a mirror. The 'art' of art is the skill by which two dissimilar objects are brought to resemble each other. It is the connection of these two different things that prompts our admiration, or, as Smith puts it, the 'disparity between the imitating and the imitated object is the foundation of the beauty of imitation'.[29] The pleasure that we experience is like the pleasure that arises from the systematic connection of ideas. We admire the skill and thought that are involved in the systematic arrangement that leads our mind from one thing to another. Moreover, our admiration is enhanced if we are able to understand how the imitation is brought about. The 'more pleasing satisfaction of science'[30] is that we are able to understand how the work of art has been produced. Like the person who saw behind the scenes of the opera, we lose our innocent wonder and gain a different sort of pleasure from understanding how things work.

It is worth drawing out a couple of the observations that Smith makes here as they allow us to understand why he presents his ideas in the way that he does. His main concern is with clarity of expression, what he calls 'perspicuity'.[31] Writers should avoid jargon and overwrought or flowery prose; they should stick to short sentences and write in as plain a style as possible. This is particularly the case in philosophy and in historical and didactic writing. Smith's reason for this is related to the account of how we develop beliefs in the *Astronomy*, but it is also crucially related to the account of the moral sentiments, to which we will turn in the next chapter.

It is worth quoting Smith's account of a successful literary style here as it will help us to understand why he constructs his books in the way that he does.

> When the sentiment of the speaker is expressed in a neat, clear, plain and clever manner, and the passion or affection he is possessed of and intends, *by sympathy*, to communicate to his hearer, is plainly and cleverly hit off, then and then only the expression has all the force and beauty that language can give it.[32]

Smith's view on simplicity of expression rather than the use of figures of speech or literary techniques represents a shift in literary style that would gain strength through the eighteenth and nineteenth centuries as history and philosophy sought to distance themselves from rhetoric. For Smith, the expert will seek to convey his knowledge rather than obscure it. As he puts it: 'One who has such a complete knowledge of what he treats will naturally arrange it in the most proper order.'[33] Facts should be clearly stated, narratives straightforwardly related, and arguments arranged in a gapless fashion around a simple core principle. Perspicuous writing arranges the expression of ideas in their 'natural' order and allows the reader's mind to flow seamlessly along with the text. The use of literary effects, metaphors, and allusions must be kept to a minimum and judged only by their success in illustrating the ideas for the reader. Overly florid prose was anathema to Smith and forms the basis of his criticism of writers such as Lord Shaftesbury (1671–1713) and Joseph Addison (1672–1719).

Writing with perspicuity meant writing in short, clear sentences whose aim was to convey ideas rather than show off literary skill. Smith believed that this was a relatively recent phenomenon. Prose was a product of 'commerce and opulence',[34] of a society where facts needed to be stated and understood. No one, as Smith pointed out, ever made a bargain in verse.[35] The obsession with clearly conveying ideas runs through his discussion of the different styles of writing and argument in the rest of the lectures. His favoured style was plain, simple, and clear – though one may wonder at the extent to which his published writings actually lived up to this ideal.

Most significantly for our interests, this view on style shapes Smith's views on how historians should write about the past. Smith distinguishes between two broad styles of argument: the didactic and the rhetorical. The didactic focuses on proving a proposition by weighing the evidence, while the rhetorical takes sides and seeks to prove a proposition by literary affect. Neither of these is appropriate for writers of history. Historians should adopt the narrative style, where facts are simply related without assessment. They may engage in a critical reflection on their sources in order to determine the accuracy of the facts that they relate, but they should not approach history with a view to 'proving' something. The best historians, and Smith here references Thucydides and Tacitus, do something else in addition: their narratives examine historical events in terms of cause and effect. An account that merely describes one thing after another is not an explanation of events. Returning to the argument of the *Astronomy*, he notes that 'we are not satisfied when we have a fact told to us which we are at a loss to conceive what it was that brought it about'.[36]

This, according to Smith, is the most promising approach to history. He also rejects the ancient habit of meticulously describing

the character of particular historical individuals and their psycho-
logical condition as explanations for events. These are literary
illustrations rather than a clear causal chain of events. Good history
provides a chain of events and shows how one leads to the other.
As such, the writing of history is like all other writing in Smith's
view: it is best achieved through a gapless narrative with a simple
principle that has great explanatory reach in accounting for a
particular chain of events. Smith refers to this as the Newtonian
method, one which is 'the most Philosophical'[37] and preferable to
Socratic didacticism and Aristotelian teleology.

In order to convince the reader, the core principle needs to be
illustrated by a series of immediately recognizable examples. In his
lectures on rhetoric, Smith provides us with the two key types of
such examples which dominate the rest of his work: the historical
case study and the generalized character sketch.[38] It is through these
two techniques that he demonstrates the plausibility of his theories.
The Newtonian ability to connect the apparently unconnected in
one chain under one principle is persuasive if the examples used are
either from common experience or from detailed empirical cases.
Through these techniques, readers are drawn along with the author
and find their imagination running smoothly from one observation
to the next until the explanatory whole is laid before them.

As we will see in the rest of the book, Smith remains committed
to the main principles of the method outlined in this chapter. He
was modest about what he expected to be able to learn from his
studies and he was very careful to arrange them around a central
explanatory principle, and to illustrate them with examples that
would carry his reader's imagination along with him. His aim was
to trace cause and effect in history.

Conjectural History

Smith saw himself as adopting a self-consciously scientific
approach to his subject matter, and in doing this he sits within the
mainstream of the Scottish Enlightenment's application of science
to social subjects. The inspiration here was the French philosopher
Montesquieu (1689–1755). Montesquieu's monumental *The Spirit
of the Laws* (1748) represented the first modern attempt to apply
something like the scientific and observational method to society as
a concept. In doing so, the Frenchman focused on how the 'spirit'
of the customs, habits, institutions, and morals of different types

of society can help us to understand them. The Scots all absorbed this approach and combined it with the natural jurisprudence that Hutcheson had drawn from Pufendorf to develop an approach that was to be more scientific than the available alternatives. The science of man was contrasted with the existing attempts to explain the origin of, and justify obedience to, social institutions. Smith, like Hume, realized that the dominant political factions in Britain, the Tories and the Whigs, had developed social philosophies which served their interests. The Tories developed a theory of passive obedience and divine right that favoured the hereditary monarchy, while the Whigs developed the idea of the social contract that grounded government in the consent of the people. The contract argument had the virtue of providing a basis for rebellion when the terms of the contract had been breached. The classic case of this was John Locke's *Two Treatises of Civil Government* (1689), which sought to justify the new British settlement after 1688 in terms of a justified removal of a contract-breaking tyrant, James II, whose supporters in turn deployed arguments about the divinely ordained nature of monarchy and the danger of anarchy. Both of these explanations served a political rather than a scientific agenda.

As we noted above, the Scottish literati were sympathetic to the politics of the Whig approach, but they were not attracted to the arguments used to support it.[39] The main reason for this was that these arguments failed to account for the reality of the nature of social life. Society, as Hume pointed out, was not a contract: there had never been a social contract, and even if there had been, it would not provide an adequate basis for the legitimacy of present governments.[40] The evidence, as Adam Ferguson pointed out, showed that humans had always been social and so there was no state of nature that they left through a contract to enter society.[41] This, as Hume noted, was obvious on a conceptual level, because the idea of a contract is based on an existing convention of promise keeping, a convention that can only exist in society. The concept of a contract is itself a product of a time when humans already lived together in society. So, if the origin of society did not lie in contracts, where did it lie? The answer for Smith and his fellow Scots lay in the examination of history. But the historical record for the distant past was at best imperfect, and in reality non-existent: history only develops long after humans have become social. What was required was a way of developing a theoretical account of the earliest stages of human society that was more closely related to the evidence that was available.

The shared methodology that the Scots developed to explore the deep past has come to be known as 'conjectural' history. The term comes from a line in Dugald Stewart's biography of Smith where he describes the method as 'Theoretical' or 'Conjectural' or 'Natural' History.[42] The example that Stewart chooses to illustrate Smith's use of the method is the 'Considerations Concerning the First Formations of Languages'. Smith attached this essay to *Moral Sentiments* from the third edition of 1767 onwards, and it is a good illustration of his more general approach to historical explanation. As Stewart points out, it is impossible for us to gain knowledge of the actual early development of language and yet, to quote him,

> if we can shew, from the known principles of human nature, how all its various parts might gradually have arisen, the mind is not only to a certain degree satisfied, but a check is given to that indolent philosophy, which refers to a miracle, whatever appearances, both in the natural and moral worlds, it is unable to explain.[43]

Theoretical history is a form of scientific explanation that provides a plausible account of the operation of some particular phenomenon by using the known to account for the unknown.

Smith's theory of language deals with an issue that was discussed by a number of eighteenth-century thinkers in just such a way. In the absence of a direct historical record, he theorizes a situation based on what we know of human behaviour and what we know of the basics of social interaction. Two 'savages' meet and very soon develop vocal signals to identify common objects. This aids communication between them and gradually evolves into a system of classification based on the association of ideas. As a result, languages develop through a 'natural' disposition to name similar objects in a similar way and then to develop this into a class of objects, and then into a way of describing the plural from the singular occurrence of the same object. So a thing (tree) becomes a word 'tree' which becomes a plural 'trees'. Similarly, the quality that marks out the class develops from a description to a quality, so green becomes greenness. Languages then develop words to describe the relation between objects and to allow us to differentiate between them. From here we see the development of linguistic categories and concepts such as numbers, gradually leading to the development of grammar and an evolved standardization of pronunciation. For Smith, languages develop from everyday use rather than abstract philosophy, and so these concepts exist before we recognize them on the level of philosophy. Languages give us the basis for abstract thought, and this continues to evolve as we develop written languages. The theoretical account of language is one based on its gradual evolution from the unintended consequences of human social life.[44]

Conjectural history also represents a desire to account for the diversity of forms of human society, and for the fact that societies change form over time. We are faced by a lack of direct evidence of the early history of our own society, so rather than create imaginary states of nature like the contract theorists do, we should instead look to the evidence of the condition of other societies. This method is based on the assumption that there are sufficient underlying universalities of human nature and human social life to make meaningful comparisons. Given what we know about human nature from the observation of human life from the historical record and contemporary societies, we can form theories about the sorts of institutions and practices that may have existed in the distant past. The aim is not to invent history, but rather to create a theoretical understanding of the likely path of human development. What is of interest here is not the history of any one society, but rather to draw on the evidence of different societies to develop a theory of the historical development of 'society' as a category of social explanation.

In the *Lectures on Jurisprudence*, Smith makes extensive use of the method. The lectures include a series of case studies in comparative law where the examples of different legal systems' responses to shared practices, such as property ownership or inheritance, are used to make generalizations about how similar types of society develop similar practices. Smith draws extensively on Scottish and European examples, but he also draws on the description of the social practices of the Native American tribes that had been provided in the accounts of travellers. This was a way of acquiring information about a society that existed in a stage of development that was similar to that of our own ancestors.

By comparing several of these accounts, we can corroborate the evidence as accurate on a descriptive level, while at the same time identifying the universal aspects shared by that type of society. We can use the historical evidence to compare and 'experiment', discounting material that contradicts what we know about human nature and generalizing from what remains. The point is not to discover absolutely similar institutions or beliefs across societies, but rather to note sufficient similarities to generalize about 'types'.

In Smith's hands, this becomes what has come to be known as the 'four stages' theory. The theory provides a schema for the identification of types of society based on the main way of securing subsistence: hunting, shepherding, agriculture, and commerce.[45] We will discuss the details of Smith's application of the theory in more detail in chapter 5, but for the present discussion a broad outline of the view will allow us to see the methodology that he adopts to flesh out his application of science to social matters. In the *Lectures on Jurisprudence*, there are a number of applications of the theory, but perhaps the clearest is the discussion of property. Smith's aim is to examine the origin and development of property as absolutely necessary to the existence of all societies. Each of the stages of society has a different conception of ownership that reflects the circumstances of that society. Hunting societies tend to have an undeveloped and immediate idea of property in what is currently to hand or in the animal that has just been caught. Later the idea of owning livestock over time emerges in a shepherding society, an idea that extends to ownership of land once agriculture has developed, and eventually property is extended to intangible things like money and shares in a commercial society. Understanding the differences between the concept of property in each type of society gives us a better understanding of the nature of property as a social category, while at the same time helping us to understand how the institution of property functions in our own society.

Another practitioner of the method was Smith's student John Millar. Millar's *Origin of the Distinction of Ranks* (1771) is a classic of conjectural history that applies the Smithian 'four stages' theory to basic forms of human social relationship, including that between men and women and parents and children. In each case, he shows how the context, the main mode of subsistence, such as hunting, shepherding, agriculture, or commerce, shapes the form that the relationship takes. In Millar's hands, this becomes one of the first sociological accounts of the development of gender inequality.

It is worth pausing to note a couple of the implications of this methodology. First, it is absolutely dependent on the idea that there is a universal human nature; that despite the wide variety of behaviour we find in different cultures, there is a shared basic model of human psychology. This means that no one form of social life is any more 'natural' than any other, and so crude ethnocentric judgements are to be avoided. The point is not that some societies are defective or corrupted according to some crude normative scale, but rather that they need to be understood in their own terms.

The commitment to a universal human nature has several further implications for Smith's thinking. Smith, unlike some of his fellow Scots, is uninterested in ideas of race or polygenesis: all human beings are the same in his view. More generally, the thinkers of the Scottish Enlightenment also had to defend the idea of a universal human nature from the possibility that human behaviour was directly affected by the physical environment. In the *Spirit of the Laws*, Montesquieu had detailed experiments with heat and cold that purported to show that the climate had a direct effect on human physical responsiveness. This could then be used to explain why different parts of the globe displayed different behaviour. David Hume, in the essay 'Of National Characters', systematically destroyed this theory and demonstrated that differences in behaviour between different social groups are due to social factors rather than differences in climate. The differences between the French and the Germans cannot be explained by radically different climates, nor do geographically dispersed people such as the Jews differ radically in the practices they maintain.

Second, the descriptive account of different types of society need not be understood as deterministic and inevitable. Smith is not saying that all societies will inevitably pass through the four stages. Indeed, he is explicit that there are examples of mixed forms of society, of societies that have moved from hunting to agriculture without being shepherds, and even that there are societies that have been commercial and are now agricultural. Lived history does not fit neatly onto the model being developed here, but that does not diminish the accession of knowledge that the science of man acquires by thinking about societies in this way. Even if we had a complete historical record of a particular society's development through time, and that record did not conform to the conjectural speculations, this would in no way discredit the approach. As Dugald Stewart observed, the systematic knowledge advances our understanding of the general phenomenon of society as such.

Social Change

In addition to being an academic enterprise, the development of conjectural history was intended to provide an account of how social change might have occurred that was more closely related to the available evidence than that of the contract theorists. Smith and his fellow Scots were not the first to attempt something like this, and it is worth pausing to consider the impact of two such influential accounts as they help to set the scene for Smith's own moral philosophy. Among Smith's first published works was a letter to the *Edinburgh Review* (1756) where he discusses contemporary philosophy, the *Encyclopédie*, and Jean-Jacques Rousseau's (1712–78) *Discourse on the Origin and the Foundations of Inequality among Men* (1755).[46] In it Smith compares Rousseau to Bernard Mandeville (1670–1733), the author of the controversial *Fable of the Bees*, and situates him in the context of a debate about the possibility of virtuous self-interest and its tension with the idea of socially directed morality.

Rousseau had adopted a deliberately contrarian attitude to the Enlightenment notions of reason, science, and progress. In his *Discourse* and elsewhere, he made the case that the development of modern civilization was not an example of progress but rather a tale of the corruption of humanity from an original innocence to a selfish and vanity-driven modernity. Rousseau's account dwelt on the idea that the process of socialization had created perverted value systems grounded in envy and self-conceit, where pride and concern for social status had transformed humanity for the worse. As Smith rightly noted, Rousseau's idea was very similar to that of Mandeville, who had extended his original satirical poem about a beehive, which charted the beneficial unintended consequences of selfish behaviour (burglars make work for locksmiths), into a theory of morality that reduced moral behaviour to a desire for social approbation and an aversion to social embarrassment (the moral virtues are flattery begot on pride). Mandeville's conclusion that private vices created public benefits signals an issue that clearly came to fascinate Smith: what happens when intentions and outcomes do not obviously cohere?

These ideas are interesting because they provide us with the initial jumping-off point of the *Moral Sentiments*. Rousseau and Mandeville had focused on how a set of shared beliefs and institutions could emerge from social interaction: for Rousseau, the result was a moral abomination and a deeply corrupted society; for Mandeville, the result was the cynical realization of the unintended generation of wealth and power. Smith had before him a mode of explanation that promised to allow a scientific, evolutionary, and naturalistic account of how human moral practice emerged as an unintended consequence of social life, but he also had before him two quite different conclusions about whether this was necessarily a good thing.

It is clear that Smith had been thinking about the relationship between self-regarding and other-regarding behaviour for quite some time. His teacher, Francis Hutcheson, devoted considerable energy to attacking Mandeville's theory and developed his own account of a unique mental faculty, a moral sense, that discerned moral truth in the same way that sight and hearing discern external stimuli. Hutcheson believed that the characteristic principle of our moral sense was benevolence, and so Mandeville's account of the generation of morality was back to front. Hutcheson was contributing to a debate within a particular strain of British moral philosophy. This strain held that morality was best understood as an emotional experience rather than a rational experience. Thinkers such as Lord Shaftesbury who stressed benevolence and self-command might have differed greatly from those like Thomas Hobbes (1588–1679) who stressed passion and self-interest, but they all operated on the assumption that it was feelings, passions, and emotions that moved human beings. The challenge for these moralists was to come up with a way to reconcile the fact that individuals were moved by feelings with the fact that morality was outward looking. Hutcheson's attempt at this involved positing a unique mental faculty or sense that was part of human nature. Joseph Butler (1692–1752), on the other hand, sought to distance human morality from self-interest through a reflective process of conscience. They were all involved in seeking an answer to the same basic challenge: how can morality be explained by the sentiments without reducing it to whatever makes us feel good? It was this debate that Smith stepped into when he published *The Theory of Moral Sentiments* in 1759.

3

Morality and Sympathy

Smith's moral philosophy is to be found in his *The Theory of Moral Sentiments*, published in 1759. The *Moral Sentiments* is a book-length development of ideas that Smith had worked on during his time as a student at Glasgow and Oxford, as a freelance lecturer in Edinburgh, and as a Professor at Glasgow. It went through six editions in his lifetime: the second (1761) and sixth (1790) of which show substantial revisions, indicating that Smith continued to work on the ideas throughout his life.[1]

As we saw in the previous chapter, Smith developed a careful philosophical methodology that was intended to explain as much as possible, in as clear a fashion as possible, and resting on as much evidence as possible. In the 1790 edition of the *Moral Sentiments*, he expanded Part VII, which assessed the existing theories of moral philosophy from the ancient and modern world. This represents the application of the account of progress in science we have just discussed to the history of moral philosophy. The aim of this section was to demonstrate that though all of the past schools of philosophy contained some elements of the truth, they failed in some vital respect to account for the actual experience of moral judgement.

Smith was dissatisfied by the existing state of moral philosophy for one overwhelming reason: he did not believe that any of the theories of ancient or modern philosophy had developed an accurate model of what it is to experience moral judgement. He set himself the task of providing an accurate theory of the everyday experience of moral thinking. What results is one of the most subtle works of moral psychology in all of philosophy. Smith's moral thought is not primarily intended to reveal the nature of the virtues, nor is it meant to identify right and wrong in a didactic manner. Instead it is intended to provide an account of how human beings come to be moral creatures. Smith's evidence is largely grounded in examples from everyday life that allow readers to follow through his points in terms close to their own experience. The vivacity of Smith's examples means that most, if not all, of them remain easily accessible to contemporary readers, who are instantly familiar with the sort of thoughts and feelings being described from their own lives.

Once again, it was David Hume who had set the agenda for this project. Hume had argued that when it came to moral philosophy, there was a distinction between those philosophers who were anatomists and those who were painters.[2] His point was that the exercise of dissecting and understanding moral judgement was different from that of promoting moral behaviour. Hume worried that the desire to paint a moral picture would lead to philosophers treating humans as they ought to be rather than as they are. Moreover, he thought that successful moral painting depended on accurate anatomical knowledge. Philosophers need to understand how humans think and feel before they can produce an effective account of what we should expect from them.

Smith's worry about the existing schools of moral philosophy was that they sacrificed accuracy of anatomical description for purity of principle. The easiest way to understand this is to look at Part VII, where the ancient schools – Platonist, Stoic, Epicurean – and the potential candidates for a moral principle identified by modern philosophers – self-interest, reason, utility – are discussed in turn, and in each case Smith shows how they fail to account for some basic element of ordinary moral experience, or that they issue in counterintuitive outcomes when applied to everyday examples. But his response to this is not to reject them all outright. Instead he believes that they all 'border' on the truth. Each of them has identified one element of our moral experience, but has failed because it has sought to make that element, and that element alone, definitive of moral philosophy. This is a fundamental critique of the discipline of philosophy. Philosophers have been working with a 'partial and imperfect view of nature',[3] leading them to develop partial accounts of moral experience. This is particularly important in Smith's view because, as he observes: 'Gross sophistry has scarce ever had any influence upon the opinions of mankind, except in matters of philosophy and speculation; and in these it has frequently had the greatest.'[4]

Smith seems to have been worried that the act of philosophy itself, the practice of retired and concentrated thought, distanced philosophers from the real world and led them to mistake their abstractions for reality. In the case of moral philosophers, this was combined with a tendency to sanctimony, such that the world became full of 'whining and melancholy moralists',[5] whose 'splenetic'[6] tendency was to deprecate the pleasures of ordinary life. Interestingly, this seems to have been Smith's attitude to the school of ancient philosophy that critics have often pointed out as the greatest influence on his thought: the Stoics. Smith was, as we will see, interested in the idea of self-command and the management of the emotions, but he clearly regarded Stoic withdrawal and emotional suppression to be a deeply unnatural school of moral philosophy. Smith observes that such 'wrong systems'[7] have the potential to mislead us, to lead us to ignore ordinary, he would say natural, emotional responses. Bad philosophy leads to unnatural behaviour that misdirects the moral sentiments. In their rush to understand the world, many philosophers seek to bend reality to fit their ideas.

Smith's commitment to empirical evidence stresses that a system of knowledge must be able to account for all of the observable features of the relevant phenomenon. The central aim of his book, then, is to provide an accurate moral psychology: a systematic theory that accounts for how actual agents make decisions in concrete, everyday situations. His system will attempt to do this not by creating a novel single principle that is able to replace the views of past schools, but rather by developing a system that is able to reconcile all of the different aspects of moral experience, including those of past schools, in one coherent whole.

We see a clear example of this at the very start of the book. Smith begins with a stark statement: 'How selfish soever man may be supposed, there are evidently some principles in his nature, which interest him in the fortune of others, and render their happiness necessary to him, though he derives nothing from it except the pleasure of seeing it.'[8] Simple observation of how people actually behave and think about morality demonstrates that humans are sometimes benevolent and sometimes self-interested, and similarly that on some occasions they regard benevolent actions as the correct thing to do and on others they regard self-interested behaviour as the right thing to do. Philosophical systems like those of Bernard Mandeville or Thomas Hobbes, who reduced all human motives to self-regarding behaviour or vanity, and also those like Smith's teacher Francis Hutcheson, who criticized Mandeville and regarded benevolence as the core of morality, are both wrong.[9] Systems that attempt to reduce morality to either of these principles will inevitably issue in counterintuitive outcomes when the appropriate decision principle lies in the other. Mandeville's or Hobbes's theory cannot provide a satisfactory explanation for disinterested pleasure in the happiness of others, and Hutcheson's cannot provide a satisfactory account of the limits of our benevolence.

Smith's objections to the dominant principles of the other schools can broadly be summarized as follows. Morality cannot be reduced to reason because it is a felt experience which moves us to action whereas reason is inert and calculative, and so the rules of morality are not derived from reason, but generalized from the repeated experience of sentimental interactions. The idea of an innate moral sense is an unnecessary complication that is not borne out by the evidence. Utility has a role to play as a philosopher's explanation after the fact, but it cannot account for the thought process of decision making because its focus on outcomes means that it cannot properly account for non-consequentialist elements of moral experience such as deservingness and motivation. Stoicism is excessively rigorous and leads to an inhuman disregard for those close to us; whereas Epicureanism cannot account for the observation of a sense of duty that leads us to accept discomfort.

Of the modern accounts of moral philosophy, Smith is most dismissive of attempts to reduce moral experience to reason. An influential school of thinkers in the generation before him conceived moral philosophy as the rational exploration of an objective moral order that existed in the world and which could, through philosophy, be reliably identified and used an authoritative guide to how we ought to act. In Smith's view, this is a complete misapprehension of the nature of moral experience: morality is a felt experience; it is the product of human emotions and passions. Reason, to the extent that it has any role to play, is subordinate to the emotional experience. Moreover, accurate moral judgement is not really the preserve of philosophers at all. It is something that emerges from feeling rather than argument and so arises from actual judgements in the real world rather than isolated reasoning. It is this that leads Smith to the heart of his own account of morality. His commitment to the scientific method leads him to reject excessive abstraction in philosophical argument. The subject matter of moral philosophy is instead to be the 'maxims of common life'.[10]

Sympathy

Smith finds the 'hidden chains' that account for morality in the notions of moral sentiment and sympathy. It is important to understand that his moral sentiments are not a moral sense like that proposed by Hutcheson: a unique cognitive capacity that is innate to all humans and allows us to identify the right thing to do. Instead his is an attempt to give an account of the nature of moral experience through human emotions combined with a human propensity for fellow-feeling. The moral sentiments are those emotions that prompt our behaviour towards others: we feel that something is the right thing to do.

It is also important to understand that Smith is not saying that there is a single moral sentiment. Instead there are a variety of ordinary emotions that play a role in our interaction with others (the moral sphere). On a basic level, these include both benevolence and self-interest, but more than that they also include a series of deeply ingrained universal human responses to the external world, including pity and grief as well as joy and admiration. Smith's project in the rest of the book is to explain how these emotions are experienced and how they come to form the basis of a set of beliefs about how we ought to behave. Some of these are crude and instantaneous, like when we recoil our arm when we see another about to be hit there, or when we feel uneasy at the sight of the sores of a beggar. Smith regards these familiar feelings as evidence for a deeper truth about human beings. Our emotions are capable of being moved by what we see and how that affects our imagination. The arm about to be hit is not our own, nor are the sores, but they have an emotional impact on us nonetheless.

Smith's model here is that of a spectator or audience member at a theatre: an observer who is affected by what he sees, is moved by it, and thus has his attitude changed. The image of the spectator most likely came to Smith from his schoolboy reading of Addison and Steele's *Spectator* and their interest in manners and morality. In order to understand how the moral sentiments operate, Smith examines how different types of feeling can be entered into by an observer. He takes care to outline different moral sentiments and the different degrees to which they affect us. His point here is to make the case that our sentimental experience is not a thoughtless contagion. Hume had developed a concept of sympathy in his writing that operated like a sort of unconscious emotional transfer, where a group of people are subject to an emotional contagion like panic or hysteria without any conscious thought. Smith accepted that this was, indeed, the case: moods can travel through groups. But he believed that there was another, more significant, form of emotional transference and that this was related to the fact that there are certain emotions that require unpacking.

For Smith, this was illustrated by the fact that we are often unable, or unwilling, to sympathize with others until we are aware of the reasons behind their emotional display. In one sense, we are made curious by seeing a person expressing a strong emotion, but that emotion is not directly transferred to us by osmosis. Instead we try to find out what has caused the emotional display, and only then are we able to 'enter into' the feeling. Strong emotions in others, like anger and love, make us uneasy and anxious to know the cause before we are willing to go along with the feeling. Similarly, we find it more difficult to enter into strong passions that arise from the body than we do from those that arise from the imagination. This is because our response to such stimuli is emotional rather than physiological: we imagine the pain of the sufferer, but we do not physically feel it. Smith believes that fact supports his view that it is the situation and the imagination that are significant rather than a direct transfer of physical feeling. This also accounts for the human propensity to attempt to hide physical discomfort from others. We know that other people are less able to sympathize with physical pain and so we downplay its significance.

Smith continues the discussion of injury and points out that one of the ways we can be certain that it is spectating rather than contagion that is behind sympathetic experiences is that fact that we are usually more affected by witnessing an external injury than an internal injury. Our imagination is presented with an image of blood and gore that moves our sentiments as a tangible marker of pain; we find it easier to enter into this person's situation than we do to imagine an internal disease. This visual element of Smith's argument is revealing because it suggests that humans find it easier to enter some emotions rather than others. Smith points out that in most cases our sympathy with sorrow is weaker than our sympathy with joy; the experience of sympathizing with sorrow is unsettling while that of sympathizing with joy is pleasant. This becomes significant for Smith because it helps to explain some universally observable human affects: the fact that we are attracted to joyful and happy situations and uncomfortable in sorrowful situations. The result is that people hide their sorrow and share their joy, because they know from their own experience that joy is more readily entered into that sorrow. As we will see below, Smith thinks that this tendency is what lies behind the human propensity to admire the rich and shun the poor.

There are, of course, limits to this sympathy for Smith. One such is the experience of love. Love is a strong emotion that has a particular object and Smith argues that we find it difficult to enter into the degree of passion and attachment of another person for their particular paramour. People in love are, then, hard to fully sympathize with and as a result can appear ridiculous and are bad company for a third, disinterested party. Another of Smith's illustrations of this is not romantic love, but rather our professions or studies. When we meet people who share our obsession, we indulge in our shared love, but when we are in the company of someone outside our profession, we easily become a bore if we drone on about our passion. Fortunately, most people are aware of the fact that others don't share our enthusiasms and are able to curb their enthusiasm.

Smith's stress on the act of spectatorship demonstrates that his interest is in the social impact of our passions. In his account, the experience of emotions brought about when we observe other people explains the origin of human sociability. We are moved by the fate of others; this is simply an observable fact about humanity. As a result, it is not something that can be ignored by moral philosophy. There is, then, a sort of two-level emotional experience when we enter into the situation of others: there is the imagined emotion generated within us, but there is also a sense of pleasure when we recognize that we have succeeded in entering into the situation of another person and of matching their emotion. We gain pleasure from fellow-feeling.

Sympathy is the mechanism by which we are able to undertake this process of understanding the emotional experience of others. What matters is not the display of emotion, but rather the understanding of the situation that has brought that emotion about. For Smith, the only way we can possibly do this is through an act of the imagination. He develops a particular notion of sympathy that he believes grounds moral experience in our imagination. Moral experience is reflective and imaginative rather than rational and calculative. We need to be clear what Smith means by sympathy. He does not mean what we today mean when we say that we sympathize with people. Smith's sympathy is not pity or benevolence: we should not let the opening line of the book mislead us into thinking that he is rejecting self-interest in favour of benevolence. Sympathy here is not the opposite of selfishness. Instead Smith has in mind a complex imaginative process where we are able to place ourselves in the position of another and come to understand how they are feeling. His notion of sympathy is not as narrow as the present usage which evokes pity or commiseration. It refers to empathetic 'fellow-feeling' with 'any passion whatever'.[11] By focusing on this empathetic propensity, Smith is able to develop a model of how it is that people come to develop normative beliefs about moral notions such as good and evil. The point that he wanted to make was that the generation of a set of shared common beliefs about ethics was possible without an (actively) supernatural apparatus and without recourse to a single overarching principle. Our capacity to imagine what other people are experiencing and for that to guide our reaction to them is the central explanatory principle of Smith's *Moral Sentiments*.

Sociability

As we noted above, Smith begins from the observation that morality cannot be reduced simply to selfishness or benevolence. Human moral experience is richer than many of his predecessors' theories would allow. While self-interest and benevolence form two of the passions that can motivate human activity, they are not sufficient to explain moral judgement. Human beings, no matter how hardened a 'ruffian',[12] are interested in their peers. They are also by no means driven by so extensive an interest in others as to render universal benevolence a satisfactory description of the core principle of morality.

Smith believes that humanity is naturally sociable and that this sociability is a fact that colours how we operate on an emotional and moral level: 'Nature, when she formed man for society, endowed him with an original desire to please, and an original aversion to offend his brethren. She taught him to feel pleasure in their favourable, and pain in their unfavourable regard.'[13] Social life is not simply the arena within which morality plays out, it is also responsible for generating morality itself. Human beings experience life as members of a group, and it is their interaction with their fellows that is the basis of Smith's account of the generation of morality. Humans are acutely aware that they are the subject of the attention of their peers; they are also universally in possession of an emotional need for approval. These two features come together to provide a theory of socialization that underwrites Smith's book. We adapt our behaviour in an attempt to gain the approval (approbation in Smith's terminology) of our peers because we gain pleasure from the concurrence of our feelings with those of others. This occurs at the same time as we ourselves judge our fellows and both parties enjoy the pleasure of 'mutual sympathy'.[14] Smith believes that this facet of the human mind explains why we feel relief in close emotional relationships and find social interaction therapeutic.

Smith's account of morality in terms of feelings is combined with his belief in the central role of imagination in human moral experience. Morality is the product of an imaginative process because, if we cannot feel what others feel, the only path to understanding we have is through observation and imagination. Morality is a felt experience, but our judgement of others is conducted through imagined experience of their situations. We are able to 'enter into' the situation of others, and to bring their case home to ourselves through our imagination. Smith regarded it as obvious that the data that we draw upon to do this is our own experience. As he puts it, 'I judge your eyes by my eyes'[15] because I have no other way of doing so. I cannot feel what you are feeling in precise detail, but I can put my knowledge of my own feelings to use to imagine your emotions. Yet while I draw on my own experience to inform my imagination, I am not imagining that it is me in the situation of another. Instead I imagine how I would feel were I that other person, with all of his feelings and commitments. I may never have had a child, but I can imagine the situation of a person who is grieving for one, and empathize with her loss.

The process of judgement that Smith has in mind is one that checks the appropriateness of behaviour against our imagination's model of how we would react in similar circumstances. If the behaviour observed fits with that which we imagine ourselves as experiencing in a like scenario, then we approve of it because it is how we would feel were we the person concerned. Moral judgement is judgement of the appropriateness of behaviour undertaken through an imaginative process allowing us to step into the situation of others. Smith stresses that there is a reflective element in this process. He does not regard sympathy as a purely thoughtless imitation; it requires reflection and even at times effort. While we can recognize and are attracted by smiling faces, it is only once we have become aware of the situation that has brought about the smile that we are able to 'enter into' the happiness of the person smiling and engage in the sympathetic process of judgement that generates approval. In this sense, the completeness of our sympathy is restricted by the level of our knowledge of the situation.

One example that Smith has of this is that of us coming across an angry person. Anger is an unsettling and 'unsocial' emotion. As such we should be repelled by displays of anger. However, if we imaginatively enter into the situation of the person, if we understand the source of their anger, we can come to feel a measure of it on their behalf and to approve of their response. The anger of the spectator, though, will never be as strong as that of the person principally concerned.

Smith's sympathy is thus capable of allowing us to enter into the position of people very different from ourselves. It is even capable of allowing us to sympathize with the dead. Obviously, the dead cannot feel, but we are capable of imagining what death might be like, the absence of feeling, removal from one's loved ones, and loss of the pleasures of life. We are thus able to conceive that this situation is undesirable and to approve of the grief felt by those who have lost someone close to them and to pity the unfortunate situation of the deceased. Continuing with the theme of bereavement, Smith gives the example of a man who approaches us weeping. Initially, we might be disturbed by this emotional display, but our approbation is forthcoming when we learn that he has just had news of his father's death.[16] We are able to conduct an imaginative process that allows us to suppose how we would feel were we him, and to pass judgement on the propriety of his reaction accordingly. Similarly, if a man approaches us weeping uncontrollably and we learn that the cause is some trivial matter such as that he has just lost a game of golf, we can undertake the sympathetic process, conclude that his behaviour is not in line with our assessment of an appropriate response, and so be disposed towards disapprobation. Judgement through imagination is the essence of moral experience.

Smith uses these examples to make two points that are vital to his understanding of moral experience. First, my ability to imagine how another person should feel in any given circumstances does not depend on the person in question actually feeling that way. To illustrate the point, Smith describes how we feel pity for the situation of a person who has lost their mind, even though that person feels no such distress. Second, it is precisely because we are assessing how we imagine someone ought to feel in a given situation that we are inclined to judge whether that person's behaviour matches our imaginative assessment. Sympathy is a judgemental process. This means that our interest in others is driven not by benevolence or pity, but by the approval or disapproval of the appropriateness of their responses in their particular circumstances.

Propriety

The extent to which we approve of another person's behaviour depends on the extent to which we are capable of reaching mutual sympathy with them: of matching our imagined feeling to their display of emotion. To say that we completely approve of another person's behaviour is to say that we are in complete sympathy with them and would do the same were we them. When we assess other people, we assess the appropriateness of their behaviour to the context in which it takes place.

The experience of reflective moral judgement demands that we attempt to exercise spectatorship on the situation of others. As attentive spectators, we attempt to assess as much of the information available to us about the circumstances of the person observed. It is only after we have done this that we are able to generate a lively picture in our mind of the complete situation. Smith's argument is not, to repeat the point we made earlier, that we imagine ourselves in the shoes of another, but the stronger claim that I imagine myself to be that other. The imaginative process invoked is intended to allow us access to how that person is experiencing their situation. The problem here is obviously that this remains an imaginative process. We never fully enter into the person of those whom we observe. Instead we can only ever, for epistemic reasons, develop a partial sympathy. We can imagine how it would feel to lose a close relative, but we 'know' that we have not. As a result, the emotions generated are of a lower 'pitch'[17] of intensity.

Smith then explains how the observed person knows this to be the case, from their own moral experience, and so restricts their outward display of emotion accordingly. They lower the pitch of their feelings to that which experience tells them will be acceptable to the spectators. This adjustment in our display of emotion is not effected with the intention of securing some material benefit: it is directed solely at gaining the approval of our fellows. We want other people to approve of our behaviour.

Smith regards this moderation process as one of the great causes of tranquillity of mind. He is aware that we are able to generate more perfect sympathy with those who are close to us, and it is in the presence and approbation of friends and family that we are able to indulge our strongest feelings and expect the greatest understanding. But we are also subject to the judgement of more distant spectators who are not partial enough to indulge our strongest feelings, and who cannot enter into our passionate experience as fully as those who are familiar with us. Such figures may enter into our experience of serious misfortunes, like the death of a loved one, but they are less willing to indulge our disappointment at matters of smaller account. This fact about humans leads Smith to observe that society and conversation have a therapeutic effect. Moreover, the society of strangers with their weaker degree of sympathy, and our subsequent desire to flatten our emotions, suggests that mental tranquillity can be restored by associating with those who are less willing to indulge our feelings.[18]

This marks the first appearance of Smith's idea of an impartial spectator. In this context, the spectator is an actual individual, one who is disinterested in the situation, but who observes and passes judgement. The weeping golfer is subject to disapprobation because his display of emotion is judged to be inappropriate by an impartial spectator. The golfer, keen to secure the approval and sympathy of his peers, realizes this and alters his behaviour. This is an important observation for Smith because it leads him to the idea that the desire to secure the approval of strangers helps us to compose ourselves. It is company, particularly the company of strangers, that calms our minds. Our friends and family indulge and condole us, but strangers force us to master our feelings. The desire to be approved of by people who have no emotional connection to us provides the playing field on which morality develops.

Society, as Smith famously puts it, is a 'mirror'[19] in which we see ourselves reflected back in the reactions of others. We want to be approved of by others, so we seek to match our emotional displays to the level we imagine that a spectator would be willing to go along with. We are 'anxious' for approbation of our appearance, actions, and emotions. What this leads Smith to is the observation that human social interaction is largely a matter of exercising control of our passions in order to acquire the approval of others. In the hands of Mandeville and Rousseau, this observation was considered problematic. This was because they felt that it was little more than a matter of conforming with social norms and masking one's true feelings. Smith's point is rather that this is simply how humans interact when it comes to displays of emotion. It is not a question of hypocrisy, or of pride, it simply is what it is.

Thus morality becomes synonymous with self-command over the passions that drive our actions. It is our restriction of our emotions within the bounds of what we regard as socially acceptable that accounts for the phenomenon of moral experience. Society is the 'great school of self-command'.[20] It is control of our emotions in line with assessments of appropriate behaviour rather than emotional incontinence that characterizes the operation of sympathy. 'Mediocrity' of 'pitch'[21] in emotional display coalesces into a set of habituated standards or expected forms of behaviour that are the basis of moral rules – what Smith calls propriety. Situational propriety differs in accordance with the circumstances of the individuals involved. For instance, Smith describes how we come to form different expectations of individuals engaged in different professions. To use an example, though not one of Smith's, we would be shocked by and disapprove of a laughing funeral director, but not a laughing barman. Appropriateness of conduct is assessed in line with the socially generated norms applied to a given situation, and these norms have their origin in the experience of passing moral judgement in specific cases.

How this applies to different sentiments is fascinating. Smith argues that humans have both social and unsocial passions and that we are aware that it is easier for a spectator to enter into the social passions. As a result, we are more anxious to exercise control over our unsocial passions. Anger, grief, and envy are subject to a greater degree of control than contentment, happiness, and admiration. But this does not mean that the social passions are allowed unlimited play by Smith. Excessive joy gives those observing it 'the spleen'[22] just as excessive displays of grief are 'disgusting'.[23] The point is that it is the appropriateness of the emotion that is being assessed. The assessment takes place in line with our learned experience of appropriate behaviour. In other words, the rules of appropriate behaviour have emerged from past experience of everyday life.

General Rules

Contrary to the moral rationalists, Smith believed that our moral rules are generalizations from our experience of previous assessments of propriety. They are not deduced from some single master principle of philosophy. This is perfectly in line with the inductive theory of knowledge outlined in the previous chapter, but it also means that Smith's account remains naturalistic. He does not suppose that such rules are 'rational' or universally applicable, or unchanging. Instead they represent rules of thumb generated from our own past experience and our socialization with a group whose traditions and customs carry with them a sort of body of knowledge of past moral experiences. Moral rules are themselves the product of cumulative acts of moral judgement and their authority as such comes from this. Smith also points out that we can form these rules for ourselves without realizing that we have done so. There is a species of moral habit that guides our judgements, and a shared set of moral habits becomes the shared traditional morality of a people.

Smith then sets out an account of the assessment of praise (merit) and blame (demerit) based on our experience of the process of judging and being judged in turn by our peers. The urge to judge explains the generation of social phenomena of punishment and reward. We see punishment as the proper reaction to behaviour that generates strong disapproval, and reward as the proper reaction to that which generates approval. Punishment is the result of 'sympathetic indignation'[24] where we enter into the indignation of the sufferer and pass judgement on the person who inflicted suffering. Our assessment must, however, be made with the conviction that the person concerned is responsible. The intervention of fortune affects our judgement of the appropriateness of a punishment in the sense that we add to our imaginative assessment a consideration of how responsible the individual is for a given set of outcomes. This in itself is also subject to a fine-grained form of judgement. The distinctions between accidents, negligence, and gross negligence are recognizable and relevant considerations in a judgement of merit and demerit.

Repeated experience of a particular set of experiences leads us to become 'used' to them, in the same way repeated experience of the sight of blood inures a surgeon to the shock.[25] Our life experiences are the source of the content of our expectations about appropriate behaviour and our moral rules are constructed from social interaction. This leads Smith to observe that such rules emerge in a very similar way to other socially generated expectations. In particular, he is interested in the similarities between fashion and custom and morality (a point we will return to in the next chapter). In a sense, this was nothing new as both Hutcheson and Hume in their own ways had linked their account of ideas of beauty to their account of ideas of morality. But Smith is aware that his account seems to leave open the possibility that morality is little more than mere social convention.

In Part V of the *Moral Sentiments*, he takes great care in showing how he thinks the phenomena are distinct. The distinction between fashion and custom, on the one hand, and the 'natural principles of right and wrong',[26] on the other, is a tricky one to plot. Smith accepts that when custom and fashion coincide with the natural principles, they support and confirm them. But what happens when they do not? Smith explores this possibility through the idea of diversity and social change.[27] It is an empirical fact for him that different societies have their own beliefs about right and wrong and, moreover, that the same society's ideas about right and wrong can change over time. This might be thought to present a difficulty for the moral philosopher intent on finding universal moral principles. The key for Smith lies in the notion of a natural sense of right and wrong. He believed in a universal human nature, and this led him to the view that all humans have the same basic emotional set-up. As a result, if we put the same human animal in the same circumstances, the same response will be forthcoming unless philosophical beliefs or socialization gets in the way.

Custom

Smith goes on to explain how such inter-subjective standards come to form the basis of custom and shape the 'general style of character and behaviour'[28] of a social group. To achieve this, he draws on a further aspect of the universal human nature: habit. Habits are acquired through practice, yielding a constant conjunction in the mind. This conjunction is strengthened, growing 'more and more rivetted and confirmed',[29] through repetition. Habits, drawn from experience, act as a non-deliberative guide to our behaviour; they allow us to form expectations around which we are able to order our actions. Sociable individuals come to form unwritten or non-deliberatively generated conventions of behaviour which develop into customary modes of behaviour as they are repeated. Smith illustrates this process in his discussion of aesthetics in *The Theory of Moral Sentiments*. He begins from the basis of the 'habitual arrangement of our ideas' and proceeds to note that our notions of 'taste' are in large part formed by the influence of custom and habit.[30]

Discussing the aesthetics of Alexander Pope, Smith argues his view that '[t]he whole charm' of our notions of taste 'would thus seem to arise from its falling in with habits which custom had

impressed upon the imagination'.[31] Smith, however, believed that
this was not sufficient. For if all of our judgements of beauty were
made with reference to past habits, then no innovation would be
possible. On the contrary, Smith believed that humans were highly
attracted to new phenomena and that these, far from depending
solely on fitting in with established tastes, drew their beauty from
their utility. As he puts it: 'The utility of any form, its fitness for the
useful purposes for which it was intended, evidently recommends
it, and renders it agreeable to us, independent of custom.'[32]

As we become familiar with an innovation whose utility is
apparent to us, we absorb it into our everyday practice. 'Custom
has rendered it habitual'[33] to us and we draw on our experience of
it habitually and non-deliberatively rather than through constant
reference to its utility. Custom shapes our behaviour and our
expectations of the behaviour of others. Ideas and practices become
general by custom, that is to say, constant repetition leads to
conventional expectations and relations developing amongst a
people. Thus generalized moral principles are drawn from the
repetition of actual, individual, moral judgements in everyday life:
the judgement is 'antecedent' to the rule.[34]

Smith writes: 'The different situations of different ages and
countries are apt ... to give different characters to the generality
of those who live in them.'[35] The moral conventions that exist in
a society are the result of a habituated balance of sentiments with
circumstances within the specific context of that society. Thus, for
Smith, a savage becomes inured to hardship and his behaviour
becomes shaped by his circumstances. As he puts it: 'His circumstances not only habituate him to every sort of distress, but teach
him to give way to none of the passions which that distress is apt to
excite.'[36] The precariousness of the savage's situation leads him to
stifle his humanity, to deaden his emotional responses, in order to
survive and to secure subsistence. So experience teaches a savage
the most profitable way to act. He is socialized by the example of
others who have similarly learned from experience those practices
necessary for survival. This is not to say that a savage lacks
particular emotional elements of human nature. Smith's point is
rather that circumstances can be such that we 'smother' or 'conceal'
elements of our nature in order to secure survival.[37]

Adaptation to external circumstances accounts for much of the
diversity to be found among peoples. But the circumstances in which
individuals find themselves are not solely physical or economic in
their nature. They are also moral. Humanity exists, as we have seen,

in a social context, and experiences those conventions of behaviour that have been formed by its predecessors and contemporaries. Individuals become socialized into a culture and habitually accept these conventions, taking on the general 'character' of their nation.[38] This process, however, does not imply either an explicit agreement with, or endorsement of, these practices by each individual. We are dealing with habitual acceptance of circumstances; thus the habits of others become part of the circumstances to which we become habituated as we are socialized. We need not have any conscious or deliberative notion of the utility of these practices, but our propensity to form habits and our desire for social acceptance lead us to accept them without any great thought.

Customary behaviour, insofar as it shapes part of the circumstances in which we find ourselves, becomes hard to change. Individuals continue to act in a habitual fashion even after the circumstances from which that habit arose have changed. There is a problem here. A custom is a habituated practice drawn from everyday experience and shared by a group of individuals in a certain set of circumstances. But the strength exerted by habit and custom on the human character, compounded by long practice, socialization, and emotional attachment, is such that even after those circumstances shift the behaviour pattern lingers on. How, then, does an individual accustomed to a savage state manage to 'progress' to civilization?

Smith's discussion of the Graeco-Roman practice of infanticide will allow us to examine his theory of moral change and how it relates to the generation of wealth. Smith considers it a matter of progress that infanticide is no longer widespread. He regards the practice as a feature of savage societies that has been abandoned in 'civilized and thriving nations'.[39] The explanation that he provides for the origin of infanticide is grounded in utility. It is a response to population growth in a situation of severely limited physical resources. This form of behaviour, which Smith believes is contrary to human nature and feeling, arose in times of 'the most savage barbarity'[40] and became habitually accepted. Individuals put aside their horror in reaction to their circumstances, and the repetition of this practice rendered it a custom which became accepted by the people as a whole. Custom, then, legitimized a 'bad' practice; indeed the continuation of infanticide leads Smith to note that custom may be able to authorize almost any 'gross' practice.[41] In his view, such behaviour is more understandable in situations of extreme indigence where the survival of the parent is also at stake. However, when the circumstances of subsistence change, the practice continues as it has become ingrained. Smith argues:

> In the latter ages of Greece, however, the same thing was permitted from views of remote interest or convenience, which could by no means excuse it. Uninterrupted custom had by this time so thoroughly authorized the practice, that not only the loose maxims of the world tolerated this barbarous prerogative, but even the doctrine of philosophers, which ought to have been more just and accurate, was led away by the established custom.[42]

What Smith wishes to highlight here is that even in what are considered civilized nations it is possible to identify anomalous practices that stand against the general character of behaviour. He illustrates this by noting that his contemporaries in Europe often criticize the Chinese practice of female foot binding as barbaric, yet just a century before it was considered normal European practice for women to wear binding corsets to alter their body shapes.[43]

Smith recognizes that a society whose general character is marked by customs such as infanticide cannot long survive, arguing that no society can 'subsist'[44] in widespread customary practices that go against the tenor of human sentiment and feeling. However, he does recognize that an anomaly such as infanticide can survive as a 'particular usage'.[45] This is because it is possible for custom to pervert our view of propriety away from our natural emotions in a limited field. As he puts it: '[T]he sentiments of moral approbation and disapprobation, are founded on the strongest and most vigorous passions of human nature; and though they may be somewhat warpt, cannot be entirely perverted.'[46]

Let us now apply this model of moral change to the 'particular usage' of infanticide. How did this custom pass out of use? How did people free themselves from socialized acceptance of the custom of infanticide? Smith's theory suggests that people gradually became aware of the incongruity of infanticide with human nature and feeling, they came to be repelled by it, and as their material condition became more secure, they rejected it as a practice to deal with issues of population. Such a process relies, at least on some level, on a deliberative calculation – a weighing up of the pros and cons of the practice – which balances sentiment with circumstance. What is significant for Smith's theory, though, is that such deliberative judgements would occur in relation to particular cases of infanticide. They do not refer to a process of the rational examination of the practice as a social phenomenon, but rather to a feeling of repulsion leading to a belief that the practice is unacceptable. Moral philosophers are of little importance in this account of moral change; in fact, as Smith shows, their rationalization of the practice is a barrier to change. Instead his model deploys an individualistic micro-level explanation to account for the macro-level change in social practices. Moral rules are developed as the unintended consequence of our everyday moral judgement of the behaviour of our peers.

As subsistence becomes more secure, we move away from the immediacy of savage times and are free to give wider rein to the sympathetic and emotional aspects of human nature. As Smith notes: 'Hardiness is the character most suitable to the circumstances of a savage; sensibility to those of one who lives in a very civilized society.'[47] With wealth comes the ease to allow our feelings a greater role in our judgement of action. As Smith puts it: 'A polished people being accustomed to give way, in some measure, to the movements of nature, become frank, open and sincere. Barbarians, on the contrary, being obliged to smother and conceal the appearance of every passion, necessarily acquire the habits of falsehood and dissimulation.'[48] Or as he notes in another passage: 'A humane and polished people, who have more sensibility to the passions of others, can more readily enter into an animated and passionate behaviour.'[49]

Individual actors make deliberative decisions to cease committing infanticide based on their examination of their changed economic position and the incongruity of the practice with the universal human emotional attachment to children. Infanticide becomes both economically unnecessary and emotionally unacceptable as people move towards secure subsistence. The specific individuals who cease to practise this custom then internalize this stance and begin to form the opinion that infanticide is neither prudent nor fitting with propriety. This internalization through conscience leads these individuals to judge the behaviour of others within the group as unacceptable when they practise infanticide. They express 'sympathetic indignation' and make actual judgements of the behaviour of those who continue to follow the old custom regarding the 'particular usage' of infanticide.

It is important to note that the motivating factor in the assessment here is not utility but rather emotion and the desire for the approbation of our fellows. The internalization of the new standard of propriety as an aspect of individual conscience results in a situation where individuals limit their actions before the deed to avoid disapprobation. Over a period of time, the practice gradually falls from use, comes to be considered as improper and anach-ronistic, and there is a gradual shift in the conventional forms of behaviour within the group. The new convention becomes habitually accepted, generalized, and forms the basis of individual emotional assessments of proper behaviour. Individuals become socialized to accept the new standard of propriety and there is a gradual change in moral attitudes. The whole model is marked by the gradual and individualistic nature of its account of changes in moral attitudes. It also provides an account of the difference in attitudes held by succeeding generations. Though habit and custom deepen the acceptance of general behaviour, they also allow for subtle shifts over time in the case of 'particular usages'. Thus when one generation cease a practice from fear of the disapprobation of their fellows, the next will internalize this as the accepted standard of decent behaviour and be repulsed by their ancestors' behaviour. As Smith notes: '[W]e are all apt to think well and commend the customs of the times we live in and to prefer them to all others.'[50]

The Impartial Spectator

However, Smith is not yet satisfied that he has captured all of the dimensions of moral reflection.[51] His next step involves examining the internalization of the process of spectatorship. To achieve this he extends the idea of *an* impartial spectator into that of *the* impartial spectator. The idea is that we internalize the process of judgement that provides us with an impartial assessment of others and apply it to our own behaviour. I am able to reflect on my behaviour while stripping out my own partiality. I imagine how my behaviour would appear to an impartial onlooker and thus am able, through my socially acquired knowledge, to generate expectations of likely reactions. I become a spectator of my own conduct.

> When I endeavour to examine my own conduct, when I endeavour to pass sentence upon it, and either to approve or condemn it, it is evident that, in all such cases, I divide myself, as it were, into two persons; and that I, the examiner and judge, represent a different character from that other I, the person whose conduct is examined into and judged of.[52]

This process of psychologically splitting into two persons and dispassionately examining our own conduct becomes habitual to us as we learn about the reactions of others. It is to 'see ourselves as others see us'.[53] We internalize a notion of propriety from the reactions of our peers and are then able to draw on it imaginatively before we act. We are thus able to restrict our behaviour to avoid real disapprobation. Once we have learned this process, we are able to exercise self-command in line with our understanding of socially acceptable behaviour.

It is this internalized habit of self-assessment that lies behind Smith's account of conscience. 'Man', he claims, 'naturally desires, not only to be loved, but to be lovely; or to be that thing which is the natural and proper object of love.'[54] This is extended into a desire to be not only praised, but also praiseworthy. It explains, together with the impartial spectator, how it is that we come not just to recognize the shared moral beliefs of our peers, but also to internalize them as standards that we regard as valuable. It would, up to this point, be possible to accuse Smith of leaving open the possibility that morality was not a truly reflective activity, but rather operated purely by social conformity. The appearance of virtue would, by this reading, be sufficient to secure approbation from our peers. But the development of the self-reflective mechanism of the impartial spectator as conscience means that, in addition to assessing our behaviour before we act, we develop a habit of passing judgement on ourselves.

It is this that represents the crucial step in Smith's account of moral psychology. We practise self-judgement to such a degree that we are dissatisfied with approbation unless we, as judges of our own behaviour, are satisfied that we are worthy of such approbation. We 'turn our eyes inwards'[55] and find that approbation that results from deception simply does not satisfy us. I may enjoy the praise of my peers, but that praise will not be forthcoming from my own conscience, which has access to the knowledge that I am undeserving. It is this notion, the desire for praiseworthiness, that underpins our nature as moral beings capable of self-reflection. Indeed, Smith goes so far as to state that it is the love of this self-approbation through conscience that is the love of virtue. Conscience will haunt someone who pursues the appearance of virtue without its substance.

The development of a capacity to see ourselves through the eyes of an impartial other is the basis of 'ordinary good-breeding',[56] but it also helps us with another key element of moral experience. It allows us to put ourselves and our concerns in perspective. A small and trifling incident might preoccupy us, but we know that we should moderate our response to it to gain the approval of the impartial spectator. Smith's account of good character dwells on self-deprecation and modesty in company as examples of polite other-regarding behaviour.

This sophisticated and naturalistic model of the development of moral thinking leads Smith to identify duty with the dictates of the 'higher tribunal' of the impartial spectator, 'the man within the breast, the great judge and arbiter' of our conduct.[57] Human psychology has produced moral reflection from the unfolding of our emotional natures, and conscience allows us to make judgements in a swift and accurate manner. Our reflections lead us to generate rules of proper conduct that are the formal rendering of our imaginative and emotional assessment. The 'general rules of conduct'[58] are the outward manifestation of our moral beliefs. They represent generalizations drawn from actual judgements and are a product of the natural propensity to assess the conduct of our peers.

Once again, though, Smith wants to distinguish his view from mere social conformity and to stress its developmental nature. He is aware that his model also helps to explain how it is that we can develop the belief that the established moral rules of our society are mistaken. We can consult the impartial spectator and form a judgement as to the proper course of action in a given situation, and this assessment can lead us to decide that existing social beliefs are in error.[59] So strong is the authority of conscience, so thoroughly have we internalized the authorizing thought process, that we accept it as the final court of appeal and are willing to stand up to established social norms if we feel they do not agree with the assessment of our internal impartial spectator.[60]

Before we move on, it is worth making two further observations concerning the impartial spectator. The first of these is that Smith clearly did not intend this to be an ideal spectator in the sense that it is all-knowing or all-wise. His point is that the voice of the impartial spectator is our imaginative reconstruction of what such a character would think. In this sense, it is a product of our knowledge and beliefs and so is human rather than superhuman. Secondly, the impartial spectator is not representative of 'reason'; rather it is a process of reflection that is still grounded in the sentiments. This is not the higher self of reason imposing its will on the lower self of the passions. Instead it is a thought process where we come to 'feel' the right thing to do. To underline this, Smith points out that our decision-making process can occur 'instantaneously',[61] allowing us to consult the impartial spectator and understand its view on an emotional level before we think through the basis of its opinion. This is a result of the fact that we have internally habituated the process such that the voice of the impartial spectator appears unprompted and points us in the right direction.

The Limits of Sympathy

We noted above that Smith was critical of his teacher Francis Hutcheson's idea of a moral sense characterized by benevolence. Smith's criticism of Hutcheson dwells on what he sees as two fatal flaws with his teacher's adoption of benevolence as the central principle of morality. First, benevolence is limited. In order to explain this, Smith points out that it is an empirical fact that humans care more for those close to them and are able to do more to affect the lives of those nearby. Familiarity and affection for those near us is a form of what he calls 'habitual sympathy'.[62] He is clear that the further away we move from ourselves, the weaker the strength of our benevolence. We shouldn't be surprised by this argument of Smith's because it is merely an extension of his central observation about the impartial spectators. His point is that it is simply a fact that our benevolence is constrained and so an accurate moral theory must accommodate this within its explanation of morality.

Smith does this by pointing out that it is not benevolence but rather the desire to do the right thing, understood as acting as the impartial spectator suggests, that lies behind moral actions. Now this is not to say that those actions are never beneficent, but it is to say that the passion of benevolence is not the motivation that leads us to act in the right way. This is important for understanding Smith's overall theory, as it reveals to us that it is the authority of conscience, rather than any of the individual moral sentiments, that is the crux of his account of normativity. Propriety is driving Smith's account forward as it gives humans a practical guide to living and benevolence is too weak to account for the universality that forms part of our notion of morality.

This leads to the second major criticism of Hutcheson's privileging of benevolence: universal benevolence is, quite literally, inhuman. Smith's discussion stresses that human beings are limited and imperfect in the extent of their benevolent feelings, and this means that we cannot expect them to act with complete benevolence. Instead we have a less stringent set of expectations which regards it as right that individuals seek to look after their family, friends, and nation. This restriction of the scope of benevolence is fortunate, in Smith's view, because it limits our engaged emotions to those areas where we are likely to be able to make a difference. He draws on this point to argue that our love of country is not derived from a generalized benevolence towards all humans; instead it grows outwards from our family, friends, and locality.

Self-command

Smith does not give up on the idea of universal benevolence. Instead he suggests that it becomes part of our conception of the deity, as an ideal form of benevolence that we would wish to see in the world, but which we recognize as beyond the grasp of humanity. Consequently, it becomes an object of our striving to be better people. As Smith puts it, '[K]indness is the parent of kindness.'[63] We want to be liked and to be worthy of that liking. But we must leave to God any hope of effecting a perfectly just and benevolent universe.[64]

What Smith is trying to illustrate here is the disconnect that can arise between our wish for a world that is perfectly just and the world that we can hope to make with our limited, human, natures. This isn't a counsel of despair, though. One way to unpack why this is not the case lies in one of Smith's most colourful examples. He asks us to imagine the reaction of a person in Europe to the news of the death of millions in an earthquake in China.[65] He tells us how such a man of humanity would reflect on the awfulness of the event, then conjecture on the causes and likely impact of the disaster. But once he had done this, he would return to his everyday pleasures no more moved than before. In contrast, Smith asks us to imagine a man who knows that he will lose his little finger tomorrow. Smith explains how such an individual will be traumatized and unable to think of anything else when faced by this small misfortune. The description is factually accurate for Smith: it is simply a truth of moral thinking that we do in fact react this way. The question is: what we can conclude from this about humans?

It is true that it confirms restricted benevolence, but Smith then goes on to show us that we are nonetheless bound by what is right rather than driven to regard our minor misfortune as more signif- icant than the fate of many. Smith asks us to imagine being given a choice: the loss of our finger or the deaths of millions. His point is to show us that no one would consider for a minute the sacrifice of millions for their minor discomfort. For Smith, this is evidence that it is duty and not benevolence that guides our behaviour here. The impartial spectator would tell us of the horror that others would feel for us should we prioritize ourselves above others in such a way. Hence it is

> that to feel much for others and little for ourselves, that to restrain our selfish, and to indulge our benevolent affections, constitutes the perfection of human nature; and can alone produce among mankind that harmony of sentiments and passions in which consists their whole grace and propriety. As to love our neighbour as we love ourselves is the great law of Christianity, so it is the great precept of nature to love ourselves only as we love our neighbour, or what comes to the same thing, as our neighbour is capable of loving us.[66]

We are able to put our own concerns, our deepest passions, into perspective by consulting the impartial spectator. For Smith, this explains how self-command becomes the central feature of our moral lives. We are capable of knowing what the right thing to do is and we can do this despite our selfish passions driving us in the opposite direction. But Smith's account also has another message. It is a message about the futile nature of excessive or 'extreme sympathy' or 'artificial commiseration'.[67] He wants to argue that it is not just our own feelings we put in perspective, but also our sympathetic feelings for others. A person who entered into complete sympathy with every misfortune or joyous occasion in the world would be literally incapable of living a functioning life of their own.

Perspective works both ways and explains why we would never cause the death of millions, but we likewise lose no sleep over it when we do hear about it. Limited sympathy does not make us bad people; in fact it is necessary for us to be able to live any kind of life. Smith's account of morality is based on the moral sentiments, but it is an account that seeks to distance itself from emotional incontinence and move towards self-command. Moderated sympathy with others is the sign of a well-adjusted and well-meaning individual: a man of humanity is both sensitive and sensible about his sensitivities. As Smith would have it:

> The man of real constancy and firmness, the wise and just man who has been thoroughly bred in the great school of self-command, in the bustle and business of the world ... maintains this control of his

passive feelings upon all occasions; and whether in solitude or in society, wears nearly the same countenance, and is affected in very nearly the same manner.[68]

Once again, the company of strangers is therapeutic for us precisely because it helps us to restore the view of the impartial spectator and exercise self-command over our stronger emotions.

Smith goes further than this, however. He suggests that much of the misery and disorder in the world is brought about by a lack of perspective, a failure to understand what should really matter to us, and a tendency to over-rate the difference between different situations. This leads us to one of Smith's own problems with his theory. He is clearly worried that the account of the social generation of moral beliefs might leave too much discretion to weak individuals. That is to say, that we might deceive ourselves and make excuses for our behaviour. In a sense there are a number of aspects of Smith's theory that are helpful in answering this: the judgement of actual spectators, the judgement of our impartial spectator, the general rules of how to act, and so forth. But he remains concerned that we might be partial spectators of our own behaviour. Smith's point here, as we will see in the next chapter, is one that he also makes in connection with the development of social rank and the corruption of the moral sentiments by the over-rating of the advantage of one situation over another.

Smith's interest in ordinary decent behaviour links back to where we began this chapter: to his distrust of existing systems of philosophy. Smith has shown us how the existing systems are partial because they focus on one feature of moral experience rather than on the whole picture. His idea of a rounded moral agent is that of a person who has lived in the world and made moral judgements. This is not something that ivory-tower philosophers have done. And it is here that Smith wants to bring that point home to us. He argues that people's natural moral responses can be warped by wrong systems developed by philosophers. His particular concern here is religious and political demagogues who, driven by a commitment to their philosophical system, seek to make reality fit their model. These 'ignorant quacks and imposters, both civil and religious',[69] seek to move the multitude to serve their own moral system. Such a man of system is an enemy to every other person who would choose how to act for themselves. Moreover, he will inevitably fail as his systems are only partial and cannot capture the rich diversity of human sentiments.[70] The man of system is a partial spectator on behalf of his own faction and his judgement is not to be trusted.

Smith, on the other hand, has provided us with an account of the social generation of moral beliefs and a sense of duty from everyday life. The result is a theory which explains how we learned to live in complex and morally diverse societies by developing an idea of the sort of agents who make the right decisions rather than seeking a model to be imposed in all circumstances. Smith's great achievement in the idea of the impartial spectator is to provide an agent who represents our better selves, whose view becomes habitual to us, and who helps us to decide what best we can do in the circumstances we find ourselves in. The spectator is both authoritative and realistic about what we can expect from real agents. Accurate moral judgements are most likely to come from people who have lived in the world and experienced moral judgement for themselves. Smith's account of self-command in ordinary life dwells on the command of our selfish emotions, but also on the fact that self-command is produced when we become impartial spectators of our own case. I control my emotions in line with the standard of propriety generated by the impartial spectator. In a sense I become the impartial spectator and its judgements are my judgements.

4

Justice and Virtue

In the previous chapter, we explored the idea that Smith should not be read as the kind of philosopher who seeks a single principle that can account for all of morality. Instead we saw that he sought an account that could reconcile all of the elements of moral judgement. In this chapter, we will move on to consider his analysis of justice and the virtues.

While Smith's main account of the virtues occurs in Part VI added to the 1790 edition of the *Moral Sentiments*, there are other discussions of them throughout his works. The main purpose of these seems to be to provide a reordering of the classical virtues for a modern society. The virtues appropriate for a commercial society are not those that were appropriate for a classical republic. This does not mean that Smith is best understood as a virtue theorist who resolves all of morality into an analysis of character traits.[1] Rather it means that he acknowledges the need for a discussion of the virtues to be part of any systematic moral theory. Discussing the virtues allows us to understand the character traits of moral actors. If we want to breed good people, we need to be aware of the traits that they ought to possess.

Part VI also has an educational role to play in Smith's thinking. By outlining the virtues and assessing their operation in everyday life, he is able to lay out his vision of what it is to be a good person in the real world. Smith's interest in pedagogy is apparent in the chapters on education in the *Wealth of Nations* (which we will return to below), but for the moment we need only note that he saw moral education as a form of character shaping. In a slightly more cynical vein, he suggests that 'The great secret of education is to direct vanity to proper objects.'[2] More accurately, his position is that moral education involves making individuals into the sort of people who want to be good.

We have two notions at work in our moral thinking: the ideal and what it is practicable to expect from ordinary people.[3] Smith's account of the virtues needs to be understood with this is mind. When he sketches the image of the idealized man of virtue, he is not suggesting that this is a character that we ever truly attain. It is, however, a useful ideal that we can approach. Smith describes this ideal character in the following terms:

> The man of the most perfect virtue, the man whom we naturally love and revere the most, is he who joins, to the most perfect command of his own original and selfish feelings, the most exquisite sensibility both to the original and sympathetic feelings of others. The man who, to all the soft, the amiable, and the gentle virtues, joins all the great, the awful, and the respectable, must surely be the natural and proper object of our highest love and admiration.[4]

Such an individual displays the perfect mixture of prudence, justice, and benevolence.

Having set this high bar, Smith moves on to the particular virtues. In order to do this, he returns to his habit of sketching character types as illustrations of good and bad character. But here again, there is a distinction between the man of perfect virtue as an ideal, and the ordinary attainable level of the virtues, in particular the new bourgeois virtues of the prudent man. The prudent man is the epitome of the new middle classes, and his virtues are those that are necessary for a happy life, but not sufficient for a great life. What Smith does do, however, is raise the profile of prudence from its relatively lowly place in the classical virtues. As he would have it: '[T]he prudent man is always both supported and rewarded by the entire approbation of the impartial spectator, and of the representative of the impartial spectator, the man within the breast.'[5] But however much we approve of prudence, we do so with a certain 'cold esteem'.[6] Smith's point here is that living a prudent life is a sort of minimal expectation for a virtuous life. Prudence provides us with the basic conditions necessary for the pursuit of the other virtues.

The prudent man is good at his job and respected by his peers, he is modest and keeps to himself, is not a 'bustler in the affairs of others',[7] nor is he a prodigal who wastes his resources or an over-ambitious 'projector' or speculator. He is careful and plans his actions to make what gains he can without endangering what he has already secured.[8] And while this character sketch of ordinary careful behaviour may be far from the heroic, Smith's point is rather that if these forms of behaviour predominate in a society, then the general course of that society will be secure. His view of prudence as the baseline virtue required for modern life is complemented by his discussion of what he considers to be the central virtue necessary for any society: justice.

Justice

Smith regards justice as the primary virtue, a moral concept necessary for the existence of society itself. Justice is the 'main pillar' that supports 'the immense fabric of human society', and without it society will 'crumble into atoms'.[9] Smith's approach is, once again, to deploy the observational method and to try to account for the actual, lived experience of notions of justice. His anatomy of the concept leads him to consider the development of the natural jurisprudence tradition and the ordinary-language use of the term 'justice'. He notes that there are three basic senses in which this term appears in all languages: what the natural lawyers call commutative justice and distributive justice, and a third, overarching sense of justice that Smith attributes to Plato. It is worth looking at how Smith distinguishes these three separate notions. In the *Moral Sentiments*, he states that commutative justice refers to the type of justice 'the observance of which may be extorted by force, and the violation of which exposes to punishment'.[10] This is the sort of justice covered by the criminal justice system. Distributive justice, on the other hand, refers to 'proper beneficence'[11] applied to charity and generosity. Finally, the Platonic notion of justice refers to some condition of absolute perfection in all the virtues, an idealized notion of the perfectly just man who estimates precisely the correct regard that everything is due.[12] We will return to the third sense in a moment, but for now let us consider the two notions of justice that Smith absorbs from the jurisprudential tradition.

In the *Lectures on Jurisprudence*, Smith suggests that the distinction between commutative and distributive justice follows that of the jurisprudential distinction between perfect (commutative) and imperfect (distributive) rights. He regards the latter as 'not properly belonging to Jurisprudence, but rather to a system of morals as they do not fall under the jurisdiction of the laws'.[13] What Smith now has to do is provide us with an explanation of how such a distinction has developed in all languages and what its significance is for moral philosophy.

Smith's discussion takes place within his account of the moral sentiments and imaginative sympathy. Commutative justice, he tells us, develops from a sympathetic judgement of propriety which raises the resentment of a spectator at the actions of some individual. The sentiment that gives rise to commutative justice is resentment at injury, and it becomes moralized when spectators issue sympathetic approval for the indignation of the victim. Justice, then, is 'sympathetic indignation'.[14] Smith uses the powerful example of what happens when we use our imagination to enter into the situation where a murder has taken place and shows how the imaginative experience moves our moral sentiments to want to seek vengeance on behalf of the slain to the extent that we would see violence used against the guilty party.[15]

Smith's discussion of justice trades on the idea that humans are able to identify tangible harm to others that has been deliberately brought about (though it is worth recalling that his account of merit and demerit allows him to develop an account of blame grounded in negligence). The point he wants to make is that we can identify forms of behaviour that raise sympathetic indignation to a level at which we regard punishment as appropriate. Justice is particularly amenable to this very specific form of identification. It is this that marks justice out from the other virtues. It is amenable to coercive enforcement because it can be precisely identified by sympathetic imagination and then regularized into rules of justice. The other virtues are more context-specific and open to discretion; they are more imprecise than justice. On Smith's account, our discretion on how we can act is limited by the rules of justice in an absolute way, whereas the other virtues are left more open. He compares this to the difference between grammar and style:

> The rules of justice may be compared to the rules of grammar; the rules of the other virtues, to the rules which critics lay down for the attainment of what is sublime and elegant in composition. The one, are precise, accurate, and indispensable. The other, are loose, vague, and indeterminate, and present us rather with a general idea of the perfection we ought to aim at, than afford us any certain and infallible directions for acquiring it. A man may learn to write

grammatically by rule, with the most absolute infallibility; and so, perhaps, he may be taught to act justly. But there are no rules whose observance will infallibly lead us to the attainment of elegance or sublimity in writing; though there are some which may help us, in some measure, to correct and ascertain the vague ideas which we might otherwise have entertained of those perfections. And there are no rules by the knowledge of which we can infallibly be taught to act upon all occasions with prudence, with just magnanimity, or proper beneficence: though there are some which may enable us to correct and ascertain, in several respects, the imperfect ideas which we might otherwise have entertained of those virtues.[16]

This is the 'remarkable distinction'[17] between justice and the other virtues, which are not as amenable to coercive enforcement because of the imprecision that arises in their application in different circumstances.[18] Society depends on a minimal level of just behaviour in order to exist, and those injuries that raise our indignation to the level where we support punishment involve clear and deliberate acts of harm against others. Smith underlines the point by asking us to think about economic competition as a race. We may engage in all activities within the rules of trade, but when we 'justle'[19] or deliberately injure the chances of our rivals, an impartial spectator will not approve of our actions. Commutative justice refers to rule-governed behaviour; it suggests boundaries of behaviour towards others with particular regard to harm. Interestingly, commutative justice also applies equally to us all, leading Smith to a commitment to the idea of equality before the law. He thinks that he has identified a naturalistic account of how we are able to distinguish between rudeness and inappropriate behaviour and injustice worthy of punishment.

Smith wants to stress that this is a better explanation than other accounts of the origin of justice. In particular, he has the theory of his friend Hume in mind. Hume's account of the origin of the artificial virtue of justice is that we gradually come to see the utility of the institutions of property, government, and justice and over time accrue a sympathy with the public good through loyalty to the institutions that uphold justice.[20] For Smith, this gets the psychology the wrong way around: it is the judgement of right and wrong that comes first and only later that we realize the utility of the institution for society. We are already judgemental creatures before we fully develop the level of abstract thought to think about things in terms of the good of society. Smith's account is a more accurate description of how we actually pass judgements on the (in)justice of a situation.

Smith agrees with Hume that the system of justice is socially useful, indeed this is part of why he thinks that justice is the central virtue, but he disagrees with his friend's account of its development. If, as Smith argues, utility is an 'afterthought',[21] an explanatory device of philosophers, then we need to be very careful about thinking that the origin or the justification of punishment has anything to do with utility. Justice cannot be reduced to utility. For Smith, the motivational factors come from quite other sentiments. Once again, his concern is with the accurate identification of the sentiments involved and the way that they shape our reactions. He makes a similar point when he explores the relationship between justice and benevolence.

Benevolence

Smith's account of the distinction between justice and benevolence leads him to suggest that we try to keep the two ideas distinct in our mind.[22] They come from different sentiments, prompt us to think in different ways, and ultimately may come into conflict with each other. It is, Smith admits, perfectly possible to talk about benevolence in the language of justice – we can say that the unfortunate have a 'right' to our aid – but he wants to be clear that applying such justice talk to the issues arising from benevolence is to speak metaphorically. As he puts it, '[A] beggar is an object of our charity and may be said to have a right to demand it – but when we use the word right in this way it is not in a proper but a metaphoricall sense.'[23]

If we look at Smith's definition of the metaphor from the *Lectures on Rhetoric*,[24] we see that it is a figure of speech designed to convey a sentiment through sympathy. The metaphor acts through the creation of an allusion between two distinct phenomena, or, put another way, saying that benevolence can be described in metaphorical terms in the language of justice is to say that they are distinct. The main point of difference is that one is justiciable while the other is not. What I feel for the victim of a crime is not the same as what I feel for a person who is deserving of charity. If a person is made poor because someone steals from them, then my indignation is raised and I regard the act as a crime, blame the culprit, and favour retribution. But if a person is poor through no deliberate action of another, then I do not blame society and wish to see it punished; instead I regard it as my duty to act with charity towards them. The two situations are distinct, and Smith takes great care in trying to separate out and analyse justice, benevolence, charity, and generosity.

Smith spends a significant part of Part II, Section II of the *Moral Sentiments* trying to distinguish between justice and benevolence, and he does this because he believes that the distinction is important for understanding how we think about our duties towards others. Moreover, he believes that the differences between the two allows us to better understand the vital nature of justice to the very existence of society, while at the same time understanding that a merely just society without benevolence is far from ideal. As Smith points out, we need justice for society to exist, but it is a 'mere' or 'negative' virtue that can be fulfilled by sitting still and doing nothing.[25] Not attacking our fellows and taking things from them is essential to society, but it is not enough to ensure a flourishing society. When we judge those who are just in the merely negative sense, we approve of them, but with a degree of merit short of those who go beyond this into active benevolence. Our sense of justice prevents us from harming others, but our sense of humanity leads us to seek to do good for them. Justice is the foundation of the 'building' of society and benevolence is its ornament.[26]

This leads us to another characteristic of beneficence (those actions prompted by the moral sentiment of benevolence). Following an extended discussion in Hutcheson's work, Smith dwells on the voluntary nature of benevolence. We cannot coerce a benevolent motive. 'Beneficence is always free, it cannot be extorted by force, the mere want of it exposes to no punishment; because the mere want of beneficence tends to do no real positive evil.'[27] In a case of deliberate injury, our resentment demands the punishment of the aggressor. In a case of absence of beneficence, our resentment is not raised to a level where we want to inflict punishment. Force is justified in cases of injury but not in cases of a lack of humanity or generosity. In one sense, we can provide a social-level explanation of this being because justice is essential to the stability of society, but for Smith this is a philosopher's reconstruction and the reality of the distinction lies in the difference between our natural resentment at deliberately inflicted injury and that at a want of beneficence.

Smith's argument that beneficence must be freely chosen from benevolent motives leads him to stress its active nature. While one may be just by sitting still and doing nothing, one cannot be inactively benevolent. For Smith, 'indolent benevolence'[28] is not the object of moral approbation. Generosity, charity, and humanity demand action from us as individuals.[29] Smith is also clear that public utility and benevolence are distinct. Beneficence is a virtue which is best understood in terms of situational propriety. We may owe particular duties of beneficence to particular others depending on their relationship to us. We have duties to our family and friends that we do not have to others. Smith underlines this point by returning to the ideas of the circles of sympathy and arguing that the love of our country does not derive from benevolence towards humanity as a whole, but rather grows outwards from our more particular duties of beneficence to those close to us. In particular, and like these, it arises from habitual sympathy. Public utility, on the other hand, since it concerns decisions of expediency directed at the good of society as a whole, refers to a quite distinct sphere from that of beneficence.[30]

Police

It is this observation of the special status of justice that leads Smith to observe that in general we should not sacrifice justice to either benevolence or public utility. As we will see below, he is perfectly aware that this might lead us to difficult situations where we have to trade off public utility and the demands of justice. Smith's earliest biographer, Dugald Stewart, underlines how important these distinctions were to Smith's moral philosophy lectures. He suggests that: 'In the last part of his lectures, he examined those political regulations which are founded, not upon the principle of *justice*, but that of *expediency*, and which are calculated to increase the riches, the power, and the prosperity of a state.'[31]

   When Smith turns his attention to questions of expediency in his *Lectures on Jurisprudence* and the *Wealth of Nations*, he does so under the heading of 'police' – what we today call matters of policy as opposed to matters of justice. His distinction between justice and police is imperfectly realized, however, and blurred by his use of a third, intermediate category of the 'justice of police',[32] referring to local patrols to discourage crime. We'll return to the details of Smith's account of police in the following chapters on jurisprudence and the wealth of nations. For the moment, it is enough to note that police refers to the 'inferiour parts of government, viz. cleanliness, security, and cheapness or plenty'.[33] These concerns are 'trifling'[34] when compared to those of justice and are in reality matters of expediency rather than of principle. This is particularly the case because the regulations of police will differ depending on the circumstances of the society. Police, for Smith, is predominantly a local matter.

Part of the confusion over Smith's discussion of the apparently clear distinction between justice and police is that he muddies the water in a number of places with an imperfect use of the terms. For example, in the *Moral Sentiments* he suggests that magistrates can 'command mutual good offices to a certain degree' that 'impose upon men other duties of beneficence'.[35] But in the same passage he also states that such action by the government 'requires the greatest delicacy and reserve to execute with propriety and judgment' and if it goes too far it will destroy 'all liberty, security, and justice'.[36] Of course, what this reinforces is that police is not justice, nor is it liberty or security.

There is another case where Smith lets his terminological distinction get away from him. We noted above that he is engaging in a criticism of his friend Hume's account of justice, and there is a classic, if difficult, passage that has become central to understanding Smith's view here. D. D. Raphael notes that Smith seems to botch his use of the example of the execution of a sentinel who falls asleep.[37] Smith seems to say that the execution of the sentinel is felt to be just because it serves public utility. But, Raphael points out, if he was being consistent, he would say that it was expedient but unjust. What is interesting here is that Smith seems on one level to be falling back into the metaphorical, everyday use of the term 'just', but on another level he is clearly maintaining the distinction between utility and justice. The case is a difficult one precisely because we are conflicted in how to balance the claims of justice and those of public utility. Smith invites us to compare the sentinel case with that of a murderer. As he would have it: 'The very different sentiments with which the spectator views those different punishments, is a proof that his approbation of the one is far from being founded upon the same principles with that of the other.'[38] The social utility of punishing the sleeping sentinel involves a very different thought process to that of the punishing of a murderer. So what are we to do when we come to problems such as this one, where our sentiments and the ways of thinking that we have developed from them leave us unsure how to proceed?

At this point, we can return to the third conception of justice, the Platonic or perfect sense of justice. This is the idea of justice understood as the character of a 'wise and virtuous man'.[39] But as we saw above, Smith's account of the virtues is undertaken on two levels:

on the ideal level and the attainable level. As a result, the Platonic notion of perfect justice is something that can exist only as an idea for humans rather than as a practical reality. This notion of justice as perfect would also involve both commutative and distributive justice. Distributive justice, as perfect beneficence, is not amenable to precise rules. So Smith's account, like that of Plato, has to be a sketch of the proper balance of the virtues in an idealized character of the perfectly good man. Smith attempted this in Part VI of the *Moral Sentiments*, where he offers us an updated version of the classical virtues aimed at the inhabitants of a modern commercial society.

Part VI is Smith painting virtue, but doing so after completing Hume's challenge to anatomize the moral sentiments. The discussion is didactic and based on the idea that we can become better people even if we can never attain perfect wisdom and virtue. In one sense, this does involve normative claims, but it does not mean that Smith is a virtue theorist. This 'exact idea of propriety and perfection' prompts us to improve ourselves and to secure 'that degree of approximation to this idea which is commonly attained in the world'.[40] The Platonic ideal of justice has didactic uses, but is not attainable in the real world. When Smith focuses on 'magnanimity' as a key virtue, he is not providing us with a single principle upon which all of moral philosophy can be based.[41] Nor is he providing a sort of new cardinal virtue (for he has already told us that justice is the most important virtue). Instead he is pointing out that self-command and adapting to the reality of the world in which we live is the truest path to a virtuous life.

As we saw above, Smith is cautious about 'men of system' who believe that they have a utopian vision of a perfectly just society and who use coercion to force others to accept their vision. Having said this, though, he is aware of the strength of this inclination amongst human beings. We are capable of developing a sense of what a just world would look like, and we are aware that we do not live in such a world. The outcomes of the real world do not match onto our beliefs about deserved outcomes. Humanity's weak powers mean that there are many times when we cannot bring about the outcomes we desire and regard as just in the Platonic sense. Sometimes fortune intervenes and is too strong for our 'impotent endeavours'[42] to overcome it. The sentinel who is put to death moves us, so Smith tells us, to wish that he finds justice in the next world. But more than this, the idea of the next world, of a world of perfect justice, allows us to deal with those cases where our modes of thinking about morality come into conflict.

Religion

It is at this point that we discover how Smith fits religion into his account of moral experience. True to his empirical approach, he accepts that religion and morality are intertwined. So his account of moral experience, in order to be comprehensive and free of gaps, must also explain how religion is related to moral judgement. When we discussed Smith's account of science in chapter 2, we saw that he provided a naturalized account of religious belief as emerging from the same sentiments as science: wonder, surprise, and admiration. His account of the natural history of religion relies on the notion that it acts as an explanatory framework that helps us to dispel wonder. When it comes to the disconnect between our conception of an ideal perfect justice and the real justice of our world, we return to the idea of the perfection of a deity. Smith provides us with a social psychology of the belief in heaven.

> That there is a world to come, where exact justice will be done to every man, where every man will be ranked with those who, in the moral and intellectual qualities, are really his equals is so flattering to the grandeur of human nature, that the virtuous man who has the misfortune to doubt of it, cannot possibly avoid wishing most earnestly and anxiously to believe it.[43]

This is a 'hope and expectation deeply rooted in human nature'.[44] Only an omnipotent and omni-competent God in a state of perfection such as heaven can make all outcomes precisely just in the Platonic sense. That we hope for this is a natural feature of humans as moral creatures. The hard decisions that we are faced with in this world are traumatic for us and we cannot but hope for a world ahead where they will be resolved. Smith's theory of the moral sentiments is an account of imperfect beings trying to do their best. Religion operates in such a system as a form of consolation and a way of coping with the reality that our judgements of merit and demerit are not realized in the outcomes of everyday life.

There is a debate amongst Smith scholars about whether he was a religious believer and the extent to which his theory depends upon the idea of God and a providential plan for humanity.[45] It is true that Smith notes that the sanction of religion supports moral rules and gives us an additional reason to obey them, but his account of where these rules come from is based on their naturalized emergence from experience. It is only once we have identified them as moral rules that we understand them as divinely ordained.[46] We recognize them as a duty before we attribute them to God. So the account remains naturalistic and the belief in the sanction of the deity is explained rather than part of the explanation.

More controversial are the various passages throughout the *Moral Sentiments* where Smith refers to Nature, to the Author of Nature, and to a designer. Those who read an active role for God in Smith's account have interpreted these as a providential underpinning to his conception of the moral order. On the other hand, those who seek to downplay the role of religion in Smith's thinking point out that these phrases are usually window-dressing which involves no active role for God in the actual generation of the phenomena at hand. Instead what Smith does is provide a naturalistic account of the phenomena and then use the references to Nature and design as a literary frame for the descriptive account.

Moral Corruption

Smith's account of the idea of a perfectly just world that acts as an inspiration to flawed human beings trying to live better lives is complemented by an analysis of the sources of the impediments to perfect virtue. In particular, this takes the form of an analysis of the operation of moral corruption.[47] Smith develops this analysis through exactly the same explanatory schema as his account of the development of the elements of the system of human morality. That is to say, the same method that explains where we get our moral ideas from also explains where the sources of immoral behaviour come from. But Smith's argument is more complex than this, because he wants to suggest that there are elements of 'bad' behaviour that might nonetheless prove useful in bringing about socially beneficial outcomes.

Smith's first foray into the theme of corruption comes during his discussion of the origin of ambition and ranks in the *Moral Sentiments*, Part I, Section III. Here he argues that because we are more disposed to sympathize with joy than with sorrow, we tend to parade our wealth and hide our poverty. Smith's observation is based on one that we discussed in the previous chapter: that though our sympathy with pain and discomfort is more pungent and lively than that with joy, it also falls shorter in degree. That is to say, our sympathetic experience of joy is closer to the emotion felt by the person principally concerned. As a result, it is easier to attain mutual sympathy with joy than it is with sorrow, and because we gain pleasure from mutual sympathy, then we are more ready to enter into what we think of as joyful rather than sorrowful situations.

This fact about our natures leads us to develop a natural propensity, a desire to better our condition, which becomes one of Smith's central analytical tools. His explanation of the origin of ambition is not that we enjoy greater utility from wealth, but rather that we gain the attention of our peers through the display of wealth and power. 'To be observed, to be attended to, to be taken notice of with sympathy',[48] is why we pursue wealth and seek to display it. Note the language here: it is the same sentimental mechanism and sociable desire for approval that operates to undergird Smith's account of morality.

The psychology of wealth and social class is examined in unflinching detail by Smith. His observation that the rich love to be the centre of attention, while the poor are ashamed by their poverty and seek to hide it, allows him to build an account of the social psychology of rank that explains why every society that has existed has displayed a system of unequal status that is accepted by its members. Once again, the account is based on a desire to explain how human beings actually behave. Smith observes that philosophical doctrines reject the idea of social inequality based on wealth and fame, but 'nature' has a tendency to bring about political order and obligation in a way that philosophy cannot explain. This, he explains, is why monarchy has such an enduring appeal to the human sentiments.

In Smith's view, this disposition to submit to rank need not be a bad thing. For him, social rank is necessary for political stability, and nature, in disposing us to admire the rich and powerful, has laid the grounds for this stability in human sentiments rather than in the doctrines of philosophy. This fact about human beings is also connected to the virtue of justice, which, as we just saw, likewise emerges from our feelings rather than from our philosophies. Justice is a virtue that is absolutely necessary for the existence of society and emerges from the sympathetic indignation at injury. Smith's claim, then, is that justice is so important to the existence of society that the urge to it is embedded in our emotional make-up. Moreover, he goes on to claim that the apparent conflicts between benevolence and justice that plague our moral decision making have also been settled in favour of justice. This is because: 'The peace and order of society, is of more importance than even the relief of the miserable.'[49] We will return to this point in the next chapter when we discuss the political institutions necessary to provide justice in a society, but for the moment we can simply observe that some of the forms of behaviour that have been the traditional target of philosophical disapproval turn out to have unexpected and beneficial consequences.

Social inequality, it transpires, is one of these. The poor daydream about becoming rich and famous, they admire the situation of the wealthy and imagine how happy those advantages make them, and this leads them to accept the naturalness of the distinction between rich and poor. Smith's discussion of this turns on the fascinating observation that it does not depend on the poor expecting some material advantage from their obsequiousness to the rich. Rather they appear to be the 'disinterested'[50] admirers of the rich.

This allows Smith to develop an analysis of the social phenomenon of fashion that runs alongside his account of morality.[51] He suggests that the propensity to admire the wealthy allows them to lead the fashion in material goods. The rich want to display their wealth and the poor want to emulate the appearances associated with the rich. As Smith puts it:

> With the greater part of rich people, the chief enjoyment of riches consists in the parade of riches, which in their eyes is never so compleat as when they appear to possess those decisive marks of opulence which nobody can possess but themselves.[52]

Scarcity enhances value because it provides exclusivity. It is this desire for ornamentation and display that drives the consumption of the rich. Again, this is very similar to our desire to be approved of by others in the operation of sympathy as the driver of morality. Smith's view is that '[t]o be observed, to be attended to, to be taken notice of by sympathy, complacency, and approbation, are all the advantages which we can propose to derive from it [the parade of riches]. It is the vanity, not the ease, or the pleasure, which interests us.'[53] The man of fashion is pleased by the attention of others, and when we seek to emulate him, we do so by pursuing the trinkets and baubles of fashionable ornament. We will return to the economic impact of this in the chapter on the *Wealth of Nations*, but for the moment let us highlight two points that are important for Smith.

First, distinctions of rank, signalled by fashionable display, come to have a social meaning. It is worth quoting Smith at length on this:

> Though it is in order to supply the necessities and conveniences of the body, that the advantages of external fortune are originally recommended to us, we cannot live long in the world without perceiving that the respect of our equals, our credit and rank in the society we live in, depend very much upon the degree in which we possess, or are supposed to possess, those advantages. The desire of becoming the proper objects of this respect, of deserving and obtaining this credit and rank among our equals, is, perhaps, the strongest of all our desires.[54]

Smith is describing the reality of a system of rank where possession of certain ornamental and convenient items is the basis of self-respect. We are not talking about the necessities of physical life here, but rather the necessities of social life. To be thought an equal member of society we must possess certain material goods. In the *Wealth of Nations*, Smith returns to this idea and suggests that the goods in question differ as societies develop. The richer the society, the more goods must be possessed for recognition as a person worthy of consideration.[55]

Second, and also in the *Wealth of Nations*, Smith suggests that social rank impacts on our moral judgement of individuals. We are, he argues, more willing to indulge dissipation in the rich as that will not lead them to poverty. A wealthy man who goes on a spree may have to tighten his belt, but he will not starve as a result. However, we are less willing to indulge such behaviour in the poor, where a week's dissipation may lead to lifelong consequences for them and their families. This is a matter of situational propriety for Smith, but it also helps to explain the social psychology of celebrity and why we continue to be fascinated by the lifestyles of the rich and famous, leading to the appearance of one set of moral rules for the rich and another for the poor.[56]

It is the desire to be observed with admiration, to be thought a person of rank, that drives ambition. And it is this ambition for status that is the source of 'all the rapine and injustice, which avarice and ambition have introduced into the world'.[57] But it is also the source of rank in a political sense, and this, Smith recognizes, is essential to the good order of society. So the disposition to admire the rich is the simultaneous source of political stability and moral corruption.

Smith goes on to examine how this creates two alternative paths to status: status achieved through wisdom and virtue, and status achieved through wealth and greatness.[58] Philosophy tells us that wisdom and virtue are the morally admirable routes to acclaim, but reality tells us that many people worship wealth and greatness. The 'mob' see the latter means as the only route to rank. This, for Smith, is the path of the 'vulgar' – whether rich or poor.[59] The desire to be admired creates a social dynamic that explains the operation of fashion, but that also gives us an explanation of the pathology of class-based envy. Many of the poor want to be thought wealthy and so conduct themselves as though they were of a higher station than is actually the case. Consequently, they become what Smith calls 'coxcombs': show-offs who affect a status that they do not deserve; figures of contempt who can be recognized as pretenders rather than of high rank.

However, it is at this point that Smith's description takes an unusual turn. In chapter 3, we discussed the influence of Rousseau's and Mandeville's accounts of the moral corruption of modern commercial societies, and from what we've read here we might expect Smith to develop a similar account. But that is precisely what he does not do. Instead he seeks to explain how the pursuit of wealth and greatness has unintended social benefits. As usual, Smith illustrates this explanation with a character sketch of an everyday individual. In this case it is the 'poor man's son' whom heaven has cursed with ambition.[60] Smith tells us how such a person forms an idea of the comfort and enjoyment that the situation of the rich brings them. This spurs his ambition and leads him to work as hard as he can, to fawn over his betters in the hope of advantage, to work long hours and never to settle for what he has. At the end of his life, when he has amassed his fortune, acquired 'greatness', and worn himself out mentally and physically along the way, he finds that the material goods that he always thought would bring him happiness are but 'trinkets of frivolous utility'[61] which bring him little in the way of ease of body or mind. All of the goods that he admired turn out to be things which were admired because they were observable, rather than from the degree of physical comfort or pleasure they bring.

Once again, Smith notes that this analysis of the apparent futility of mistaking wealth for happiness is something which is the result of philosophical consideration: it is apparent to us if we stop to think about it, but we rarely do so. It is only when we are melancholy or in low spirits that we resent the material goods enjoyed by the wealthy. And this, Smith suggests, might actually be a good thing. His account of the poor man's son is not a simple morality tale. He wants us to grasp the fact that what drives this process is the desire to emulate the wealthy, to acquire the material situation that they are in, rather than any genuine acquisition of happiness. The point is that it is the social dynamic that matters rather than any objective notion of happiness. As a result, this process will be insatiable: it will apply in wealthy societies as well as poor societies. Ambition to improve our situation is ubiquitous and ineradicable from human life. This is a point that Smith returns to in some detail in the *Wealth of Nations*, but for the moment let us simply note that his detached explanatory account allows him to agree with Mandeville that the social goods of political stability and wealth are unintended consequences of the pursuit of the illusion of happiness in wealth and greatness.

Smith calls this a 'deception',[62] but he recognizes that it is a useful one because it produces material advantages for the whole of society. The way in which the poor man's son makes his fortune is by manufacturing or trading with others: by creating wealth which in turn is enjoyed by the society as a whole. The deception that the situation of the wealthy makes them happy is what rouses human industry. It is the deception that drives economic development. Material progress depends on vanity and ambition.

The Invisible Hand

Smith's discussion then moves on to the unintended distributive impact of the pursuit of display by the rich and the desire for improvement of the poor. The account marks the appearance of his metaphor of the invisible hand in the *Moral Sentiments*:

> The rich only select from the heap what is most precious and agreeable. They consume little more than the poor, and in spite of their natural selfishness and rapacity, though they mean only their own conveniency, though the sole end which they propose from the labours of all the thousands whom they employ, be the gratification of their own vain and insatiable desires, they divide with the poor the produce of all their improvements. They are led by an invisible hand to make nearly the same distribution of the necessaries of life, which would have been made, had the earth been divided into equal portions among all its inhabitants, and thus without intending it, without knowing it, advance the interest of the society, and afford means to the multiplication of the species. When

Providence divided the earth among a few lordly masters, it neither forgot nor abandoned those who seemed to have been left out in the partition. These last too enjoy their share of all that it produces.[63]

The unequal distribution of goods provides for a near equal distribution of necessities. And because we have seen that true happiness does not come from the possession of these trinkets, we can see that the deception is useful, as it generates economic growth and serves to provide the necessaries, and increasingly the conveniences, of life to all of society. Smith's unpicking of the normative criticism of inequality from the empirical account of the generation of improving living standards represents his advance on Rousseau and Mandeville. He is able to recognize the generation of wealth from vanity, but at the same time remind us that it provides increasing levels of wealth for society as a whole.

Smith argues that:

> In what constitutes the real happiness of human life, they are in no respect inferior to those who would seem so much above them. In ease of body and peace of mind, all the different ranks of life are nearly upon a level, and the beggar, who suns himself by the side of the highway, possesses that security which Kings are fighting for.[64]

He is not really being complacent here, nor is he retreating into some sort of Stoic rejection of interest in the material world. Instead he is pointing out that the restless ambition for status can never be shaken off by most of us, and that once we go beyond the basic necessities of life, we do so in pursuit of a deception driven by the desire for status rather than by anything that will really add to human happiness.

Smith returns to this idea and argues that:

> What can be added to the happiness of the man who is in health, who is out of debt, and has a clear conscience? To one in this situation, all accessions of fortune may properly be said to be superfluous; and if he is much elevated upon account of them, it must be the effect of the most frivolous levity. This situation, however, may very well be called the natural and ordinary state of mankind. Notwithstanding the present misery and depravity of the world, so justly lamented, this really is the state of the greater part of men. The greater part of men, therefore, cannot find any great difficulty in elevating themselves to all the joy which any accession to this situation can well excite in their companion.[65]

This seems to be a startlingly complacent passage. Smith appears to be saying that the existence of vast inequality is ultimately of little importance. But we need to put this claim in context. The first thing to note is that Smith's entire account of rank is supposed to show us that most of our pursuit of wealth is for ornamental display rather than material necessity. The pursuit of frivolities rather than necessities is the true engine of economic growth. Smith's point is that the desire for ornament creates the conditions where the poor are able to secure both the necessities and some of the conveniences of human life. This is important to grasp. Smith is perhaps the first to develop a notion of poverty that is focused on the meaning of status in a society. His argument is that to have social status, the members of society must possess a certain level of material goods, and this level of goods differs in each society. However, this is not quite like our modern notion of relative poverty, where we measure poverty through unequal access to goods. Instead what Smith is pointing out is that because our ambition to improve our situation is insatiable, what counts as conveying status in a society will likewise continually change over time. He is far from complacent, but he does observe that in most societies the 'wages of the meanest labourer'[66] can supply the basic necessities.

The Implications of Inequality

Before we leave our discussion of the virtues, we should examine one final feature of Smith's account. As we have seen, there are apparently two paths laid before us: the path of wisdom and virtue and the path of wealth and greatness. Wealth and greatness are more visible than wisdom and virtue and so they attract the attention of the bulk of humankind. We have seen how Smith thinks that this need not be too much of a disappointment as there are unintended socially beneficial outcomes in terms of wealth and political stability that follow from them. But what about the man who pursues wisdom and virtue: how is he to fare in a society where the rich are driven by vanity and the mob glory in fame and fortune?

Smith approaches this question from two different directions. First, he notes that the 'man of spirit and ambition'[67] is subject to different incentives than the 'man of rank and greatness'.[68] The former pursues the approval of society, fame, and status through achievements in the arts and sciences, whereas the latter is content with displaying the material and social graces expected of his station.

Such individuals, from what Smith calls the 'middle and inferior'[69] ranks, generally run the administration of the country. Their industriousness and ability are their means of advancement. This group of individuals rise through talent and serve as a bridge between the ranks of the rich and the poor. It is tempting to think of Smith and his fellow Scottish literati as the model for this passage. They were neither politically powerful, nor poor and marginalized, but instead sought advancement through merit acquired in service to society.

But Smith also cautions us about ambition. He suggests that the love of applause is such that it becomes addictive, and this is particularly dangerous in politics. This means that men of ability can contrive situations to show their skills and acquire renown. Smith even goes so far as to suggest that they welcome war as a chance to show their ability.[70] More seriously, the desire for fame in politics leads to the danger of the demagogue: the politician who seeks the approval of the mob and threatens the balance between the ranks in society. In general, Smith believes that the partiality of each class, rich and poor, to their own interest creates a balance in society that can be managed by the middling ranks, who serve as the personnel for the institutions of the state. In such a situation, there is a balance of interests, while the actual running of the state is left to men of ability whose status depends on their wisdom and virtue in fulfilling their office.

The problem arises when someone seeks to undo this balance and to manipulate the factions that exist in society to rise to power. Smith was distrustful of such figures, even when they acted from benevolent motives, and believed that they were susceptible to self-deception in a way that was dangerous to the peace and order of society.[71] These individuals might be moved entirely by a desire to serve the public, but they inevitably come with a view about what is in the public interest that may differ from that of the rest of the public. Smith's criticism of the man of system suggests modesty in what we can hope to achieve from the reform of society.[72] In general, he prefers gradual reform to revolutionary change.

There is, however, a final and powerful check against the dangers of moral corruption and ambition. The voice of the impartial spectator, the man within who speaks for our conscience, is always with us. And so, no matter how much we may deceive ourselves and pursue wealth and fame, there will always be a voice on hand to remind us that we are seeking praise rather than pursuing praiseworthiness. This, for Smith, was the ultimate check on moral corruption.

In the next chapter, we will examine how Smith moves from a discussion of the evolution of ideas of justice and virtue and their internalization in our conscience to a discussion of the institutions and rules that embody justice in society. Smith's natural jurisprudence links his moral and political thinking and shows how societies embed a moral idea of justice in their political institutions.

5

Jurisprudence

In the previous chapters, we have seen how Adam Smith develops a naturalistic and evolutionary account of the development of morality. His account is based on the human emotions and a series of universally experienced reactions to the fact that other people observe and judge our behaviour. Part of his account established a very clear divide between the virtue of justice, which was necessary for society to exist, and the other virtues. In this chapter, we will examine how the institutions associated with justice emerge in human societies. In particular, we will look at the institution of coercive force and government. Our main source in this chapter will be the student notes on Smith's Glasgow *Lectures on Jurisprudence* and Book III of the *Wealth of Nations*, where he discusses the evolution of the modern state.

Smith divided his Glasgow *Lectures on Jurisprudence* into two main parts: as we noted above, the division occurred along a line that Dugald Stewart identified as that between matters of commutative justice and matters of what Smith called police (policy issues governed by the principle of expediency). Jurisprudence, Smith tells us, refers to the 'rules by which civil governments ought to be directed',[1] whereas police refers to 'whatever regulations are made with respect to the trade, commerce, agriculture, manufactures of a country'.[2] Both of these are distinguished from the realms of distributive and Platonic justice that we have just discussed in the previous chapter. In this chapter, we will examine Smith's account of justice and natural jurisprudence, and in the following two chapters on the *Wealth of Nations*, we will turn to questions of policy or expediency in the pursuit of the 'conveniencies and necessaries of life'.[3]

As we saw above, Smith's *Moral Sentiments* provides us with a naturalistic account of the origins of commutative justice through the sympathetic indignation generated when we see deliberate injury being done to others. The sentimental origins of justice are the basis of all punitive legal systems. Public utility might be the effect of this human proclivity, but the origin of our legal system lies in the moral approval of restitution for injury. Smith's project now moves on to an attempt to understand how this basic moral urge develops into complex systems of rules and institutions designed to enforce them.

Smith's approach to these lectures follows that adopted by his predecessors at Glasgow, Gershom Carmichael and Francis Hutcheson. They had developed a curriculum based on the Protestant natural law theories of Hugo Grotius and Samuel Pufendorf.[4] At times, Hutcheson's account almost verbatim tracks that of his predecessors. The framework may have been that of a natural jurisprudence, but Smith blended the inherited structure with his own scientific account. The lectures are a master class in the Scottish Enlightenment's conjectural historical method. Smith's aim is to provide a systematic analysis of the basic principles of law that is both analytical and historically informed. The end result is a theoretical explanation of the gradual evolution of the basic features of the shared legal order of the European nations.

The method is comparative: examples are drawn from around Europe and throughout history. By far the majority of these are drawn from Scottish and English law. There are good reasons for this. First, Smith's audience would be more familiar with these illustrations, and would also find them more useful when, as was often the case, they went into the legal profession. And second, his account represents a study of how the legal and governmental institutions of commercial society develop over time. This is an account of the rise of what he thinks of as a modern sense of liberty. This liberty had reached its most perfect form in the constitution of Great Britain, and so this example was of particular interest to him.[5] Smith is also taking part in a wider eighteenth-century debate about the different nature of freedom in the modern world. He was well aware that the representative governments and freedom under the law of modern Britain represented a very different understanding of what it meant to be free than the idea of active citizen participation in the political life of the state that characterized the ancient notion of liberty. As we will see, his account of the rise of modern freedom is also an account of the superiority of this sort of freedom to its ancient precursor.

Smith's approach to the subject does not involve a narrative history of Britain. The method does not proceed by a detailed study of the history of English law and government, as Hume's *History of England* does; instead it is a general, sociological, account of the basic social forces that brought about modern liberty and the rule of law. Smith's explanations downplay purposive actions by particular individuals. Instead the focus is on the unintended consequences of the interaction of individuals as they adapt to each other and their material circumstances. Smith's aim is to provide a systematic analysis of the basic features of a legal and political order as they are likely to have proceeded. The jurisprudence is 'natural' in the sense that it provides a realistic account of how institutions and practices arise and function to manage particular aspects necessary for social life. The approach is the same as Smith uses to account for science, language, and morality. Along with this comes the opportunity to identify 'natural' justice and principles of equity that emerge as social life develops.[6] Throughout the focus is on social explanation rather than particular history. The desire is to provide a scientific account of history freed from the interests, biases, and superstitions that absorbed many historians.

We see a very clear example of this when Smith comes to discuss the dominant ways of thinking about politics in the generations immediately prior to his own. As we saw in chapter 2, he rejects the idea of a social contract, arguing that there is no historical evidence for such a concept, and, moreover, that it is only really popular in Britain.[7] His evidence for this is empirical:

> Ask a common porter or day-labourer why he obeys the civil magis-
> trate, he will tell you that it is right to do so, that he sees others do it,
> that he would be punished if he refused to do it, or perhaps, that it is
> a sin against God not to do it. But you will never hear him mention
> a contract as the foundation of his obedience.[8]

This, Smith argues is because contract theory is a normative argument that has developed from British party politics. No self-respecting scientist would start his account of government from a partisan rhetorical device. Smith has a similar attitude to the principles of utility and authority which characterize the respective platforms of the Whigs and the Tories. Both of these no doubt have some role to play in an explanation of the development of law and government, but neither one alone will suffice. As Smith points out, all government rests on consent, but even in Britain, with the freest constitution and the most representative system, that consent is 'metaphoricall'.[9]

Submission to law and government, Smith argues, is the result of a long process of habit, socialization, and the development of customs. Nations develop their institutions through a gradual process of balancing interests and reacting to material circumstances. A natural jurisprudence, a systematic account of the underlying principles that unfold as part of this process, is possible because we are observing a universal human nature dealing with universally ubiquitous social problems. The evidence is drawn from particular examples in particular legal codes, but these are then compared and generalizations are developed about types of response to specific legal and political problems.

Stadial Theory

Smith, as we noted in chapter 2, was hugely influential in the development of the Scottish Enlightenment's approach to historical writing, and it is in the *Lectures on Jurisprudence* that we see it in its classic form. Here he provides us with the classic statement of the 'four stages' – hunting, shepherding, agriculture, and commerce – that for him, as we saw in chapter 2, characterize the dominant economic model.[10] It is important to note that Smith is not providing us with an account of some sort of inevitable material theory of history, like that later provided by Marx. Instead this is an explanatory and systematic presentation of the main 'types' of social order arranged around a universally experienced human function: the way a people provide food for themselves.

Smith points to two significant features that lead to a change from one type of society to another. The first of these is population. Animals and humans multiply in direct proportion to the available 'subsistence'[11] and the demand for food, and the natural reproductive drive leads to a growth in population that gradually places pressure on societies to find ways to expand food production. Hunting societies have small populations, and we can track a 'natural' growth in the numbers that can be supported through the development of more diverse and more productive ways of providing subsistence.

For Smith, this leads to the second significant feature: humans gradually develop knowledge of more and more ways to secure food. The course of this knowledge can be arranged in a 'natural' order. The first human societies were hunter gatherers and they would remain as such so long as the resources of the hunt were sufficient to feed the population. Hunting societies become shepherding societies when the skills of animal husbandry are developed. These skills arise from the hunter's observation of and familiarity with animals. Shepherding societies become agricultural societies when the familiarity with the food of animals leads to experiments with vegetables and crop-raising skills develop. As agricultural societies develop, the concentration of population in towns eventually leads to the development of the division of labour and the rise of commercial societies.

What matters for Smith are not so much the particulars of what happens in any one society or in any actual transition from one type of society to another. Instead the point is that by identifying the types of society, we are able to systematize our examination of social institutions. This allows Smith to develop his account of the origins of property and government as the key institutions of justice in society.

Property

Smith's aim is to examine the origin and development of property as absolutely necessary for the existence of all societies and at the same time to provide a 'natural' account of the development of the idea of private property in commercial society. The need for property is an underlying universal of human experience that can be observed in different forms in different societies. There are basic modes for the development of an idea of ownership: most basic perhaps is occupation, or occupation over time. Smith then examines how notions of property change, and become more complex in different forms of society. Property evolves with subsistence, and it is disputes about property that act as a particular spur to the development of law and government. Injury to the person, reputation, or property are tangible harms in the sense that Smith thinks motivate our assessments of justice. To infringe upon them is to deny our 'rights'. As human beings evolve shared beliefs about morality, they also develop a shared sense of what constitutes an injury, so these become 'evident to reason'[12] and identifiable by every individual in society. As a result, they are basic to the development of the institutions that allow us to live together in society.

In a hunting society, there is no abstract notion of property. What ideas of property do exist refer to immediate holdings: this is my spear; this is the animal I have just hunted. Hunting societies are incapable of direct notions of futurity and ownership beyond the moment. Of course, this provides Smith with yet another ground on which to reject contract theory: the earliest human societies have no notion of ownership or contract. The idea of property really develops in shepherding societies. The idea that I own particular animals gives birth to the abstract notion of ownership. My animals are mine, and as I depend on them to feed myself and my family, theft of them has very serious repercussions. The sympathetic indignation of a spectator who sees a family starve rises to such levels that it will license the most severe punishment. In shepherding societies, theft of animals results in the death penalty. As Smith proceeds through the lectures, he also provides us with an account of how norms of punishment change through time.[13] In a hunting society, there are no settled ideas about punishment; gradually we see the development of parallel systems of compensatory punishment for minor offences and brutal, indeed lethal, punishments for more serious matters. In general, though, Smith's account of the development of punishment is one of a decrease in the brutality involved as life becomes less precarious and humans are able to indulge their sentiments more fully. This parallels the account of the increasing scope to indulge the moral sentiments that we saw in the case of infanticide in chapter 3.

Alongside the recognition of property claims over time comes the notion of property claims beyond immediate physical contact: my flock is mine even if I am not beside it. This in turn leads to notions of title and ways of distinguishing who owns what. Accompanying this are ideas about inheritance[14] and contract.[15] For Smith, the immediate consequence of the development of these conventions is the expansion of inequality within shepherding societies.[16] The ownership of particular animals prevents others from accessing them and introduces the distinction of ranks between rich and poor. Those who first develop the skill of animal husbandry become powerful and those without animals of their own become dependent on them. Along with the concept of ownership comes a series of recognized origins of rightful claims which Smith also analyses and traces through the historical development of law. For Smith, property claims can be based on: occupation; voluntary transfer or tradition; accession (where something is produced by something that I own, such as the milk of my cows); prescription (where something has been abandoned by another and held by me over time); and succession or inheritance.

In shepherding societies, the nomadic nature of the people precludes the idea of property in land. But they do allow for more extensive groups to form. Shepherds group together for mutual security and their 'hordes' are able to support larger populations than the hunting 'bands'. Defensive concerns also lead shepherd societies to develop strongholds where they can retreat for security against attack.[17] These locations become important centres for the adjudication of the customary rules that govern the shepherds. In time, they become the centres for trade and for the development of the arts and are the origin of cities.

This is something that develops in agricultural societies when shepherds begin to settle in fixed communities. At this point, we see the development of legal concepts that manage the social conflicts that arise from fixed habitation. In Smith's account, the key step in the development of the modern notion of private or 'several' property comes when these regulations are extended as a result of the experience of living in cities and towns.[18] This is a result of the continuation of the growth of population and its concentration in particular locations, leading humans to develop ways to demarcate ownership and settle disputes. Towns become centres of trade and of adjudication. As a result, the rule of law develops there first. This leads to Smith's account of the development of modern commercial societies. We will look at this in particular detail later in the chapter, but for the purposes of the present discussion we should note that the impact of the development of commerce on notions of property is a continuation of the process of growing complexity that we have seen so far. In a commercial society, we see property reach a level of complexity and abstraction that supports notions such as it being possible to own a share in a company. Contract and commercial law develop to meet the needs of commerce and we see the development of increasingly sophisticated legal orders.

Government

Smith's account of the development of conventions surrounding property is accompanied by an account of the growth of government as a device to resolve conflict and delineate property. As he details it, governments have three major roles: to preserve justice, to protect property, and, once these are secured, to promote opulence. The 'first and chief design of all civill government'[19] is the preservation of justice.

The idea is that the story of the evolution of government can best be understood in the 'four stages' schema. In hunting societies, there is no formal government structure. The hunting tribes may defer to a temporary chief to lead them in war, but the notion of a permanent hierarchy or subordination of ranks means that such eminence is limited to the single task of war leadership. The absence of a concept of property means that there are no rules to delineate property and there is no need for an institution to enforce property claims.

Government in any recognizable form arises in shepherding societies. The development of property in flocks and the subsequent inequality that arises leads Smith to the stark, and unsentimental, observation that the initial invention of government was to protect the rich from the poor and its powers were unformalized and exercised precariously:[20] 'Civil government, so far as it is instituted for the security of property, is in reality instituted for the defence of the rich against the poor, or of those who have some property against those who have none at all.'[21] Smith observes that '[w]herever there is great property, there is great inequality',[22] and what he means by this is that when a few people own all of the property (as they do in a shepherding society), the mass of people become dependent on them. The first developments of law and government arise at the same time as the first development of inequality and social subordination relating to property ownership. Government is a device that 'naturally' arises to answer the problems created by the development of ownership and inequality.

In the *Moral Sentiments*, Smith tells us that our belief in social rank and our tendency to defer to those we consider to be our superiors is not driven by material dependence. Rather it is based on us forming an opinion that they deserve our obedience. So, although the origin of status may be wealth, the social psychology of deference is based on some other and disinterested opinion on the right to superior status. Smith suggests that there are a number of such distinctions that develop in society. These might be personal attributes such as strength, or age (which suggests wisdom), but they are often difficult to discern and so wealth and nobility soon replace them in the shepherding era not because of direct economic dependence, but rather because they provide more stable bases for assessment of rank. At this point, Smith returns to the idea that the ability of the few who govern to command the many is based on a mixture of reasons grounded in authority and utility. Age, strength, wealth, and nobility are reasons why we attribute authority to individuals, but we also need government to provide justice in society. Smith is quick to note that we do not submit to government because it is in our personal interest. Instead we do so because we recognize that it is necessary for society and we value it as such. It is the public utility of having a system of government and law that we identify with rather than the prospect of individual gain, and we come to associate this with being a part of a society and recognizing the authority of its leader. The whole social psychology of subordination links seamlessly to the account in the *Moral Sentiments*.

Smith's theory of how this process takes place parallels that of his friend David Hume. Smith sees a 'natural' inclination to turn to war leaders or powerful individuals in society to act as judges in disputes between members of the society. These judge-chiefs are then able, over time, to expect the loyalty of the people who are dependent on them for subsistence, law, and protection from external foes.[23] In its earliest stages, the claim of authority is precarious and can be based on physical strength, intelligence, age, or wealth.[24] But over time wealth and inherited status come to be the most stable means of securing a system of rank in society. Smith's point is not so much that this is a morally desirable account of the origin of our governments, but that it is a more historically plausible account than contract theory.

In the *Lectures on Rhetoric*, Smith returns to this idea of the development of judge-kings from war leaders and refers to them as 'umpires'.[25] He then suggests that the decisions of these umpires come to form a set of precedents or expectations that are the origin of law. Alongside this, Smith suggests that this system, a common law system, is more 'equitable' than a statute-based system because the law arises from actual judgments in cases and so its equity can be demonstrated to the people. As he puts it: 'What is founded on practise and experience must be better adapted to particular cases than that which is derived from theory only.'[26]

When societies begin to settle geographically in the agricultural stage, the government becomes attached to a particular physical territory rather than a nomadic people. Over time, the institutions of government develop in complexity alongside the range of problems that come from social life lived by numbers of people in close proximity. Government is more certain and developed in the towns and cities, and gradually, as we will see, spreads to the rest of the country. In a commercial society, government becomes more extensive still as the grounds for dispute enlarge with the scope of property and lead us to the rise of the modern legal state. The rule of law extends its scope and becomes the characteristic mode of regulation. The arbitrary personal authority of the earlier rulers is replaced by a rule-governed system of institutional authority.

Smith also provides an account of the evolution of the different offices of government. He points out that all of these would initially fall to one individual, but over time that judge-king would begin to delegate the enforcement and judging function to other people. This division of labour between executive and magistrates would develop over many centuries and eventually lead to a situation where it is possible to make analytic distinctions between the different branches of government. There is a very important unintended consequence of this for modern liberty, which Smith describes in the following terms:

> This separation of the province of distributing Justice between man and man from that of conducting publick affairs and leading Armies is the great advantage which modern times have over ancient, and is the foundation of that greater security which we now enjoy both with regard to Liberty, property and Life. It was introduced only by chance and to ease the Supreme Magistrate of this most Laborious and least Glorious part of his Power; and has never taken place until the increase of Refinement and the Growth of Society have multiplied business immensely.[27]

Smith's account dwells on the development of inequality and this has important economic and moral implications, as we saw above in our discussion of the corruption of the moral sentiments. The idea that, from the point of view of political economy, there is a 'useful inequality in the fortunes of mankind'[28] will be explored in subsequent chapters. But for the moment we should consider it from its political perspective. Smith is quite clear that this inequality is socially necessary and socially useful. The few must lead the many, but the development of rule-governed societies and the decline of arbitrary exercises of power create a security and stability of expectation that is crucial for the development of civilized society.

Warfare

Government continues to have a role in protecting the group from outside threats, and Smith also uses the 'four stages' theory in his account of the development of warfare between human societies. In Book V, Chapter 1, Part 1 of the *Wealth of Nations*, Smith makes a contribution to an ongoing eighteenth-century debate about the value of citizen militias versus professional standing armies. There was a strong tradition in British political thinking that saw the lesson of the decline of the Roman Republic as a morality tale about the dangers of replacing citizen militias with professional armies.[29] The worry was that when war is professionalized, it opens the space for the army to become a distinct political actor whose interests are at odds with the rest of the citizens and who will use force to take control of government. It was widely thought that only an army of voluntary citizens, willing to do their duty when called, could guard against this. The argument was accompanied with an argument about the superior virtue and moral motivation of such soldiers. Ancient liberty was the liberty of citizen soldiers. Smith's friend Adam Ferguson was a particular defender of the superiority of citizen militias and an active campaigner for a Scottish militia, and Smith's analysis of the development of war within a 'four stages' schema annoyed him.

In a hunting society, there is no developed sense of government or property and so war is undertaken by hunting tribes only from quarrels or retribution for injury. In such societies, all are warriors and fighting for the tribe is a mark of honour. The small scale of such societies means that the numbers involved will be small, and the absence of technology means that the expense to the tribe will be in terms of manpower. In shepherding societies, the reasons for war expand to cover access to animals and grazing land. The conflicts occur between larger groups and the structure of the military maps onto the structure of rank that has developed within the tribes. Shepherds are nomadic and rely on their animals, so when they go to war the whole society moves with them and all able-bodied men fight.

In agricultural societies, wars take place over land disputes. Here, though, the nature of the military changes. Agricultural production demands that some of the population remain at home to tend the crops. This means that only a section of the population fight, and that wars tend to be limited to the period between sowing and harvesting the crops. The campaign season and the conventions of war develop at this stage and manifest themselves in the codes of chivalry that map military service and rank onto social status. It is this model that gives birth to the concept of the gentleman militia that Ferguson so admires. The image of the Roman general laying aside his ploughshare to lead the army and then returning to it when the campaign was over generated a powerful idea of the virtues of military service and public duty.

In Smith's view, it may well be the case that there are particular virtues that are promoted by having a citizen militia. The citizenry are kept from becoming cowardly and prey to laziness, but in a commercial society the social and economic conditions suggest that a standing army will be preferable for national defence. There are two sides to the analysis. First, Smith points out that a commercial society that wants to raise an army will have to pay its soldiers. This is because a merchant or a manufacturer who is fighting has to stop selling or producing in a way that farmers and shepherds did not. Armies will have to be paid even if they are composed of citizen volunteers. This leads to Smith's second observation. Commercial societies are characterized by specialization and the division of labour. For Smith, this applies just as much to the military as it does to other parts of society. The role of soldier becomes a particular occupation, and as the amount of technology used in warfare develops, we develop a group of individuals in society who have the skills and training in modern weapons and tactics. Ferguson's argument that an army of motivated citizens would defeat an army of hired soldiers misses this point. Smith is clear that if a modern professional military meets a group of motivated but unprofessional amateurs, the result will be slaughter. Indeed the events in 1746 at Culloden, where the Highland clan militia of the Jacobite army faced professionally drilled Hanoverian forces with modern artillery, provided brutal empirical evidence of his argument.

Driving his point home, Smith notes that the success of the Roman Republic's citizen army was less to do with the virtue of militias and more to do with the fact that near-constant warfare made it into a professional army in all but name.[30] While it may be true that '[t]he arts and improvement of sciences puts the better sort in such a condition that they will not incline to serve in a war',[31] the only role a militia can have in responding to this is in encouraging virtue. In military terms, a commercial society needs a professional army to defend it. Smith's final argument against militia republicanism is to point out that in modern commercial states the sovereign feels secure because he has his standing army and as a result is willing to grant wider freedoms to his people.[32] A turbulent and armed population would be a constant threat to a government without a standing army, and as a consequence they would see any public clamour as the start of a possible revolution to be met with by force. So long as the laws and the constitution limit the arbitrary use of the army by the sovereign, the inhabitants of a modern commercial society have no need to fear the fate of the Roman Republic.

It's worth pausing at this point to dispel another of the myths that have arisen about Smith. In the study of international relations, he has come to be associated with a particular view that is often (illiterately) labelled 'liberalist'. This is a view that believes that countries who trade together under a system of international laws are unlikely to go to war with each other. As an understanding of international relations, it grows out of Montesquieu's idea of *doux commerce*, the idea that commerce civilizes and softens our manners and reduces violence. Smith clearly thought that this was true of the relationships that hold within particular societies, but he is wary about extending this to international relations.[33] This is because he could see a series of incentives and pressures that might lead to trade becoming a cause of war. We will see more about this in chapter 7 when we discuss Smith's criticism of mercantilism, trading companies, and imperialism.

The Fall of Feudalism

Smith's 'four stages' analysis provides him with the basis for an account of the historical evolution of property, law, and government. It also forms the backdrop to his more detailed account of the move from agricultural to commercial societies. Book III of the *Wealth of Nations* explains how commercial societies emerge as a result of a process of historical change. Smith argued that the change of political system from the medieval model to the modern model was entirely the product of unintended and chiefly economic causes. In the title of the chapter he calls this analysis an account of the 'progress of opulence in different nations', but it is also an account of the evolution of the legal and political institutions that are necessary for the development of commerce and wealth.

Smith begins by noting that economic growth and subsistence are driven by the relationship between the town and the countryside.

The 'natural' relationship between the two is that the growth of towns is constrained by the capacity of the countryside to provide food to support the urban population. However, Smith goes on to observe, this is not what actually happened in the history of Europe after the fall of the Roman Empire. The 'natural course of things' was disturbed by 'human institutions'.[34] What Smith means by this is that the rise of the feudal order disturbed the natural relationship between countryside and town.

Smith's explanation rests on the incentives that develop in feudal landholding. Again, the point is not that the position of some legal order known as 'feudalism' causes the change, but rather that the change is driven by the economic and political incentives of the circumstances of Europe at that time. Smith looks at how the feudal landowner becomes a 'sort of petty prince'[35] able to demand loyalty from his dependants and to exercise legal authority over them. In such a system, the degree of power of a particular lord would be measured by the number of his dependants, which would in turn be limited by the extent of his estates. In response to these incentives, the practices of primogeniture (inheritance by the oldest son) and entail (inheritance in the male line conditional on maintaining the estate) develop. These practices are designed to ensure that an estate remains intact and passes to a clear heir. In terms of the basis of wealth and power in a feudal society, they make complete sense, even if, as Smith suggests, they offend against our 'natural' concern for our other children and our desire to manage our own property in our own way.

The owners of these great estates are seldom great improvers and instead live dissipated lives based on constant feasting and entertaining; the hunt rather than the farm is their chief interest, and the hunt itself has become a sport rather than a necessity.[36] After the fall of Rome, the lords lived on estates surrounded by dependent serfs and jealously eyed their neighbours. What merchants and manufacturers there were lived in the towns and cities. The granting of status to these urban centres allowed 'freemen' or 'burghers' privileges that freed them from dependence of particular lords. The people of the towns secured 'liberty and independency'[37] before the countryside. They did this by way of grants and charters from the Crown. In return, the Crown expected their loyalty and left them alone to raise taxes for the treasury. The absence of a predatory lord in this process led to the development of authority structures within the towns, and the town councils and guilds became independent seats of government and sources of law.[38] The kings were keen to encourage this system as they saw it as a way to extend central authority in the face of opposition from the powerful regional magnates.

Smith's analysis of the dynamics of this process is a fascinating study in incentives. The lords despised the burghers, envied their wealth, and would plunder the towns if they could. The burghers knew this and so hated and feared the lords. The king despised the burghers as beneath him, but he did not fear them and so was willing to ally with them to frustrate the lords. As Smith puts it: 'They were the enemies of his enemies, and it was his interest to render them as secure and independent of those enemies as he could.'[39] The unintended result of this was that the first 'regular government' arose in the towns. It was this stable legal environment that created the space for economic growth. As we saw above, this was a historically sensitive account of the decline of the arbitrary use of authority.

While 'order and good government'[40] rose in the towns, the countryside remained mired in violence and poverty. There was no incentive to improve agriculture beyond bare subsistence because of the fear that you would be subject to predatory lords. It was only the towns that allowed this, and so the 'natural' course of the development of the country before the town was reversed in feudal Europe. As Smith observed, when town dwellers 'are secure of enjoying the fruits of their industry, they naturally exert it to better their condition, and to acquire not only the necessaries, but the conveniencies and elegances of life'.[41] The first place to see this were the cities of Italy and those of the Hanseatic League. Trade arose in these cities and they took on the role of importing goods from abroad and finishing the product of the countryside in manufactured goods. The growth of the cities was thus freed from the constraint of dependence on their immediately local countryside because they were able to develop trading relationships with other countries. This sets the scene for the dynamic that Smith believes explains the decline of feudal institutions and the spread of commerce beyond the towns.

Smith's account of how commerce leads to the improvement of agriculture is a masterclass in the analysis of unintended consequences. He begins by noting what he regards as the two main features that drive the improvement of the country: first, the towns provide a market for rural produce and the existence of such a market is an incentive to the rural population to improve output; and, second, merchants often buy estates in the countryside and seek to turn a profit from them by introducing agricultural improvement.[42] Over time, these introduce the habits of the town into the country and gradually order and good government spread from urban to rural areas.[43] Smith then goes on to analyse the dynamics of this process.

In a feudal society, the powerful have nothing to do with their wealth except use it to dominate over their serfs and engage in competition with other lords. All of the product of their land goes on supporting retainers, not because they are benevolent but because they need the security that they provide and, at the end of the day, because they have nothing else to spend the wealth on. The incentive structure in place in a society like this prevents the development of a single unified legal system across the nation. Each landowner is judge over his own dependants and so disorder and violence remain endemic between these petty jurisdictions. Smith cites the Scottish example of Cameron of Lochiel, who exercised judicial authority in his part of the Highlands as a clan leader and raised over eight hundred men to fight in the 1745 uprising.[44]

There are no developed manufactures or foreign goods to buy. But when these goods become available from the towns, the lords have something that they can spend their wealth upon that they themselves can consume. This alters their incentives. They can now indulge their selfish desire for ornamental and luxury goods, and so they do so. As Smith points out, it is the 'silent and insensible operation of foreign commerce and manufactures'[45] that gradually brings about the decline of the feudal system. In a vivid example, he explains how a feudal lord will expend the price of the maintenance of a thousand men on a pair of diamond buckles and that the lords' vanity leads them to dissipate the great estates on which their power depends.[46] So from their selfishness they begin to cease to support serfs, who in turn, deprived of their living in the country, move to towns and find employment in the manufacturing of goods bought by their former lords.

It is important to note that Smith still thought that the feudal lord was supporting the people, but he was supporting them indirectly. The workmen and merchants involved in the production of the buckle are supported by the wages they earn, and these wages ultimately come from customers such as the feudal lord. This is crucial for Smith because it explains what he calls 'freedom in our present sense of the word'.[47] The account of this revolution that was, in his view, 'of the greatest importance to the publick happiness'[48] is brought about by two different orders of people who are pursuing what they think is in their own interest. The lords see the consumer goods as an improvement to their situation and a way of displaying their power and status, while the merchants and manufacturers are improving their situation by seeking to profit from the market for luxuries and conveniences. As Smith would have it: 'Neither of them had either knowledge or foresight of that great revolution which the folly of one, and the industry of the other, was gradually bringing about.'[49]

Smith ends his discussion by returning to the relationship between the town and the country. The wealth generated by trading cities can rise to immense levels, but it is also prey to sudden destruction. This can happen because trading routes change, or wars prevent safe transport, but it can also dissipate quite quickly because, as Smith observes, capital is mobile and a merchant is 'not necessarily the citizen of any particular country'.[50] Once capital has been physically invested in a particular place, such as in the improvement of an estate in the countryside, it becomes more stable and lasting. Smith's point is that the long-term impact of the fall of feudalism and the spread of law and commerce to the country will be a growth in the output of the countryside.

Modern Liberty

The selfishness of the lords and the desire of the former serfs to better their own economic condition destroyed the personal authority of the lords by robbing them of the basis of their power. This is the origin of the modern liberty that Smith sees as both morally and economically desirable. A former serf is now freed from dependence on a single lord and instead works to sell goods to many wealthy people; the lords lose their power to command military service from the serfs and so lose their power to disrupt the social and political order. The lords no longer have the power to assert themselves against other lords and thus the basis of arbitrary local power disappears, to be superseded by the modern centralized state and legal system.

The argument is that commerce and trade lead to stable government and the rule of law, because trade needs stability and because the means of disturbing the social order are gradually diminished in the pursuit of wealth and consumer goods. Commerce and industry, as Smith would have it, 'gradually introduce order and good government' and 'with them liberty and security of individuals'.[51] Primogeniture and entail survive as a sort of residue from an earlier age and they will die out in most cases. The same, Smith points out, is also true of many of the special privileges that were enjoyed by the inhabitants of the towns. As we will see below, the power of guilds to prevent access to the market in a town falls away as the legal system becomes a national rather than a local one.

Smith fleshes out his discussion here with two additional analyses: a critique of slavery and an explanation of the rise of tenant farming.[52] Slavery, according to him, is widespread in poor societies and less common in wealthy societies. The reason for this is economic rather than moral. Slave economies are inefficient. Freemen work for wages and will exert effort in proportion to the return expected. They will then use their wages to support themselves and their families. Slaves, on the other hand, are an expense for their master, who must cover the whole of their maintenance and shelter.[53] More than this, the incentives for slaves militate against hard work. As Smith would have it: 'A person who can acquire no property, can have no other interest but to eat as much, and to labour as little as possible.'[54] By contrast, 'A freeman who works for day's wages will work far more in proportion than a slave in proportion to the expence that is necessary for maintaining and buying him up.'[55] In the face of such a stark set of unproductive incentives, the only reason why slavery persists is because it flatters the weak-minded's idea of superiority.

The inefficiency of slave economies led to their abolition in Europe for Europeans. But, as Smith was well aware, the use of slaves in Britain's American colonies was widespread, a practice that he deplored as an expression of a pervasive 'love of domination'[56] that corrupted the passions. Smith's argument against slavery is economic, but his criticism of it is clearly moral as well.[57] His defence of modern liberty against the charge that it was not the true liberty of the Roman Republic focuses on slavery. Roman freedom was bought at the expense of mass slavery and so the freedom of its citizens was, in Smith's view, inferior to modern liberty, where the freedom of the subjects of a modern state depends on other people being customers rather than slaves. In a modern society, the working poor are free to choose their own occupation, to choose where they live, and are as secure in their property as any member of society. In addition to being a good thing in itself, this improved situation for the working poor is also beneficial to the rest of society. Smith argues that independence and decent wages are the best preventatives of crime and disorder.[58]

Smith's second analysis is of the rise of tenant farmers in post-feudal Europe. The feudal lords realize that they can generate a secure income by leasing their land on a long-term basis. The cash income from these rents is preferable to the direct provision of food that characterized the dependent relationships of the past. Tenancy gradually replaces serfdom and there is the rise of an independent class of tenant farmers – the yeomanry.[59] These tenant farmers now have security of tenure and are willing to invest effort and capital in improving their farms. This model of farming leads to more efficient production and increases the pace of development in the countryside. These farmers are also more likely to improve every possible aspect of their own land because it is a workable size of farm. Smith was intimately familiar with this process since he advised his former pupil the Duke of Buccleuch on how to make just such changes to his vast estates in the Scottish Borders.

Smith's conception of the moral value of independence also finds expression in his preference for independent labour. He was worried about the social impact of large numbers of servants in society. Servants are servile, and servility is a form of mental dependence. Smith thought that this debased the mind and character and led to oppression. Indeed he thought that his own country, Scotland, had been subject to particular oppression by its aristocracy.[60] It was obvious, in his view, that the independence and the decent wages available in a commercial society tended to support public order and higher living standards.[61]

Smith's discussion of the advantages of the 1707 Union of Parliaments to Scotland stresses not just the economic access to English markets, but also the improved situation of the Scottish people. The spread of the rule of law, the extension of the power of the central government, and the suppression of the feudal jurisdictions were a good thing, in Smith's view, because they encouraged independence. In comparing Edinburgh to Glasgow, his criterion for preferring the latter was the greater level of independence and hence industry that held there. The remains of the former court and Parliament meant that dependence was greater in Edinburgh and, as a result, that disorder and crime were more widespread there.

Smith clearly shared the view that the British mixed constitution had developed a legal and political order that secured individual rights to person and property in a way that no previous constitutional order had managed. Like his friend Hume, he thought that it was a historically evolved accident. And also like Hume, he recognized that it was far from perfect and, moreover, that it was precarious. These were values that he shared with the Whig party in the British Parliament. But Smith's support for these features of the British system did not come from the mainstream social contract or mythical-historical arguments of the 'vulgar' Whigs. Instead he is better understood as what Duncan Forbes called a 'sceptical' or 'scientific' Whig.[62] Smith's aim was to provide a generalized theoretical account of the evolution of the modern commercial state that had arisen from the accidents of British history. The mixed institutions and, crucially, the rule of law had created a new type of freedom that he considered to be superior to that of the ancients. He thought that understanding the actual historical origin of these institutions would allow them to be better defended.

Smith's account is a theorized version of the rise of what he sees as the system of government of Hanoverian Britain: a historically evolved 'system of liberty'[63] which, though far from perfect, had nonetheless created the institutions of the rule of law, habeas corpus, jury trials, and an independent judiciary, divided executive, legislative, and judicial functions, and limited the power of the king and the church at the same time as the lords had lost their powerbase with the fall of feudalism. Smith's argument against the legal instantiation of feudalism in entail and primogeniture is simultaneously about economic efficiency and about promoting independence. The whole thing is set against the backdrop of an evolutionary account of the historical development of the modern commercial state, and in the rest of the *Wealth of Nations* he goes on to analyse the development of commerce. This arose 'from the fall of the feudal system, and from the establishment of a government which afforded to industry, the only encouragement which it requires, some tolerable security that it shall enjoy the fruits of its labour'.[64]

6

The Nature of Wealth

Smith's second great book was published in 1776. The *Wealth of Nations* is an enormous text and it is packed with detail, theory, and evidence. The work is divided into five books. We have already covered the contents of Book III, which outline the evolution of commercial society and government out of the feudal era. In this chapter, we will cover the contents of the first two books, which set out the basic concepts that Smith uses to analyse political economy. In the next chapter, we will examine the final two books, which criticize alternative theories of political economy and discuss the appropriate role of government.

Before we begin, it is worth pausing to consider the full title of the book: *An Inquiry into the Nature and Causes of the Wealth of Nations*. This reveals a number of important things to the reader. First, it is an *Inquiry*, and, as we saw earlier, this meant a systematic and scientific examination grounded on empirical evidence. Second, the book is interested in the *Nature* of wealth. This is important because it tells us that Smith was going to develop an argument about what wealth really was. This understanding of wealth would be in sharp contrast to the established understanding of wealth held by the merchants and politicians of his day. Wealth, Smith will tell us, is not to be understood as gold or silver, or a positive balance of trade; rather, it is to be found in the living standards of the people of the country. A country is wealthy when its people have access to the necessities and conveniences of life. If this is the true understanding of wealth, then it is clear that the features which bring that about are the *Causes* of the wealth of nations. Smith's project is both scientific and policy-related. If those in power think wealth lies in amassing gold and silver, then the policies that they adopt will be directed at this rather than at raising the access to the necessities and conveniences of life for the people at large. We will return to Smith's critique of the mercantile understanding of the nature and causes of wealth in the next chapter, but for now we will concentrate on his systematic analysis of the causes of wealth.[1]

The Division of Labour

As with the *Moral Sentiments*, Smith starts the *Wealth of Nations* by stating the central explanatory principle that he will examine through the rest of the book. The division of labour is the cause of the great improvement in productivity that is found in commercial societies. Smith uses the example of pin manufacturing to illustrate his point. One individual working on each step of the process of making a pin could produce barely 20 pins in a day. A small pin factory, by dividing the making of pins into 18 distinct operations, and then dividing these tasks between 10 individuals, is capable of making 48,000 pins in a day. So one man alone can barely make 20, but one man co-operating with others can make 48,000. This, according to Smith, is the cause of the great increase in production in societies that have discovered it. He points out that the division of labour is more applicable in some industries rather than others. For example, agriculture does not lend itself to the division of labour in quite the degree that manufacturing does. This is because agricultural production is divided throughout the year, so the same farmer ploughs the field, sows the crops, tends to them and harvests them. While an individual might specialize in being a farmer, the activity of farming cannot be broken down into specific operations like the pin-making process.

Smith then analyses the grounds for the improvement in production. He suggests that there are three main reasons for this. Each worker specializes on a single simple task and so becomes more skilful at that task. The movement from one task to another is removed, so workers can no longer saunter or avoid work as they move from one task to another. Finally, the invention of machines greatly improves production. These machines are often invented by the specialist workers themselves in order to make their lives easier. Smith gives the wonderful example of a young boy employed to operate a hatch in a steam engine who invents a way of doing this automatically so that he can spend more time playing with his friends. Machines are also invented by a dedicated group of scientists who specialize in inventions. This, Smith suggests, is a further example of the division of labour, as the professions separate out alongside the division of tasks within particular industries.

So the division of labour is the cause of what Smith calls universal opulence. But how he seeks to illustrate this is particularly interesting. He points out that this opulence extends to all ranks of society and that, in terms of the improvement it makes to people's lives, it is most apparent in the lives of the poor. His example is a woollen coat worn by an ordinary labourer. Smith asks us to imagine the great web of interdependence that lies behind the making of this modest garment: the farmer, the weaver, the carrier, the dyer, the tailor, and, more than that, all the people whom those people depend upon for their goods and tools. All of these people have to co-operate through trade and exchange to bring about the production of the coat. No one of them is aware that the end product of the labour is that particular coat destined for that particular worker, but all are nonetheless able to work together. The result, Smith tells us, is that the ordinary labourer has access to affordable clothing. It is worth quoting how he describes this, because this is, in effect, what he means when he talks about wealth: '[W]ithout the assistance and co-operation of many thousands, the very meanest person in a civilized country could not be provided, even according to, what we very falsely imagine, the easy and simple manner in which he is commonly accommodated.'[2] Smith contrasts this to an African king, a man who is the absolute sovereign over 10,000 people, but who enjoys fewer necessities and conveniences than the ordinary worker in a commercial society. The point is clear: in terms of the basic necessities and comforts of human life, societies with the division of labour are better than societies without it. This is not just a matter of material comfort. As Smith points out in the introduction to the book, societies that lack the necessaries of life are deeply unappealing places. People have to watch their children die of starvation, or, perhaps even worse, are forced to kill those children they cannot hope to support. There is nothing noble about poverty. Rousseau's naïve nostalgia for an innocent natural state was deeply wrong, in Smith's view.

Trade

Having identified the division of labour as the cause of the improved production of commercial society, Smith then tries to explain its origins. He argues that the division of labour gradually evolves from human experience of social life. Like language, property, law, and government, it emerges rather than being invented. Smith thinks that we can trace this back to an original feature of human nature that he calls 'the propensity to truck, barter, and exchange one thing for another'.[3] He does not go into much more detail on this but simply points out that everywhere we see humans we see this form of behaviour. The observation is empirically confirmed, but beyond that Smith hazards a suggestion that it may well be a product of the wider human sociability and urge to persuade that he had discussed in the *Moral Sentiments*.

In Smith's view, deliberate trade and exchange was a uniquely human propensity. Dogs don't make deliberate exchanges or agree contracts; only humans do that. When a dog wants something, it begs for it. But as Smith points out, this is an inefficient way of getting what you want. You cannot assume that your appeals will be met, but you can much more reliably assume that someone may give you what you want in exchange for something that they want. When it comes to the division of labour, we rely upon so many people who are unknown to us that begging or appeals to their humanity are not going to work. As a result, Smith famously tells us: 'It is not from the benevolence of the butcher, the brewer, or the baker, that we expect our dinner, but from their regard to their own interest.'[4] The point here is not that all human behaviour is selfish; instead it is that in economic exchange, trade, by appealing to self-interest, is an effective way of interacting beyond the circles of sympathy we saw in chapter 3. Exchanges are mutually beneficial and voluntary: we exchange because we are able to supply our needs by serving the needs of others. Smith underlines the point by returning to the example of the beggar. Even the successful beggar must then go into a shop and exchange the donation for the goods that he requires.

This trucking propensity gives rise to the division of labour in simple societies. An individual who is good at making bows specializes in that task and exchanges his bows for food secured by a hunter who is skilled in using the weapon. This basic form of the division of labour develops in all human societies, but it is only able to develop if the individuals concerned are able to produce something that other people want. There needs to be a demand for our good. Smith then goes on to make a particularly innovative move in his argument. He suggests that beyond very basic societies, the differences between individuals have little to do with natural talents. Instead he argues that most humans are the same when they are children, and that the differences between them only begin to emerge through education and different career paths. The philosopher and the street porter are very different kinds of people, but they are so because of the division of labour. The division does not depend on natural differences between people; it creates social differences as it develops.[5]

Smith is not only deflating the pretensions of the philosopher here; he is also reminding us of the argument that we saw above, that rank is necessary to society, but that it is based on opinion rather than natural differences. What Smith also wants to point out is that the differences between humans, unlike the differences between breeds of dog, can be brought into a 'common stock'[6] through co-operation. Philosophers and street porters can be useful to each other in a way that greyhounds and mastiffs cannot be. This is only possible through trade.

This leads Smith to observe that the division of labour is only possible when we are able to expect that there will be sufficient customers for the good that we specialize in making. The division of labour is limited by the extent of the market. Smith's example is someone who lives in isolation in the Scottish Highlands and must act as butcher, brewer, and baker to himself because there is no one near with whom he may exchange and thus specialize. The extent of the market is determined by the proximity of people to trade with, and so we find a greater division of labour in towns, and by the ease of transporting goods by road or water. Smith's account of the rise of towns and cities stresses how the market there encourages specialization and industry. The greater the extent of the market, the greater the scope to enjoy the benefits of the division of labour. As Smith observes, we see wealth and production reach the highest levels in places where people have congregated and, especially, where sea and river navigation allows them to extend their market by trading with other towns and cities. This is a key observation in the *Wealth of Nations*. When we move on to look at Smith's arguments in favour of free trade, we should bear in mind that it traces back to this observation. The division of labour produces the rising standards of living that we see in commercial societies, and the division of labour is limited by the extent of the market, so things that limit the market limit the division of labour, and reduce the wealth of the nation.

Markets

Once the division of labour has spread through society, we all come to live by trade. This, according to Smith, is a commercial society. Commercial societies also develop a medium of exchange to facilitate trade. As Smith points out, in simple societies I rely on someone wanting the good I produce when I want to trade it. This is not effective, and societies gradually come to develop money as a medium that facilitates trade. Smith provides a brief conjectural history of money and shows how it evolves over time to become more functional in the form of coinage. He is also clear that in commercial societies the generation of an agreed medium of exchange facilitates an even greater deployment of the division of labour.

At this point, Smith begins one of the lines of argument that run through his theory – one which ultimately generates one of his greatest failures: the attempt to identify a universal and scientifically measurable form of value. He discusses the water/diamond paradox to illustrate the problem that he is grappling with.[7] Water is useful and plentiful, whereas diamonds are useless and rare. If value was determined by usefulness, then water should have a higher price that diamonds, but this is not the case. Circumstances influence our valuation of a good. The value of water in terms of diamonds is negligible when there is ample water to be had. The value of diamonds in water is different where there is little water to be had. The 'natural' value of water is not the same as the value it possesses in exchange. This leads Smith to develop a technical distinction between the 'natural' price of goods and the 'market' price of goods, a point we will return to shortly.

Smith is trying to find a universal measure of value that he can build into his theory of how commercial societies operate, but he is trying to do this while acknowledging that there is another notion of value dictated in monetary terms in the actual exchanges in a commercial society. In this, Smith is setting off in pursuit of the great chimera of eighteenth- and nineteenth-century economics, a labour theory of value. He hits on labour as the source of value for quite obvious reasons that come straight out of the account of the division of labour. It is labour that changes a material object from its natural state into its useful state. Labour makes things useful, so a measure of labour will be technically useful in understanding how the exchange of goods operates.

Each individual is rich or poor, so Smith says, 'according to the degree he can afford to enjoy the necessaries, conveniences, and amusements of life'.[8] And his ability to do this involves him being able to secure those goods. If the goods are the product of labour, then wealth is our capacity to command labour. The problem then is that the value in terms of labour is hard to measure. Money does not really help because the money price of a good takes into account a range of features beyond the amount of physical labour involved in production. Also, as Smith points out, money has different values in different places and so the same amount of money will command different amounts of labour in different places. The example here is London and China.

The 'higgling and bargaining of the market'[9] mean that attempts to find a measure of value in labour are practically impossible. One idea that Smith hits on is to look for a proxy for this. This leads to his interest in the significance of the price of corn – as the staple food of working people – as a possible alternative to a physical measure of labour. But even here the price of corn is affected by conditions other than its role in feeding labourers. This puzzle leads Smith to try to disaggregate the various different parts of the price of a good to understand their relationship to labour. In doing so, he provides a set of concepts (wages, profits, rent) that form the building blocks of subsequent economics. They are, in Smith's view, the three original sources of revenue and exchange value.

In a simple society, the price of a good will be closely related to the amount of labour involved in producing the good. If it takes twice the labour to kill a beaver as it does to kill a deer, then one beaver will exchange for two deer. But the problem remains: how does one measure the level of effort or skill involved? A skilled beaver hunter will be more productive than an amateur, so does this mean he is expending less labour? Smith suggests that this sort of problem means that political economists move very quickly away from the idea that we can in practice find an accurate measure of labour.

In a commercial society, production costs are broken down into the cost of the material, the wages of the workers employed, and the profits of the person who advances the 'stock' necessary to arrange the production. The measure of labour is found in the wages of the workers, but again this is not the same thing as a physical measure of the skill or effort involved because it is subject to its interaction with the other costs.

At this point, Smith develops his analysis of the difference between the 'natural price' and the market price. The natural price is a theoretical construct based on the price that goods cost to bring to market: that is, the cost of the rent, wages, and profit required to bring the good to market. But the market price may be either higher or lower than this depending on the condition of the market. As Smith puts it:

> The market price of every particular commodity is regulated by the proportion between the quantity which is actually brought to market, and the demand of those who are willing to pay the natural price of the commodity, or the whole value of the rent, labour, and profit, which must be paid to bring it thither.[10]

Smith points out that when he talks about demand here he means 'effectual demand' and not 'absolute demand'.[11] This is because someone must have the resources to back their desire for the good for them to be able to influence the conditions of trade at a given time in a given market. We then see a basic model of the market: if the quantity is short of demand, then prices will rise above the 'natural' price; if the amount brought to market matches effectual demand, then the market price matches the natural price; if too much is brought to market, then the price will fall below the natural price. In the final case, this means that costs will not be recouped. Smith provides a simple model of the operation of supply and demand in a market and he uses the idea of a natural price as a theoretical construct that illustrates what the bargaining of the market moves around.

The natural price is what Smith calls the central price: the thing that the other prices are gravitating around as the producers and consumers seek to match supply to demand. He is well aware that the market price will rarely hit exactly onto the natural price, as what he calls 'accidents' will prevent it from doing so, but he thinks that thinking in terms of the natural price allows the theorist access to the component parts of price and a better understanding of the operation of the market. Smith can also use this concept as a way of understanding how particular events or regulations affect the market, allowing him to assess different policy proposals – a point we will return to in the next chapter.

It is worth pausing at this point to emphasize two of the basic principles that lie behind Smith's analysis here. First, the account of the operation of a market on the abstract level allows a central role for competition. It is competition that drives the market price towards the natural price. Consumers compete with each other to secure products, and producers compete with each other to secure customers. This is in stark contrast to a situation where there is no competition among producers: a monopoly. For Smith, monopolists are able to keep the market under-stocked and never fully meet effectual demand. As a result, they are able to maintain higher profits by selling their commodities much above the natural price. In an efficient market, the profits are lower because competition between suppliers lowers the price. For Smith, this analysis of the distinction between a competitive and a monopolistic market would become vital in his assessment of rival economic theories. Smith's second basic principle is a broad schema of types of economy that informs the rest of his analysis. He distinguishes between 'advancing, stationary, or declining'[12] economies. This is significant because the operation of markets in each type of economy is different.

Wages

One feature of the economy that is strongly affected by the three types of economy is the wages of labour. The money price of labour is determined by the demand for labour and the price of the necessities and conveniences of life for the labourer. Smith describes a situation where in an advancing economy wealth is rising and wages are rising. The operation of the division of labour increases productivity and that means that goods become cheaper and that they are produced by smaller quantities of labour. One significant impact of this is that populations rise. Populations becomes a useful proxy measure of the advancing nature of an economy. Countries 'people up' to their resources, and easier access to the necessities and conveniences of life allows ordinary workers to have larger families: these are the benefits of the 'liberal reward of labour'.[13]

However, wages are not the only component of price. In order to produce, we need somewhere to produce and the materials to work with. As a result, the division of labour presupposes the input of the owners of 'stock'. This leads Smith to analyse the nature of the relationship between employers and employees. These two orders of people have their own interests. The workers want to get the highest wage that they can, and the employers want to give the lowest wage that they can. This leads the two into a sort of conflict, but one which is defused by the operation of the labour market, where free competition among workers and employers determines the wage. In an advancing economy, this process is characterized by a scarcity of workers, which leads to employers raising wages to attract them. In a declining economy, a surfeit of workers means that employers are able to rely on competition for jobs to drive down wages. Smith also points out that this sort of clash of interests leads to workers combining in trade unions to raise wages and employers combining as a cartel to drive down wages. Smith is clear at this point that the combination of workers is understandable and not something that is to be discouraged. However, the combination of employers is anathema to him. The idea of employers deliberately plotting to force down wages for their own profit is utterly contrary to his conception of the nature of wealth in a society. Recall that the wealth of a nation is the living standard of the population as a whole. Wages must, at a bare minimum, allow a worker to live and maintain his family. If they do not, as is the case in a declining economy, the result is misery.

Scarcity of workers forces the employers to raise wages above bare subsistence. In growing economies, like Britain's American colonies, labour is scare and so wages are high. This in turn drives up population through larger families and through immigrants attracted by the high wages and cheap land. In a stagnant economy, Smith's example is China, the poor struggle to survive, while in a declining economy, here the example is Bengal, we see the population fall. Smith is then able to apply the model to Great Britain and argue that the slower growth experienced there suggests that we should see wages which are closer to subsistence than in the American colonies. The circumstances are different in each example and this leads to the differences in outcome. Smith's approach here is to point, in particular, to the institutional differences as a way of understanding the different outcomes.

This discussion of population is important because it once again illustrates the moral principles behind Smith's assessment of different economic conditions. Smith rejected the view advanced by some political economists that wages had to be kept low to force the poor into work. He dwells on the appalling impact of poverty on the population: people watching their children starve, or even being forced to commit infanticide because they cannot feed another child. For Smith, these things are moral evils, and the further that an economy can distance itself from them the better. But it is also important to note that, despite this, he was dubious about attempts to regulate wages. As he puts it: 'Where wages are not regulated by law, all that we can pretend to determine is what are the most usual; and experience seems to show that law can never regulate them properly, though it has often pretended to do so.'[14]

There is a further important impact of attempts to regulate wages. Wages, like prices, have a signalling role in Smith's thought. A competitive market draws new providers to it in the hope of securing their share of the high profits to be had. Wages, as the price of labour, have a similar function. High wages attract workers to a particular country or industry. The result of this is that the demand for labour falls and the advantages of that industry in terms of wages are gradually reduced, allowing other workers to decide not to enter the industry as wages equalize with other industries. There are, of course, exceptions to this. For example, some occupations are unpleasant or risky and they will always by their nature prove unattractive to some individuals. Wages in such occupations will reflect the hardness and disagreeableness of the labour involved. In other occupations, there might be compensations in addition to wages, while the regular or seasonal nature of the work will also feature in determining the wage level. Smith is perfectly aware that the division of labour means that there are employments that require particular skills and that these can also have an impact on the wages in that field. There may be costs associated with acquiring the necessary skills to gain admission to a profession, just as there may be a snob value in being a member of a particular profession.

Smith also makes a particularly interesting observation about another propensity of human nature that affects our choice of career. He refers to this as the 'over-weening conceit'[15] that people have about their own abilities and the likelihood that they will have good fortune. This widespread tendency leads people to focus on the prospect of success and ignore the chance of loss. Risk is always a part of the choice of profession, but the hope of higher returns tempts many into trying. Smith thinks that this is a general truth about profit in a competitive market. The level of profit reflects the certainty or uncertainty of the returns. Some are more prone to gamble than others, but as we saw in chapter 4, Smith was particularly interested in the prudent man who would resist such temptations.

In Smith's view, there is no contradiction between a growing level of industry and improving the condition of the poor – an argument that would be criticized by some of his nineteenth-century successors, as we will see in the final chapter. It is worth quoting his argument here in full as it represents a significant departure from much previous thinking on the place of the poor in the economy.[16]

> The liberal reward of labour, as it encourages the propagation, so it increases the industry of the common people. The wages of labour are the encouragement of industry, which, like every other human quality, improves in proportion to the encouragement it receives. A plentiful subsistence increases the bodily strength of the labourer, and the comfortable hope of bettering his condition, and of ending his days perhaps in ease and plenty, animates him to exert that strength to the utmost.[17]

It is at this point that we need to bring in yet another of Smith's core theoretical assumptions. The analysis above of wages and prices depends upon what he calls perfect liberty. What he means by this is that if no regulation or intervention takes place, then prices and wages will adjust in the way that he suggests. One such regulation that he discusses in relation to wages is apprenticeships. Some professions are organized around a guild or corporation that admits members based on them having served an apprenticeship under an established member. The ostensible justification of this is to ensure the new entrants have the skills necessary. But Smith is sharply critical of the practice, pointing out that they are in reality an attempt to control the supply of a particular skill in order to allow the members of the corporation to keep their wages higher than they would be under free competition. His point is that this harms customers, but also that it harms the poor by preventing them entering a potentially lucrative profession. Moreover, he is deeply suspicious of the claim that apprenticeships promote skills in practitioners. Instead he believed that the incentives required to encourage practitioners to apply themselves came directly from competition for customers. Reputation rather than occupational licensing is the best guarantor of decent service.

Corporations and guilds tend to be features of towns and cities and they are attempts to exclude new entrants to the labour market. Smith's argument is that this is a form of monopoly, and that it can only persist if the corporation in question is able to enforce the restrictions on entry to the market with the support of the political authority of the town council. This leads us to another interesting feature of his argument, one which shows us quite how far the real Smith is from the public caricature. He observes that: 'People of the same trade seldom meet together, even for merriment and diversion, but the conversation ends in a conspiracy against the publick, or some contrivance to raise prices.'[18]

Smith's political economy is characterized by a distrust of merchants and manufacturers – a feature of his thinking that will prove central to our discussion in the next chapter. Narrowing competition is always against the public interest when we come to see that the public interest is the interest of the whole of the public in their capacity as consumers.

Capital

In Book II of the *Wealth of Nations*, Smith moves on from his outline of the basic concepts for the analysis of political economy to their particular application to commercial society. His argument that 'a great society naturally divides itself'[19] as we move from a hunting society to a more interdependent commercial society leads him to examine the preconditions for the division of labour. We have already seen that it requires the gradual development of a particular set of legal and political institutions and that it is limited by the extent of the market, but he now moves on to consider the other preconditions necessary for the division of labour to develop.

Smith begins by noting that for labour to divide, we must first accumulate 'stock'. This stock can be divided between what we require for our immediate consumption and what we require to invest in specialized production. Each of us then possesses gross revenue and net revenue. The gross revenue is our total income, and the net revenue is that part of it left over when we have deducted what is necessary for immediate consumption. Our capital is the funds we have available to engage in economic activity. Capital can raise a profit by buying goods or manufacturing them and then selling them at a profit, or it can be used to improve the land, or buy machines or instruments of trade. We can better understand the operation of capital by noting that it comes in two forms: fixed capital and circulating capital. Fixed capital is the machinery, buildings, land, and human capital that we keep a hold of to improve production. Circulating capital are things like a stock of goods that a merchant buys and then resells or the wages which move between employer and employee. Smith also understands money as a part of circulating capital – a point we will return to below. In secure economic conditions, everyone will deploy their capital to secure the greatest return. As they do this, they will gradually increase the level of revenue that they enjoy, and over time this allows for both greater consumption and greater accumulation of capital.

Saving

Smith believes that capital arises from saving and reinvestment. The great source of capital is not speculation but rather the frugality of ordinary people. By living within our means, we slowly and gradually build up our capital and, unintentionally, add to the capital available for investment in the country. To illustrate his point, Smith sketches two characters: the frugal man and the prodigal. A frugal man lives within his means and saves something of his revenue for future needs and profit. A prodigal lives on his capital, and as a result he slowly eats away at it. This means that a prodigal will in the end beggar himself by removing a source of future revenue from investment of his capital. At the same time, he will reduce the amount of capital available to the society as a whole. This is interesting because it is a direct criticism of a view that was common at the time, particularly in the satirical writing of Mandeville. This view held that a rich prodigal, by expending his capital, added to the economic activity of the nation. Smith himself had acknowledged the reality of this in his account of the decline of feudalism. However, in this part of the book, he is interested in the productive employment of capital, and the use of existing capital for immediate consumption reduces the overall amount of capital available for investment in increased production. As a result, he sees the prodigal as an enemy of the public and a frugal man as its friend. Injudicious prodigals squander capital.

This might have been a matter of concern for Smith, but he believes that we shouldn't really worry about it because, taken at an average across a nation, more people are careful and frugal than are prodigal. The prodigality of some private individuals will have serious consequences for them individually, but will not threaten the whole of the society. Society can continue to accumulate capital and improve production despite the odd prodigal. Most people are prudent and so the profligate need not concern us. Smith states this as one of his central observations about commercial societies: the 'principle which prompts to save, is the desire of bettering our condition, a desire which, though generally calm and dispassionate, comes with us from the womb, and never leaves us till we go into the grave'.[20] He believes that this desire to improve our situation is insatiable. We are never entirely happy with our lot and are always looking for ways to improve it. Left alone, all individuals will pursue it to the best of their understanding. Sometimes this will lead them to make mistakes, and injudicious investments will squander capital, but in the longer run the preponderance will lie with careful and prudent investment by the bulk of the population. Smith is setting up a distinction between risky speculators and careful investors. The idea is that most people will accept a smaller return to avoid the risk of losing their original capital. Safe investment over time drives the growth of the nation's capital despite the failure of risky enterprises.

Private prodigals may not be a problem, but prodigality does pose a threat to the general growth of capital when it is a feature of the government. Smith is concerned with government prodigality because it takes place without the incentives of private ownership of capital. The government is spending other people's money and often does so without regard for the consequences – something that is far rarer when an individual is investing their own capital. Once again, while Smith is critical of this, he is not too pessimistic. This is because he believes that the historical evidence of the development of commercial societies shows that capital has continued to accumulate from private saving despite the depredations of government. The desire to improve is so strong that it finds a way to power along regardless.

This gradual improvement is often insensible, by which Smith means we do not notice it until it has accumulated over a long period of time. Again, it is worth quoting him on this:

> The uniform, constant, and uninterrupted effort of every man to better his condition, the principle from which publick and national, as well as private opulence is originally derived, is frequently powerful enough to maintain the natural progress of things toward improvement, in spite of the extravagance of government, and of the greatest errors of administration.[21]

This formulation is important because it reminds us that Smith has developed a new measure of the wealth of a nation: that wealth lies in the living standards of the people as a whole and not, like the mercantilists (see below) thought, in the amount of gold hoarded by the government. He reiterates this by pointing out that the debts accumulated by the government to fund its wars with France have led to increased taxes which have in turn reduced the amount of capital available for productive investment. Yet the British economy has continued to grow as the individual subjects have persevered in saving and investing. 'Capital has been silently and gradually accumulated by the private frugality and good conduct of individuals.'[22]

In policy terms, this leads Smith to question government attempts to encourage private frugality and saving. He believes that governments are always and 'without exception'[23] the greatest spendthrifts and so any claim for them to be an appropriate body to regulate private saving is ridiculous. Accumulation of capital invested in increased productivity facilitates the division of labour, which in turn makes more and better goods available to more and more people.

Productive and Unproductive Labour

Smith continues his analysis of the circulation of capital in the economy by adapting a distinction that he takes from the Physiocrats. The French economists whom Smith met in the 1760s had developed a theory that focused on the centrality of agriculture. This led them to develop a distinction between productive and unproductive labour. Productive labour produced subsistence from the land, whereas unproductive labour was everything else, including manufacturing. In Smith's hand, this becomes a distinction between productive labour which produces physical goods and unproductive labour which consumes them. To illustrate his point, he notes that a man grows rich by employing many manufacturers, but he becomes poor by employing many servants.

What Smith is getting at here is that the labour of a servant is spent in the act of serving. It leaves no tangible good that may be sold or enjoyed. It's important to note that Smith does not just apply this term to servants; it also applies to the government, to the professions, and even to himself. Soldiers, actors, lawyers, judges, and professors are all unproductive labour in his terms. But this is a technical term for Smith; it is not value-laden. These professions are necessary to society; the point is simply that they have a different relation to capital than the agricultural and manufacturing labourers. In the case of farmers and manufacturers, part of the return goes to replace the capital advanced in production, and we cover this first before we expend money on non-productive labour. The productive output of the division of labour means that the productive sectors of the economy must reach a level of output where unproductive labour can be supported. A society that can barely feed itself cannot support a mass of actors and lawyers.

Smith's point is analytical. In a commercial society, most of us make use of both unproductive and productive labour. As Smith puts it: 'The rich merchant, though with his capital he maintains industrious people only, yet by his expence, that is, by the employment of his revenue, he feeds commonly the very same sort as the great lord.'[24] We have seen this argument before in his account of the fall of feudalism. In a feudal society, the lords have nothing to expend their surplus on other than the support of retainers. The existence of greater funds devoted to productive industry in a society increases the revenue available to be enjoyed by its people. Smith is arguing that this is an encouragement to industry. Our ancestors were idle because of a want of capital being put to work, and in our own society we can see different types of economy in different places. The example that he cites here is of Glasgow and Edinburgh. Glasgow is the seat of industry in Scotland and there we see capital put to industrious use. Edinburgh is the seat of the law courts and the aristocracy: there we see a greater expenditure on unproductive labour. Capital is generated in Glasgow and expended in Edinburgh.

Banking and Money

Having identified the central role played by capital in supporting productive activity and the development of the division of labour, Smith moves on to consider how this is facilitated in a commercial society. His focus is on circulating capital. This leads him to notice the role of merchants. Merchants are unproductive labour in the sense that they produce nothing material, but they have a key role to play in the circulation of goods through the economy. The role of the merchant is to ensure the flow of goods from the producers to the consumers. Their profit comes from the successful anticipation of demand and organizing the conveyance of supplies to meet it. This opportunity-spotting and facilitation role is vital in the circulation of goods through the economy. We will return to Smith's discussion of merchants in the next chapter. For the moment, let us turn to another element of circulating capital: money. Smith saw money as a part of the circulating capital of a nation that behaved in some respects like fixed capital. Money is an instrument of commerce, a 'wheel of circulation'[25] that facilitates exchange. It is part of the capital of a society but not part of the revenue. Smith's point is that money signals wealth but does not embody it.

Money can be understood as paper promissory notes or as gold and silver. Paper notes are based on trust and confidence in the credit of individuals and banks, and this leads Smith to an analysis of the innovative banking system that had developed in Scotland. Scottish bankers had developed a system of overdrafts, cash accounts, and privately issued notes of credit that was far in advance of anything in operation in England. This was because Scotland lacked the levels of gold and silver held in England. As a result, it had developed a system of paper money that allowed the 'dead' gold and silver held in banks to circulate in the economy and support productive investment. Such paper money does not generally travel outside the country where it is issued and it is limited by the holdings of the issuing bank, but if operated in a prudent fashion, it allows for the more effective circulation of capital. Smith distinguishes the paper notes of private banks from the operation of the Royal Mint and the Bank of England. The Bank of England is not a private enterprise; it is an arm of the state. Its stability is equal to the stability of the British government and it operates in a way that is quite distinct from the private banking sector. But here too the Bank of England does not add to the capital of the state; it merely facilitates its circulation.

Smith spends a significant amount of time analysing the Scottish banks. He suggests that they succeeded because they were careful in their investments. They required regular repayments from known customers and their employees developed a system of credit assessment that reduced the risk of bad loans. The Scottish banks generally avoided over-issuing paper notes from a fear that it would lead to a potential bank run. This would occur when large numbers of note bearers demanded the realization of their notes in gold and silver when the bank did not have the funds to hand. However, there were cases of the over-issuing of promissory notes and there were also cases of over-trading and of poor lending. Smith discusses one particular case of this: the failure of Douglas, Heron and Co. or the Ayr Bank in 1772. This enterprise was backed by many of the wealthiest people in the south of Scotland, including Smith's friend and former pupil the Duke of Buccleuch.

The Ayr Bank over-issued notes and invested unwisely in large-scale improvement projects; over time they lost the confidence of those who held their notes. The collapse of the Ayr Bank directly affected the whole of the Scottish economy. Many of the richest individuals in the country, such as the Duke, fell liable for the bank's losses. The result was that capital that might have been put to productive use ended up being redirected to cover the failed speculation of the bank.

This leads Smith to a consideration of the role of speculators and 'chimerical projectors'.[26] These two groups are dangerous to a banking system in a way that a prodigal is not dangerous to the overall economy. The failure of a prodigal harms only himself so long as most people continue to save responsibly. But the failure of a speculator or of someone who undertakes a grand, but doomed, enterprise will harm both them and the bank, and through the bank, the prudent savers. While Smith accepted that the incentives created by the market in banking would reduce this threat, they would not eliminate it. As a result, he proposed a series of regulations to reduce the risk of such systemic problems. Among these were the ban on small bank notes, a ban on the 'option clause' which allowed a bank to delay repayment on a note to avoid bankruptcy, and a limitation of excessive rates of interest. Smith believed that a system where there was competition between a variety of small banks would encourage responsible lending and note issuing while at the same time preventing systemic failure if one of them should fail. Such 'judicious operations of banking'[27] would provide a stable system for the circulation of capital to productive enterprises. Smith was aware that these policies were a restriction on the liberty of individuals to act as they please. But he thought that the danger of systemic disaster was sufficient to warrant the restriction of liberty. Smith compares this to the regulation that forces builders to place fire walls in city buildings to stop the spread of a fire.

Two final points are worth noting before we leave Smith's discussion of capital. First, he observes that interest rates decrease as the amount of capital increases and profits decline. This is a function of the operation of the market. Where capital is scarce, it can command a higher rate of interest; this falls as it becomes more plentiful and investors compete for returns. Similarly, as competitors enter an industry and profits are driven down, the rate of return on an investment falls. Placing upper limits on the rate of interest does not prevent this from happening: it merely encourages more sober lending within the existing conditions.[28]

Second, Smith is particularly interested in investment in agriculture. This was a widespread concern in the Scotland of his time as the famines of the late seventeenth century were still in living memory. However, Smith has in mind another feature of investment in agriculture. Investment in land is fixed in a nation. This is in contrast to the capital of a merchant, who is mobile and may move to another country. Merchants do not have a home and they might on that account be considered as suspicious and lacking commitment to the country. As we saw, Smith clearly thought that merchants served an important function in the economy. If there are no merchants to ease the connection of producers and consumers, then both groups will be worse off. But the merchants as a class have their own interest, and this becomes central to Smith's analysis of the mercantile system of eighteenth-century Britain.

To summarize, Smith has developed an understanding of the nature of wealth that stresses the access to necessities and conveniences by the population as a whole. He explains how specialization and trade allow for increased output of these goods as individuals attempt to better their condition. When he discusses the capital of a nation, he adopts a similar view. It is the capital of the individuals who live in a nation. National capital is increased through the increase in individual capital, and this can best be achieved by creating the conditions where capital can flow to where it is most productive. The positive case for commercial society is the rising living standards of the ordinary people.

7

Government and the Market

Having laid out his analysis of the operation of the division of labour and the role of capital accumulation and circulation, Smith turns to a historical account of the 'natural' progress of opulence. We discussed the details of this account in chapter 5, where we saw that Smith regarded the development of the rule of law in Europe as an unintended historical evolution that transformed a feudal agricultural society into a commercial society. In Books IV and V of the *Wealth of Nations*, Smith explores political economy as a branch of the 'science of a legislator'. His aim is to apply the theory of commerce outlined in Books I and II to the sort of social and legal order that is outlined in Book III. Smith claims that political economy has two objects: to provide a plentiful revenue or subsistence for the people, or more properly to enable them to provide such a revenue for themselves, and to supply the commonwealth with a revenue sufficient for public services. Book IV is aimed at two 'false' theories of the economy and by implication provides a defence of Smith's preferred system of 'natural liberty', while Book V outlines the proper role of the government.

The Mercantile System

By far the greatest part of Book IV is taken up by Smith's attack on the dominant understanding of the economy that prevailed in Britain at the time. This 'theory' has come to be known as mercantilism. Mercantilism is not so much a 'theory' of international trade as it is a set of attitudes and prejudices that developed in Europe with the growth of trade in the early modern period. The main points of the mercantilist worldview were that wealth is national and that nations compete through trade in a form of warfare. Wealth is understood as the amount of treasure in the form of gold and silver that a nation holds. For the mercantilists, trade is a zero-sum activity: if I gain, then you lose. Importing goods means sending treasure to rivals, so I 'lose', whereas exporting goods means acquiring treasure from rivals, so I 'win'. This developed into the doctrine of the 'balance of trade', where restrictions were placed on goods that were considered too valuable to export, and tariffs and duties were introduced to protect home producers and prevent treasure leaving the country. Mercantilism was closely related to the expansion of European colonies and the first age of European imperialism. Colonialism and empire secured a captive market for a nation's goods and at the same time allowed its merchants sole access to the raw materials of the colonies. Governments granted exclusive trading privileges to powerful trading companies such as the British East India Company. With monopolies of the colonial trade in place, vast profits were secured to the company.

One of the few mercantilist thinkers whom Smith addressed directly in the *Wealth of Nations* was Thomas Mun (1571–1641). Mun was a director of the East India Company and his posthumously published book *England's Treasure by Forraign Trade* (1664) is a defence of the mercantile system. Mun is more sophisticated than some mercantilists because he sees that the crude view of wealth equalling money is mistaken. He argued that the example of the East India Company shows the profit in goods to be made if treasure is deployed in India and profits are returned home. Moreover, he was also aware that increasing the amount of gold in a country could have an inflationary effect on the price of other goods. Gold, though, did have one abiding value. It could be hoarded and used to fund wars. If trade was war by other means, then the possibility of conflict between the European powers was very real as they competed for access to and control of trade.

Mun was still an advocate of the central mercantile attitudes. The wealth of a country's merchants was the wealth of the nation. Trade should be a constant attempt to sell more than you buy and to compete by any means with your foreign rivals. There were particular profits to be made from carriage and re-export of goods between colonies and the home country and this should be secured through giving British ships a monopoly on carrying British goods. For Mun, it is the job of the government to enforce such monopolies and to use customs and taxes to advance the merchants' interests.

Smith's response to this represents a systematic debunking of all of the central tenets of the merchant's worldview.[1] It sometimes comes as a surprise to people familiar with the caricature 'Adam Smith' when they discover that Smith was a fierce critic of the dominant business interests of his day. He believed that the merchants advance their own interest and claim that it is the national interest. They are able to do this because the country gentlemen in Parliament don't understand trade and can be persuaded to enact laws and impose taxes that enrich the merchant class.

His main observation is quite straightforward: wealth is not money. Recall the full title of the *Wealth of Nations*. It is an inquiry into the 'Nature and Causes' of wealth. The mercantilists have misunderstood the nature of wealth and so the policies that they advance are misdirected. Smith has already explained that the true nature of a nation's wealth is its people's access to necessities and conveniences. 'Goods can serve many other purposes besides purchasing money, but money can serve no other purpose besides purchasing goods.'[2] By hoarding gold and granting monopolies, the mercantile policy limits the two most powerful drivers of increasing wealth. It limits the size of the market, thus limiting the division of labour, and it encourages dormant rather than circulating capital. Smith's point is simple: if gold and silver are understood as commodities, then we should trust the freedom of trade to supply us with what we can afford of them as it does with any other good. As he puts it: 'The quantity of every commodity which human industry can either purchase or produce, naturally regulates itself in every country according to the effectual demand.'[3]

Where the level of gold imported into the country exceeds effectual demand, nothing can stop it leaving. Smith discusses the example of Spain and Portugal, who imported South American gold and silver to the home market. The result was a fall in the price of gold at home, which led to gold leaving Spain and Portugal for places where it fetched a higher price. Attempts to keep the gold in the country led to smuggling and piracy. Smith argues that the real impact of the influx of gold has been to make it more available to a greater number of people. The desire for gold led to a distorted trade between South America and Europe: rather than a mutual exchange of new goods, we saw imperial exploitation. The cruelty of such policies was clearly something that struck Smith, but his argument remains empirical here. The policies are economically inefficient.

The final defence of hoarding gold was that it is necessary to pay for wars. But Smith points out that modern wars are financed by debt. Britain was able to spend upwards of £90 million fighting France when there was barely £30 million of gold in the country. Armies need supplies, and trade in manufactured goods generates the ability to buy those goods. The cost of the war was defrayed through exports of goods. Countries who export a large annual surplus of manufactured goods can fund a long-term foreign war without diminishing the amount of gold in the country. The benefit of foreign trade is not gold and silver – it is the ability to better secure our material wants and desires. Extend the market, extend the division of labour, increase the wealth of the nation.

Mercantile Policy

In the following chapters of Book IV, Smith launches detailed attacks on each of the main planks of mercantile policy. Before we look at the content of these arguments, it is worth pausing to consider the way in which Smith is arguing. He has provided us with a principled theory in the first three books and he is now applying it. But his application is a pragmatic one. Smith does not think that the policy of free trade, or the system of natural liberty, as he calls it, will ever come to full realization on account of the interests of particular groups in society being harmed by it. But he also realizes that there are other political concerns that need to be taken on board when moving from theory to practice.

Smith begins his analysis by looking at restraints on imports through high duties or outright prohibition. There are two broad types of these: those that prevent the import of goods that can be made at home, and those that are used to correct for an 'unadvantageous' balance of trade. Smith's language is revealing here. He says that merchants who support these policies secure 'a monopoly against their countrymen'.[4] The point is that the monopoly benefits the merchant, but not the rest of the country. Smith's argument is that the annual revenue of a society is equal to the exchange value of the goods it produces. This in turn cannot exceed what the nation's capital can support. No regulation of commerce can increase it beyond this. Such regulations merely divert capital and industry in an 'artificial'[5] direction. Using tax to prevent imports harms free trade and reduces revenue.

At this point, we find Smith deploying his famous notion of the invisible hand. He suggests that every individual wants to improve their situation, and they invest their effort and capital in the way that strikes them as most likely to do this. The result of this, Smith argues, is that the total industry of the nation is directed in the most efficient fashion. The individual unintentionally enriches the nation. In Smith's example here, he suggests that most people prefer to invest close to home to avoid risk. The result is that the home economy grows without the need for mercantile restriction.

This natural flow of capital and industry is more effective than any policy developed by merchants or politicians.

> As every individual, therefore, endeavours as much as he can both to employ his capital in the support of domestic industry, and so to direct that industry that its produce may be of the greatest value; every individual necessarily labours to render the annual revenue of the society as great as he can. He generally, indeed, neither intends to promote the public interest, nor knows how much he is promoting it. By preferring the support of domestic to that of foreign industry, he intends only his own security; and by directing that industry in such a manner as its produce may be of the greatest value, he intends only his own gain, and he is in this, as in many other cases, led by an invisible hand to promote an end which was no part of his intention. Nor is it always the worse for the society that it was no part of it. By pursuing his own interest he frequently promotes that of the society more effectually than when he really intends to promote it. I have never known much good done by those who affected to trade for the public good. It is an affectation, indeed, not very common among merchants, and very few words need be employed in dissuading them from it.[6]

Telling people how to use their capital is futile because statesmen will always have less knowledge of the specific circumstances of each individual and less incentive to invest the capital effectively than those individuals have themselves. Creating a monopoly in the home market directs people to use their capital in an inefficient fashion. Smith's simple dictum is that, like any sensible family, we shouldn't make at home what we can buy cheaper abroad. The unintended consequence of such monopolies is to reduce the wealth of the nation by directing capital to uneconomic activity.

Smith offers us a deliberately stark example. He points out that we could, if we wanted, produce wine in Scotland. But the amount of resources in terms of greenhouses, heating, and labour would make such an attempt ridiculous when there is the option of buying from France or Portugal, where such investment is unnecessary. It would obviously be in the interest of the Scottish wine producers to have a monopoly of the home market, but could it ever really be in the interest of the rest of the population if the government were to enforce tariffs to exclude foreign wine? All that would happen would be that we would have wine of low quality and would pay a high price for it. The monopoly would be held by the wine producers against their own people.[7] Smith illustrates this idea, what has come to be known as absolute advantage in trade, by comparing it to the ordinary lives of individuals living in a commercial society. Why try to make something at home when it is cheaper to buy it from someone else and you can save your time and energy? This is a proper policy for the interactions of a tailor and a shoemaker, and the same logic applies to the trading relations of nations.

At this point, Smith adopts a more pragmatic approach. Rather than damning all restrictions on trade on principle, he considers cases where they may be justified on some consideration other than economic efficiency. He points out that the Navigation Act, which gave the monopoly of British trade to British ships, is not favourable to commerce, but accepts that there are sound military reasons for it. The Act ensures that Britain has a ready supply of ships and sailors that can be drawn upon in the event of war. Smith extends this to a more general exception on matters of national defence. A country needs the means to defend itself in time of war, and so there are sound political reasons to subsidize or protect the home production of military materials.

Smith also considers it permissible to level a tariff on foreign imports when the home industry is subject to a tax. This simply equalizes the market conditions produced by the domestic tax. But this point also prompts Smith to reiterate another of his central arguments. He is against any taxes on necessities, for both home production and imports. These taxes raise the cost of subsistence and make it harder for the population to enjoy a comfortable standard of living. They also make labour dearer as a worker has to pay more for the necessity in question and this in turn will affect wages. Smith suggests that such interference with access to necessities acts like a natural handicap, similar to barren soil.

Smith's third exception is more carefully worded. He considers whether it is a good idea to impose a tariff in retaliation for a restriction on your own trade in the hope of persuading the removal of the original tariff against you. Smith regards this as a matter of political judgement, but notes that if there is no hope of the tariff being removed, then all that you are doing is compensating one group of people by injuring all of the people. This, in his view, is not the role of a statesman, who must look to the good of the people as a whole when deciding policy.

Finally, Smith considers how we should move towards freer trade. He argues that this should be gradual to prevent sudden shocks in the affected industry. Slowly opening domestic markets allows time for the affected industries to adjust. Smith qualifies this gradualism by noting that he thinks these shocks will be less than imagined as they will not impact on efficient industries and the capital from the defunct industries will flow to more profitable industries. At this point, he makes a specific policy recommendation. He points out that the current laws concerning welfare for the poor are based on a localized parish system which insists that the poor must stay in their own parish to secure support. However, such a policy prevents people moving to places where they might find better employment opportunities. Internal migration would allow people to adapt even more quickly to the changes that would be brought about by removing protections. This observation becomes a general theme in Smith's analysis where he points out that well-intentioned policies sometimes turn out to produce unfortunate unintended consequences.

Smith then moves on to consider the barriers to trade that are defended on the basis of an 'unadvantageous' balance of trade. This is the idea that we are 'losers' if we have a negative balance of trade with another country. Smith clearly thinks that this is a product of nationalistic prejudice. Moreover, such restrictions are often the result of political rivalry. His example here is the restrictions on French wine and preferences for Portuguese wine that arise from political alliances. The result of this is that the British pay more for poorer wine. But Smith does not stop there. He points out that this way of viewing trade is 'absurd'.[8] It ignores what we do with the goods in question and why we might want them. It also ignores the possibility of importing goods to re-export them (the basis of the success of the Dutch economy).

Trade is not zero sum, and so no goods are sent abroad except those whose value abroad is greater than at home. Profit made from exports adds to capital of the home country and can then be reinvested. Such restrictions always come from the capture of the political system by interested parties. Merchants and manufacturers are to be distrusted and their influence on politics to be resisted because they will always seek to use political prejudice to secure policies that favour their profits. The idea that we are engaged in competition with our neighbours is nonsense. Rich neighbours are good customers, so the mercantile idea of a balance of trade between countries is self-defeating. The only 'balance' that matters is between production and consumption – we must live within our means. For Smith, it is an empirical fact that free trading nations are wealthier than nations who restrict trade, so the science of a legislator suggests that such restrictions harm the nation's interest.

Having dealt with barriers to trade, Smith then moves on to the other side of the mercantile policy agenda: the attempt to encourage exports and secure foreign markets. He moves through a number of such policies and assesses their impact on the economy as a whole. The least objectionable are drawbacks. A drawback encourages exports by allowing the merchants to drawback, or avoid, the tax on a particular good if it is imported in order to be re-exported. The clearest example of this in Smith's day was tobacco, and his familiarity with the Glasgow tobacco 'Lords' made him well aware of the role of drawbacks in their business model.

More contentious are bounties, or subsidies on exports. Smith argues that all they do is allow an unprofitable industry to survive at the expense of the rest of the population who fund the bounty through taxation. Bounties misdirect capital away from efficient industry and in extreme cases they result in an industry whose 'profits' are the bounty itself. Smith notes that merchants like bounties on exports, where they can make a profit, but oppose bounties on production as a whole, which would reduce their profits.

The most detailed discussion of bounties leads Smith into a more general discussion of the regulation of the corn market. Corn was the staple food of the working population and it was subject to regulations that were intended to guarantee security of supply. Smith points out that because corn is the staple food of working people, the price of corn regulates the nominal price of other goods (including labour). As a result, the impact of interventions in the corn market is potentially felt throughout the economy. Smith believes that the vital nature of corn has led to a series of beliefs about the exploitation of the poor by corn dealers. He begins his discussion by questioning the central purpose of the corn regulations. The corn market is regulated to prevent dearth, but, he argues, these regulations do not prevent dearth, and in some extreme cases they actually lead to a dearth becoming a famine. According to Smith, the empirical evidence shows that corn dealers are not the cause of a dearth of corn. This is the result of genuine drops in supply rather than hoarding to exploit the poor through higher prices. The policy responses driven by this prejudice, attempts to restrict exports, control prices, or manage domestic production, interfere with the 'natural' operation of the corn trade. A rising price allows people to reduce consumption and prompts the corn dealer to seek new supplies from overseas. A world free trade in corn would allow the dearth in one country to be met by the excess of others. Restricting the market means that in times of poor harvest, the shortage worsens and famine results. This is a bold claim by Smith: well-intentioned governments cause famines by attempting to manage the corn market.

Smith then moves on to trade treaties. His argument here is interesting. One might have expected him to be a strong advocate of trade treaties as a way of fostering trade between countries. Instead he argues that a treaty between two countries can act to misdirect industry because it leads them to focus on the two-way trade between them rather than wider market opportunities. Trade between Portugal and Britain is brisk, but the treaty it is based on means that overall trade for Portugal and Britain may be brisker if allowed to flow naturally to other countries.

Empire

The final mercantile policy that Smith addresses is colonialism. He is deeply opposed to colonies and empire because he sees them as potentially the most dangerous of the mercantile errors. He begins his analysis by noting the modern European colonies do not follow the ancient model. In the ancient world, colonies were a response to over-population at home and generally involved settling a new city in a sparsely populated area which over time became an independent community. Modern colonies have arisen from quite different motives. The earliest European empires, those of Spain and Portugal, were a result of greed and the desire for gold. The idea that a great empire is a sign of great wealth and power was beginning to develop into a competition for prestige between the European powers. The pride in holding an empire and the avidity for gold led the Europeans to think that markets could be extended through conquest and settlement.[9]

Smith's discussion is informed by the dispute with Britain's American colonies that took place in the 1760s and 1770s when he was working on the book. He discusses why colonies become successful. They tend to grow more quickly than the native economy because they import knowledge of methods and political and legal institutions from their home country. Smith wants to suggest that it is these institutions that actually drive growth. In such colonies, land is cheap, population is low, and so wages are high. These opportunities draw people to the colony and further drive growth. The British colonies in America were the most economically developed, but this was not because they had any natural advantage in terms of fertility of land. Instead their success came from the fact that the British enforced a stable legal system and left the people to direct their own economic activity.

Smith does appreciate the irony that slavery is pervasive in the British American and Caribbean colonies, and this raises the interesting thought that the rule of law that protects property in the British colonies has the unfortunate unintended consequence of allowing slave owners greater power over their slaves. If the right to do what you want with your property is respected, then the magistrate is less able to intervene to restrict the treatment of slaves. As we saw above, though, Smith had already provided us with an economic argument for the inefficiency of slavery, and while it seems clear that he disapproved of it on moral grounds, he also wanted to understand how the institution operated in the British colonial trade.

Smith clearly had some sympathy with the complaints of the colonists. They were rightly unhappy with the restrictions placed on their ability to trade with other countries, and the complaints about taxation and representation carried some weight. But Smith adopts a conciliatory approach, accepting some of the American complaints and rejecting others. He points out that even though the Navigation Act forced the American colonies to trade through Britain, the Act itself did not provide a monopoly to any one company and so competition between British ports and ships meant that the damage of the monopoly was reduced.

What is perhaps more interesting about the argument here is that Smith thought that the colonial trade also harmed Britain. It forced

British trade in unnatural directions and prevented the British from seeking other sources for the goods that were derived from the colonies. The influence of those involved in the colonial trade had become the most powerful interest in directing colonial policy. Smith believes that the colonial trade distorts the British economy and that the supposed gains that come from it are in reality less than would be had from allowing free trade with all countries. Such a policy would also save Britain the expense of defending the colonies and the political bother of dealing with complaints about tax and representation.

In general, the colonial trade diverts British trade in an unnatural direction. It misdirects capital and it perverts prices. The trade of Britain has been forced down a narrow colonial market rather than flowing to many smaller markets as it would if left to follow its natural course. Such is the distortion of British trade that a 'small stop' in the 'giant blood vessel' of North Atlantic trade may wreck the whole economy. The public pride in the supposed scale of Britain's empire was driving the government to oppose the colonial demands. Smith argued instead that Britain should devolve powers to the colonial assemblies, guarantee representation in the British Parliament, and open up both home and colonial markets to free trade. In time and with further economic growth, he even went so far as to speculate, the capital of the empire might move to the Americas.

The mercantile arguments that were used to support imperial expansion were entirely wrongheaded in Smith's view. Perversely, the attempts to secure the colonial market are actually harmful to the home nation. If this was somewhat mitigated by the preservation of the rule of law in Britain's colonies, it was entirely lacking from the expanding influence of the East India Company. Trading companies not only had a monopoly of the trade with a particular country, they also tended to have a monopoly of the carriage as well. Moreover, they had begun to expand their influence over the political systems of the countries they were involved with. Smith accuses the East India Company of blurring the role of company and government and so failing at both. What he means by this is that the interest of a government should be in the two tasks that we began this chapter with: providing the conditions for the people to secure their living; and providing the revenue to fund the necessary activities of the state. A hybrid company-government is faced with the contradictory interests of the people and the company. The political system is corrupted and misdirected by the interests of the company. The company will use the law and the political institution to advance its interests and harm those of its rivals; its interest is in its revenue rather than in the revenue of the people.[10]

Overall, Smith is suspicious of merchants and manufacturers, and as the arguments in Book IV show, their attempt to pass their own interests off as those of the nation are sophistry. In a particularly powerful passage he notes that: 'Consumption is the sole end and purpose of all production; and the interest of the producer ought to be attended to, only so far as it may be necessary for promoting that of the consumer.'[11] A system of 'natural liberty' in international trade would allow nations to take advantage of each other's natural advantages through trade. Just as the positive case for the division of labour within a society is based on the advantages of specialization, so international trade allows the surplus of one place to fulfil the dearth of another.

The Agricultural System

At the end of Book IV, Smith devotes a single chapter (Ch. IX) to attacking the 'Agricultural System' which is supported by the French economists known as the Physiocrats. Smith had met many of the leading figures in this school when he travelled through France in the 1760s. He thought that their work was interesting and it seems to be something that he engaged with while writing the *Wealth of Nations*. The chapter on the Physiocrats is short not because Smith is being dismissive, but because many of his central arguments up to this point have directly contradicted the ideas of this school. Smith believes that the Physiocrats were wrong to assert that agriculture is the sole source of wealth. He has shown how it is the division of labour that is the chief engine of growth. Moreover, the account of the fall of feudalism in Book III suggests that the Physiocrats had underestimated the role of commerce and the towns in the particular historical development of Europe. Wealth flowed from the town to the country in the story of the development of commercial society, not the other way around.

Smith was also worried by the Physiocrats' approach to understanding the economy. They seemed to believe that it was possible to develop a detailed and systematic model of the operation of the economy that could serve as the basis for economic policy. Smith refers to them as 'speculative physicians'.[12] They are too keen to arrange the economy into a system rather than generalize from the observation of how it actually operates. As a result, they tend to be ideological rather than pragmatic in their political economy.

Smith closes his discussion of the Physiocrats by making the clearest statement of his view on the role of government. The government should not engage in directing trade; instead it should provide the conditions in which trade might take its 'natural' course. These, it turns out, are the conditions of modern liberty that we have seen Smith emphasize in his moral and legal writings. Remove restraints and privileges and 'the obvious and simple system of natural liberty establishes itself of its own accord'.[13] In Book V, Smith moves on to discuss the proper role of government and the means by which the sovereign secures the revenue to provide its core services. His discussion takes place under three headings: Defence, Justice, and Public Works and Institutions.

Defence

As we noted above, Smith's discussion of defence takes place as part of his 'four stages' schema of types of society. But it is also part of a wider debate in eighteenth-century Scotland about the military effectiveness and political danger of a professional army. Smith's central observation is that in all types of society the sovereign or government has the responsibility of defending the society from its external enemies. In a civilized society, where manufactures have begun to advance and the division of labour has taken place, we see the rise of a professional class of soldiers. According to Smith, this is a natural reaction to two features of commercial society. First, the division of labour encourages specialization as the art of war becomes more complex. The introduction of firearms and the application of technology to warfare means that experts who specialize in this task have an advantage over amateur militias. Second, the other divisions of labour in society mean that people focus their attention on particular tasks, creating the need for a government-funded army whose personnel are paid to specialize in military matters rather than in any other occupation.

The size of a country's standing army is no longer dependent on the size of its population. Instead it becomes dependent on the size of a country's economy – or on the amount of tax revenue that can be expended on permanent military expenses. Defence also becomes more expensive as society advances. This is partly because of the rising wages of the general population, meaning that army wages must also rise to retain personnel, and partly because the arms required by a modern army are more technologically advanced. Moreover, civilized countries with professional armies are no longer threatened by less advanced countries of hunters and shepherds. This, then, is Smith's central observation on the paramount role of the government in a commercial society: it must above all else defend the country from external threats. As he puts it: 'It is only by means of a standing army, therefore, that the civilization of any country can be perpetuated, or even preserved for any considerable time.'[14] To the charge that a standing army might itself become a threat to political order, Smith responds by observing that if the sovereign is the head of the army and the ranks map onto the class structure of the society, then the interest of the state and the army are the same. A government that feels secure in the possession of a loyal standing army, far from being a threat to the liberty of the citizens, in fact turns out to be its greatest guarantor. A weak and ill-supported sovereign will see every potential disturbance in society as a threat to their rule, but if they feel more secure, they will be less oppressive, safe in the knowledge that, should they have to, they can defend themselves.

Justice

In chapter 5, we discussed Smith's account of the historical evolution of the legal and political order necessary for a commercial society to succeed, and this 'exact administration of justice'.[15] His account was based on the development of property, inequality, and rank in society. Civil government requires subordination – recall Smith's claim that strength and age give way to birth and fortune as the basis of rank in more developed societies. A side-effect of this is the development of a system that protects the person and property of all citizens. Smith pointed out that the increasing complexity of the role of adjudication led the sovereign to devolve judicial power. Over time, this division of labour separated the task of making law and the task of raising revenue from the task of the judiciary. This, according to Smith, is one of the most important (though unintended) consequences of commercial society. His argument is that the judicial system should be separated from the executive function of government and have an independent career structure and an independent revenue base. Though this was initially a historical evolution, Smith is able to draw policy conclusions from it. As he would have it: 'When the judicial is united to the executive power, it is scarce possible that justice should not frequently be sacrificed to, what is vulgarly called, politics.'[16] Even when politicians mean well, they may be tempted to interfere with the impartial administration of justice in the pursuit of policy goals. But this would undermine the stability of expectations provided by a secure legal order, and result in a disincentive to invest labour and capital in productive activity. The independence of the judiciary is a key barrier to this. Independent and impartial judges provide a reliable guard against a predatory political elite using the law to favour itself or its desired policy outcomes. As we noted above, without justice, society cannot exist, so the more secure and certain the justice system, the more stable the society. This becomes the second task of government: the protection of citizens from each other.

Publick Works and Institutions

Smith's third category of government activity is the provision of certain public works and institutions that are advantageous to society, but which would not generate a profit sufficient to motivate private individuals to provide them. These fall under two broad categories: things that facilitate commerce and things that provide instruction for the people. In both cases, Smith adopts a basic rule of thumb when discussing what should be provided – that it would not be provided by private individuals for profit – and a basic rule of thumb about the most effective way to procure that good. Here it is perhaps best to quote the man himself: 'Publick services are never better performed than when their reward comes only in consequence of their being performed, and is proportioned to the diligence employed in performing them.'[17]

Some services, such as the Post Office, are straightforward enough and can be funded directly by charges to use the service. Smith accepts that the Post Office is a mercantile project run by government, but he regards it as a sort of self-funding service. In other words, the government provides the infrastructure and takes the profit to cover its outlay. While this may return a profit above the outlay, the motivation for engaging in the activity is not this profit itself; rather it is the idea that the service itself is a useful public work that facilitates social and commercial life. Beyond these sorts of limited activities, Smith is very suspicious of governments who get involved in trade. As we saw above in his discussion of the East India Company, the clash of incentives created by governing and trading almost always harms both activities.

Most public services that facilitate commerce can be managed and funded from local revenues. Smith's support for local provision is often overlooked in discussions of his views on the role of government, but by far the greatest number of the public works that he advocates are to be arranged and provided on a local basis. Bridges, roads, and canals may require initial investment by local councils, but they will in time be repaid by tolls on these transport routes, which will fall on those who benefit from them within the locality. Smith clearly thought that local taxes should pay for local goods and wanted to see a clear line between the goods provided by national government and those provided by local councils. London, he argued, should pay for the lighting of London's streets. But he was aware of the charge that local government was open to the danger of corruption. His view was that such corruption will only ever be petty as the sums involved would pale against a national government that involved itself in local service provision.[18] Petty corruption was a risk, but a risk that could be managed by the reputational effects of holding office in small communities: a point that fits neatly with the account of the origins of moral corruption that we discussed above.

The national government should provide the highways between towns and collect the tolls upon them.[19] Although the toll will fall on carriers, this will be passed on to the general population through raised prices. This, according to Smith, is not necessarily a problem in itself as the provision of better roads will reduce the cost of transport to an extent that will cancel out the modest tolls necessary to fund the upkeep and repair to the road network. Smith is more worried by the fact that such tolls come to be considered as part of the general revenue of the government and so may be raised beyond the levels necessary to maintain the road network as they become an attractive source of additional income for the government. He believes that this will, over time, lead to such tolls discouraging trade, limiting the size of the market, and slowing economic growth. In examining this danger, Smith reveals how subtle his policy analysis can be. He observes that tolls based on the weight of the vehicle might seem reasonable – as they do most to damage the road surface. But the actual impact of this will fall more on the poor than the rich, because the bulk transport of large weights of goods is usually mass-produced goods that are more likely to be consumed by the poor. As a result, Smith prefers a system where tolls fall more heavily on the luxury carriages of the wealthy, who travel for leisure, and the vehicles that transport luxury goods.

In addition to public works that facilitate trade in general, there are actions that governments have taken to advance particular industries. Here Smith returns to the issue of the dangerous relationship between the merchant class and the political system. He discusses the role of trading companies who open up new trade routes with other parts of the world. As we saw above, Smith was keenly aware of the political and economic danger of such enterprises as the East India Company, and in this section we see him make the case that any extraordinary expense needed to support a trade should be defrayed by a tax on that trade. The goal must be to prevent the companies drawing on the general revenue of society to support their particular interests. Merchants have sought the support of the sovereign to open a trade route, and Smith accepts that this might warrant a temporary monopoly on that route. But in the longer term the expense associated with that trade should be funded by it. Smith also notes that such international trade relationships create more general expenses for government, particularly through an expansion of the role of ambassadors.

Smith's analysis of the trading companies focuses on the incentives created by their structure. Regulated companies, he observes, act like guilds. Once admitted, each member makes his own profit from his own investment. He has no real common interest other than in restricting the number of members of the company to avoid competition. In the case of joint stock companies, on the other hand, all partners share from a common profit of the enterprise and this alters the incentives that guide their behaviour. In joint stock companies, the share of the profit and the liability for the debts of the company are determined by the shareholding of the individual. Smith believed that this encouraged risky investment strategies. Moreover, joint stock companies are run by managers on behalf of their shareholders, and as a result the managers are not investing their own money and so have even less of an incentive to make careful investments. The third type of possible model for such companies is what Smith calls a private co-partnery. In a partnership, each partner shares in the profit of the enterprise, but is bound for the debts of the enterprise to the full amount of his fortune. He is more likely to be involved in the direct management of the enterprise and so the incentives and risk structure of the business line up. Smith clearly preferred co-partner models, but he was willing to acknowledge that small joint stock companies could mirror the advantages of co-partnerships. However, he believes that over time the joint stock companies will lose out to the more careful investment of the partnerships. It is worth noting that subsequent developments proved this to be one prediction where Smith was very wrong.

There are some exceptions to this, and these mirror the problem of public works in the sense that there are some enterprises where the level of investment required would deter any small number of individuals from taking the risk. Smith lists banking, insurance, and canals as examples of this. In such cases, it is only through the risk limitation offered by the joint stock model that the good in question is likely to be provided. But Smith is cautious here as well. His dim view of the East India Company was discussed above. But he returns to the theme here and reiterates his view that it is both a 'bad steward' of investments and a 'bad sovereign'[20] for the people over whom it rules. The monopoly granted to such companies should be temporary. It should act like a patent, and when it expires, the forts and garrisons that it developed should revert to the government. Creating open-ended trade monopolies is a recipe for abuse.

Education

Smith follows his discussion of the public works that facilitate trade with the discussion of public works that facilitate the instruction of the people. This in turn falls into two categories: the education of the young and the education of people of all ages in religious institutions. In both cases, Smith is heavily influenced by the institutional structure of the Scottish system that he had grown up in. He begins with the education of children and observes that, as in Scotland, this should be organized and funded on a local level. His experience of the University of Glasgow and Balliol College, Oxford, had persuaded him that teaching would only be of a high quality if it was funded through a direct fee relationship between the professor and the student, as opposed to the endowed fellowship system at Oxford.

Smith's discussion of the universities is grounded in his experience at Oxford, which led him to the view that endowments, even if watched over by some external authority, failed to encourage diligence in teaching. As a result, the Oxford colleges were organized for the ease of the masters rather than the education of the students. Compared to these sham lectures where lazy lecturers repeated out-of-date material, Smith saw that the cutting-edge curriculum and diligence of his Glasgow professors was a direct result of the fact that their payment depended on their skill as teachers. Depending on the quality of one's teaching to make a living made one a better teacher. Smith believed that this was confirmed by the fact that the subjects taught by freelance tutors, such as fencing and dancing, were usually better taught that those where the instruction came from salaried teachers.

This was particularly the case in the teaching of philosophy in the universities. Moral philosophy was at the heart of the Scottish university curriculum, but elsewhere it was largely taught through the rote learning of 'sophistry'[21] or 'exploded systems'.[22] Smith clearly felt that the careful systematic account of moral philosophy that he developed in his Glasgow lectures avoided this accusation and instead provided a useful system of thought for his students. Moreover, his own experience had taught him that good teaching was popular and attracted students who were willing to pay the modest fee to attend his lectures. Smith's own experience also informs his views on Grand Tours, the eighteenth-century equivalent of our 'gap year' where students travel to educate themselves. As we saw in the opening chapter, Smith himself had acted as companion to the Duke of Buccleuch on his travels in France, but the verdict he draws on this as a model of education is damning. He thought that the students would lose the discipline of the classroom, and return more indulged and dissipated than they left. Smith was also against boarding schools, which he saw as an unnecessary separation of the child from the influence and affection of his family. Smith practised what he preached and in the education of his young heir David Douglas, he ensured that he had the best of schooling in Edinburgh, the benefit of the best tutors, and that he planned to move directly from university into a career in the law.

Smith's discussion of education turns to the Burgh school system for the education of children. The way he frames this discussion is particularly interesting. Smith begins by noting that the division of labour that is the mainspring of the wealth of commercial nations has a set of dangerous moral and physical effects on ordinary workers. The lack of mental stimulation experienced by the pin factory workers led to a sort of mental torpor. Boredom and lack of variety meant that these workers did not experience the range of stimulation experienced by people who lived in other types of society.

Aside from this being a regrettable situation for the individuals concerned, Smith also seems to have had a wider concern that such individuals might fall prey to the vice of drunkenness or to the charms of religious or political extremists. Education, combined with other suitable public entertainments that Smith believed would be provided by the market, was necessary to prevent people's escape from a boring work life threatening the social order. The educated, Smith argued, were less likely to fall prey to demagogues and religious cults, because they would be better placed to see through them and also because they would be better socialized.[23]

The impact on the individual and the potential danger to society at large meant that education became a matter that should concern the government. Again, like the universities, the model that Smith advocates is essentially that of the Scottish Burgh schools. In this system, small locally managed schools were funded from a mixture of subscription by the wealthier inhabitants of the town and a small fee charged for each child. Smith argued that such education should be compulsory and that the public should facilitate it by supporting the building of schools and the employment of teachers. The fees for such schools should be so low that the poorest would be able to afford it. The teachers would be paid directly according to the quality of their teaching.

Smith's discussion of the content of the education that should be provided closely matches the content of the Scottish system. The focus should be on literacy and numeracy and then on useful subjects such as geometry and mechanics. Latin, the backbone of the higher-level classes in Smith's own education, should not be imposed on all, but rather reserved for those who were likely to move on to the universities. Children should be encouraged to achieve excellence in the basic subjects through the award of medals and badges of distinction, and all would be expected to leave with a basic level of literacy and numeracy that would equip them for their working life.

Smith trusted that such an education would inoculate the working population from the 'delusions of enthusiasm and superstition'.[24] This leads us on to the second set of instructional institutions that Smith discusses. These are the institutions for religious instruction. In this section, Smith is responding to an argument made by David

Hume on the question of whether there should be an established national religion. Hume's *History of England* had made the case for a national church to secure the state from religious conflict driven by ambitious and fanatical preachers. Hume took the view that such a church could control the education and career prospects of the ministry and, ultimately, 'bribe their indolence'[25] by providing them with a secure living. Smith takes a very different view from his friend, and in doing so he provides a masterpiece of social scientific analysis. Smith's basic argument is to call for a system similar to that which existed in the Scotland of his time, but without the secured status of the Church of Scotland.

In Smith's time, the Kirk had a special legal protection, but did not have any financial or political means to enforce that against other denominations. The Scottish Kirk was too poor to promise much in the way of largess. But it was also based on the Presbyterian model whereby each congregation was responsible for funding the living of its Minister. In Smith's view, the clergy in Scotland were the best educated and the most diligent in Europe. They were the best preachers and were the most peaceful and committed to the existing social order. This was, of course, quite a change from the religious fanaticism that characterized Scotland in the seventeenth century, but it was an achievement secured by Smith's many friends among the Moderate establishment of the Kirk. The exception to Smith's belief in religious toleration was Roman Catholicism, which Smith, in line with the usual view of the time, regards as an oppressive and superstitious danger to the political order that can reasonably be excluded from toleration on political more than religious grounds. His claim is that the Kirk does everything that a national church is expected to do at a fraction of the cost and without the political danger of competition to secure the religious monopoly.

Smith's argument is based on religious toleration and the existence of a marketplace of churches. The approach is basically a development of Voltaire's observation that religious toleration in Britain has worked precisely because there are a vast number of small groups who have found that they need to find a way to coexist. Smith develops this observation into an examination of the economics of a competitive market for churches. He points out that the danger of having a national church is that it binds together politics and religion and encourages different churches to seek the security and wealth that come with national establishment. If the state had never adopted a national church, then there would be no political conflict over which church should have the state-backed monopoly.

National religious monopolies are also subject to all of the problems that come with other monopoly providers. The clergy are not dependent on the congregation for their living and so become lazy and neglect their duties. For Hume, this was a positive feature which discouraged fanaticism in the clergy, but as Smith points out, the real effect would be that people abandoned the dull established church in favour of charismatic and extreme sects. This would eventually lead to a conflict between the strongest of these sects and the state as they sought to take over the national church and enjoy its political and economic advantages.

Smith's plan, then, is not a model of ecclesiastical government so much as it is a call for 'no ecclesiastical government'.[26] A vast number of small sects will not prove dangerous to the public and they will instead compete against each other for members. Preachers will be diligent in their ministry because they will depend on the size of their congregation for their living. The only role of the sovereign would be to keep the peace between the different churches and to ensure that people might move from one to the other as their conscience directed them. Lest we worry that some of these sects might prove to be 'enthusiastic' or extremist, Smith suggests that the state might impose an educational qualification for preachers. But he does not see the content or the provision of such an education as a role for the state. Each church would provide something of the sort for its own clergy.

Smith's account of the marketplace of religion is also connected to his concerns about the division of labour. Here the issue is urbanization rather than mental torpor. Smith worries that individuals who are used to living in small rural communities where their behaviour is observed by their neighbours will fall into dissipated lives when they come to the city and find themselves robbed of an intimate peer group that provides them with socialization. To recall our discussion in chapter 3, we lose the mirror of society that we need to refine the impartial spectator of our conscience. But Smith thinks that many of these small religious communities will take on that function for the urban population, a truth that he sees as borne out by the austerity of the beliefs of many of the sects that were popular amongst the poor.

Before he moves on to a discussion of the different ways of raising revenue to support the activities of government, Smith pauses to consider a final expense relating to government. This is the expense of 'supporting the dignity of the Sovereign'. In Smith's day, this was no inconsiderable element of the politics of the royal court and one which appeared to continue to grow as the nation became wealthier. The simple reason for this, as Smith observes, is that the sovereign is expected to be raised above his subjects and to be a focus of national life. This is as true of presidents and ministers as it is of kings, but, as Smith notes, kings expect and are expected to display greater splendour.

To summarize, Smith sees the first task of government as defence, the second as the preservation of the internal system of justice, and the third as the provision of public works. Most of the public works that he discusses were to be provided at the local level. They would be most efficiently and diligently performed from a mixture of public support through voluntary contribution and local taxes and direct fee payment by those who benefited from the service. As a general rule, local revenue should be used for public works and the general revenue of society reserved for defence and justice.

Taxation

In the final chapters of the *Wealth of Nations*, Smith moves on to a discussion of how the government is to secure the revenue to cover the tasks that he has outlined. He begins by observing that many of the traditional sources of revenue are likely to prove insufficient in a commercial society. The rent from public lands will form a part of the revenue of the state, but it will not cover the necessary expenses. Where such lands exist, they should not be managed by the government, as Smith believed that they would end up being neglected. Instead they should be offered for let on long tenancies to secure the effort and investment of tenant farmers. Similarly, profits from investments in stock may form a part of the revenue of the state, but these cannot be relied upon for regular outgoings and are subject to fluctuations. Finally, Smith argues that the traditional tax on land will not, in itself, be sufficient to cover the expenses of the commercial state.

Like many in the eighteenth century, Smith was concerned about public debt. While he accepted that sudden public dangers, such as wars, could only effectively be funded by debt, he worried that once such a method of raising funds was opened to a government, they would find it too tempting to limit to emergencies. The governments of commercial societies were wealthy enough to be able to borrow from their own citizens through bond issues and loans and they were also stable enough and operated under certain legal systems to an extent that made them attractive borrowers. This, in Smith's view, led to a dangerous situation where governments might be tempted to make use of borrowing to fund their activities, while at the same time failing to save to repay for their debts. The mortgaging of future tax revenues and other such financial instruments were a genuine worry for Smith. Government financial innovation was likely to be managed by spendthrifts or 'projectors' like John Law, Smith's fellow Scotsman, whose speculation led to the near ruin of the French state. In addition to the possibility of corruption and mismanagement, such schemes had another fatal consequence: capital that might be lent to productive enterprises from the economy and passed into the unproductive hands of the state.

In response to this Smith, proposes to look at a variety of the sorts of revenue-raising methods that modern states have deployed. As he points out: 'There is no art which one government sooner learns of another than that of draining money from the pockets of the people.'[27] This means that Smith has a wealth of empirical evidence about the impact of different forms of tax and different models of tax collection. Moreover, he was the son of a customs officer and in the later years of his life acted as a member of the board of customs for Scotland. His observations were based on first-hand experience of the management of the inland revenue and customs and excise system of eighteenth-century Britain.

In order to assess these tax systems, he proposes what have come to be known as his canons of taxation:

1 That every subject 'ought to contribute towards the support of the government, as nearly as possible, in proportion to their respective abilities; that is, in proportion to the revenue which they respectively enjoy under the protection of the state'.[28] Smith's observation here is based on the idea that the rich should pay not only in proportion to their revenue, but 'something more' than that proportion.
2 That taxes should be certain and not arbitrary.
3 That taxes should be levied at a time when they are most convenient to pay (for example, a tax on luxury goods should be levied at purchase rather than by later inspection).
4 That taxes take as little as possible out of the pockets of the people (otherwise they obstruct investment and hence limit growth).

In addition, there are two more general observations that apply to the overall cumulative tax burden. Smith objects to excessive taxation as oppressive. The reason for this is that he understands that all taxes are drawn from revenue (which is made up of wages, profits, and rent) and either 'mediately or immediately'[29] fall on consumers. If taxes become too high, they will lead to political unrest. As Smith notes elsewhere: 'No doubt the raising of a very exorbitant tax, as the raising as much in peace as in war, or the half or even the fifth of the wealth of the nation, would, as well as any other gross abuse of power, justify resistance in the people.'[30]

Smith goes on to apply these rules to a variety of taxes. In several cases, he finds against a tax because it fails the proportion test – such as a capitation or poll tax – or because it has an impact on economic growth – such as a tax on the wages of labour, which reduces the demand for labour – or because it discourages investment – such as a tax on the profits of stock. Taxes on the capital value of land, houses, or stock also have an impact on the value of the property in question. In such cases, Smith argues that a tax in the form of a stamp duty paid at the point of purchase would provide a more certain form of tax that would be raised at a convenient time. Liquor licences and occupational taxes are a possibly reliable source of income, but the number of professions over which they might be safely rolled out without their impact being passed on to the public is limited.

This leads us to Smith's central observation about the care with which schemes to raise revenue ought to be enacted. The additional cost represented by a tax will be passed on by the vendor to his customer. In the case of non-essential goods such as alcohol, Smith is comfortable with this as a source of revenue. But where he is very much against them is where such taxes, or other direct taxes, are applied to the 'necessaries' of life. Taxing necessities unfairly impacts on the poor and at the same time drives up the cost of living in a way that has negative impacts on economic growth. Such taxes are unfair and potentially inhibit growth. Smith is critical of the existing taxes on salt, leather, soap, and candles as they are ordinary necessities and making them more expensive impacts unequally on the living conditions of the poor.

Smith advocates a tax on luxury items: fashionable clothing, tobacco, and alcohol. These non-essential items are choices. Moreover, they are choices that are indulged in more by the wealthy, who can afford both them and the tax upon them. They are paid at point of purchase and so seem to fit with all of Smith's canons. Having said that, he does observe that even these luxury taxes have their limits. Heavy taxes encourage tax evasion and smuggling. As Smith would have it: 'High taxes, some times by diminishing the consumption of the taxed commodities, and sometimes by encouraging smuggling, frequently afford a smaller revenue to government than what might be drawn from more moderate taxes.'[31]

In the background of these concerns was Smith's worry that tax would misdirect labour and capital and put up barriers to imports. He is clear that the point of a tax is to raise revenue to fund the necessary expenses of government. Taxes should not be used to deter imports or to dissuade the population from indulging in certain goods. The government must be very careful in how it applies these taxes. As we saw, Smith was writing the *Wealth of Nations* in the 1760s and 1770s and he had a very good example of that before him in the dispute between the British Crown and its American colonies. The heart of this dispute was a series of complaints about arbitrary and excessive taxation. In Smith's view, the basis of these complaints was not particularly convincing, but he nonetheless sympathized with the political claims of the colonies and closes the *Wealth of Nations* by returning to the idea of reconciliation between Britain and America. Smith's argument was that free trade between Britain and America was the soundest policy, and that if this could not be achieved with the existing British Empire, then it was in Britain's interest to let the colonies go and to trade freely with them.

Smith's discussion of the role of the government in the economic life of the nation is a pragmatic and evidence-based one. He is not the doctrinaire defender of laissez-faire that he is often supposed to be. More than this, he is a downright sceptic about the motivations of merchants and the effectiveness of corporations. But at the same time he is also a sceptic about the ability of government to act effectively in the day-to-day management of the economy. As we saw, he is also adamant that public works should be provided as close to the local level as feasible and where possible make use of market-like incentives. It is this scepticism about the prospects for successful economic policy that leads him to observe:

> The statesman, who should attempt to direct private people in what manner they ought to employ their capitals, would not only load himself with a most unnecessary attention, but assume an authority which could safely be trusted, not only to no single person,

but to no council or senate whatever, and which would nowhere be so dangerous as in the hands of a man who had the folly and presumption enough to fancy himself fit to exercise it.[32]

8

Legacy and Influence

In this final chapter, we will turn our attention to Smith's legacy and the influence of his thinking on subsequent generations of philosophers and economists. By now it should be clear that the 'Adam Smith' of popular caricature bears little relation to the complex and thoughtful thinker revealed in the writings we have examined thus far. But Smith is a member of that unusual club of world historical figures: his face appears on banknotes, his statue adorns Edinburgh's High Street, and the office I'm writing this in at Glasgow University is in a building named in his honour. In the popular imagination, Smith is still the father of economics and the patron saint of capitalism, the preacher of laissez-faire and the prophet of the invisible hand of the market. In this chapter, I want to address this problematic reputation that seems so far from the ideas the actual Adam Smith actually held.

On one level, we should not be surprised by the popular caricature. After all, the same is true of Karl Marx, of Charles Darwin, and others whose names are better known than their writings. Smith wrote big books about difficult subjects, so it is little wonder that a few misleading tropes are popularly held to be his main ideas. In what follows, we will look at Smith's reception in his lifetime and his influence on the development of moral philosophy and economics in the centuries since his death, before surveying some of the current issues of debate among Smith scholars. In the conclusion, we will revisit the case that this book has been making for reading Smith as a cautious social scientist with a particular interest in unintended consequences and the conditions of modern commercial liberty, and a proponent of pragmatic policies based on the evidence of his research.

'Das Adam Smith-Problem'

Before we turn to our discussion of Smith's legacy, it is worth pausing to reconsider one of the contradictions that some readers thought existed between the ideas outlined in Smith's two great books. In the opening chapter, we referred to this as the Adam Smith Problem, a term coined by the members of the German historical school of economists in the nineteenth century.[1] The problem they pointed to was that Smith's stress on sympathy in the *Moral Sentiments* seemed to contradict his focus on self-interest in the *Wealth of Nations*. The thinkers of the German school made a number of attempts to explain this. One idea was that Smith changed his mind between 1759 and 1776. This won't work, as Smith revised the *Moral Sentiments* in 1790 without substantively changing the account of sympathy and so obviously remained committed to its main arguments after 1776. Moreover, the discovery of the *Lectures on Jurisprudence* in the late nineteenth century, together with an appreciation of Smith's own comments in the final version of the *Wealth of Nations*, clearly shows that he considered both works to be part of a single system of thought.

Part of the aim of this book has been to show that this system of thought is characterized by a methodological commitment to a particular scientific approach to social phenomena. Smith begins his arguments from observation and it simply is a fact that human beings are both self-regarding and other-regarding in their motives. There is only a contradiction between these two modes of behaviour if one assumes that humans can or should only ever act on one principle. But as we have seen, this is precisely the view of philosophy that Smith rejects. Instead he sets out to examine how human beings act from a variety of motives in different areas of their lives. The same human beings who pursue their own interest in their economic life act benevolently towards others in other areas of their social life. And the most benevolent and charitable individuals also act in their own interest in other aspects of their daily interactions with others. The Adam Smith Problem is not a problem. Instead it reveals the problem with a non-Smithian approach to social explanation that attempts to explain the world by means of a simplistic single principle.

Moral Sentiments

Smith's first book was well received and formed the basis of his reputation. As we observed in chapter 2, it was an intervention into a particular debate in British moral philosophy at the time. It quickly garnered favourable reviews and was widely admired for its style and use of examples. The first edition of 1759 generated quite detailed criticism from some of Smith's friends, among them David Hume and Gilbert Elliot of Minto (1722–77). Smith responded to these by making significant revisions to the text and publishing a much expanded second edition in 1761. However, it is also clear that he thought that these revisions did not make any fundamental change to his theory; they were merely elaborations required to resolve objections.

Hume's criticism appears in a letter to his friend. He notes that 'if all sympathy was agreeable[, a] Hospital woud be a more entertaining Place than a Ball'.[2] Smith responded to this by adding a footnote, by extending the discussion of the tendency to prefer sympathy with joy rather than sorrow, and by developing the distinction between the pleasure that arises from mutual sympathy which is always pleasurable, and the uneasiness generated by the imaginative act of entering into another's position when that position is unpleasant.[3]

Elliot's criticism is a version of a criticism that would haunt Smith's theory.[4] He pointed out that Smith's account of propriety was an account of the generation of social norms through conformity, and that as a result the content of our moral views is shaped by the norms of our society. Smith, on this reading, looks like he could be some sort of moral relativist who believed that morality could be reduced to the contingent beliefs of each society. His response to Elliot was to develop the sections on the impartial spectator and on praise versus praiseworthiness. As we saw in chapter 3, Smith believed that the impartial spectator provided an independent authority that allowed us to move beyond mere conformity to established practices. The extent to which he can escape the charge of moral relativism remains a topic in the contemporary scholarly literature on Smith. Charles Griswold has argued for Smith's impartial spectator as a device with the power to allow us to transcend parochial beliefs. In response to this, Fonna Forman-Barzilai has pointed out that even though the spectator allows us to reflect on our society and its beliefs, it still does so from the vantage point of a consciousness developed within that society. The problem of relativism remains.[5] It seems certain, though, that Smith did think he could avoid it. The reason for this is straightforward. Smith believed in a universal human nature that meant that variations in sentimental responses existed within a range of possibilities that limited the danger of relativism. Unlike most contemporary moral philosophers, he was comfortable with the fact of differences in moral belief between different cultures and in the same culture over time.[6] As we noted before, he views the attempt to fit reality to a systematic principle of morality as a failing of moral philosophy. As a result, in Smithian terms, a moral philosophy that left no room for the possibility of differences of opinion is, by its very nature, a failed philosophy. But this still leaves Smith open to the charge that he has provided a sociological explanation of morality, but not a normative criterion for guiding moral judgements. This, however, is a mistake. It is to impose a distinction of a kind of argument upon Smith that he simply did not recognize. He does express judgements and preferences. When he makes judgements about one type of behaviour being preferable to another, however, it is always with reference to some underlying feature of human nature that can be identified through empirical research. Wealthy societies are 'better' than poor societies because people are not forced to watch their children die from starvation. This is a fact that has normative weight.

Smith's friend Adam Ferguson was still not convinced. He worried that sympathy was too changeable a basis upon which to ground morality.[7] Ferguson argued that Smith was providing what was in effect a circular argument. Rather than do the heavy lifting of coming up with a normative theory, Smith simply reduces morality to the sympathetic judgement of the impartial spectator. For Ferguson, this amounts to little more than saying that a good man (agent) approves of what a good man should approve of, and we know what that is by imagining what a good man (spectator) would approve of. As such, the whole complicated account of imaginative sympathy and the impartial spectator is little more than a detour from the main question for moral philosophy: the provision of a reliable criterion for moral judgement. Ferguson's own moral philosophy is characterized by the attempt to provide such a criterion from an empirical observation of human nature. This links the scientific and empirical science with a more detailed normative moral philosophy centred on benevolence. However, the result is little more than a survey of the generally held views of his time. This suggests that Smith's more open account was intentionally light on prescriptive moralizing precisely because he wanted his readers to examine their own consciences in the light of his explanation of how the impartial spectator operated. Smith was not providing us with a list of dos and don'ts. Instead he was giving us clarity about how we might reach our own view on morality through critical engagement with the beliefs of our society.

For Smith's successor in the Moral Philosophy Chair at Glasgow, Thomas Reid, the problem was more basic than this. Reid thought that Smith had failed in his central task. Smith wanted to develop a theory of morality that did not reduce all of moral experience to self-love. But, argued Reid, what else is at the basis of Smith's account than the pleasure of mutual sympathy felt by an agent, and the approval of that by the impartial spectator: what is that if not a refined version of the selfish system? Reid used his objections to Smith's theory as part of the argument in his later work on his own theory of common sense, and, in the hands of Dugald Stewart, Reid's and Smith's theories are merged into a system of thought that dominated British philosophical education in the early nineteenth century. This distinctive approach rested on an empirical psychology that identified basic principles of the human mind and built upon them to create a system of normative ethics.

Smith was also closely read in France. The standard translation of the *Moral Sentiments* into French became the 1798 edition translated by Sophie de Grouchy (1764–1822), the wife of the *philosophe* Condorcet. De Grouchy provided a translation of Smith that imposed her own interpretation of his ideas. In particular, she seems to have had a quite distinct notion of the relationship between emotion and reason that is some distance from that found in Smith. She also appended eight letters on sympathy to the translation that move beyond Smith and into her own understanding of the relationship between sympathy and morality. The Smith experienced by nineteenth-century French scholars was in many respects as much de Grouchy as it was him. De Grouchy also stressed the nurturing role of sympathy and its potential role in education. She read Smith in parallel with Rousseau's thinking on education, and this provides an interesting bridge to another thinker who was clearly influenced by comparing Rousseau's and Smith's thinking on education: Mary Wollstonecraft (1759–97).

Wollstonecraft is often considered one of the first feminist thinkers and she was at the heart of radical politics in Britain in the late eighteenth century. A friend of the leading reformers, she married the philosopher William Godwin (1756–1836) and supported radical causes in print. Wollstonecraft's reputation is based on her *A Vindication of the Rights of Woman: with Strictures on Political and Moral Subjects* (1792). The book is an argument for women's rights and one of Wollstonecraft's central themes is the idea that freedom is necessary for moral improvement. Giving women legal rights will improve both them and society. Part of Wollstonecraft's strategy is to suggest that the apparent disparity in moral development between men and women, the basis of the objection to women having equal rights, comes from their very different social and educational experiences. It is here that Smith comes in.

Wollstonecraft was a close reader of Smith and cites him extensively on the idea that our moral nature is a product of our experience in society. Women, because they were excluded from much social life, were robbed of the means of developing their moral characters. They lacked the mirror that society gives them and so their impartial spectators remained undeveloped. As she puts it, citing Smith's authority: '[T]he heart would expand as the understanding gained strength, if women were not depressed from their cradles.'[8] Smith's moral psychology becomes a key support to Wollstonecraft's argument: 'Let woman share the rights and she will emulate the virtues of man; for she must grow more perfect when emancipated, or justify the authority that chains such a weak being to her duty.'[9]

In the later nineteenth century, Smith's moral philosophy fell out of fashion. This was partly because what was considered to be philosophy shifted. The disciplinary distinction between empirically based psychology and analytically based philosophy took hold in the wake of Kant. Smith was dismissed as a quaint and descriptive writer who played some role in influencing the development of utilitarianism through his economic writings. This tendency of seeing his philosophical significance through the *Wealth of Nations* rather than through the *Moral Sentiments* continued until the middle years of the twentieth century. The Smith of the *Moral Sentiments* was forgotten with the rise of Smith the 'father of economics'.

The Famous Dr Smith

The *Wealth of Nations* was a very successful book. It sold well in Britain and, as noted in chapter 1, this led to a second edition in 1778 and a third revised edition in 1784. It was quickly translated into the major European languages and soon eclipsed its only serious rival, Sir James Steuart's *An Inquiry into the Principles of Political Oeconomy* (1767). Smith makes no direct reference to Steuart's book in the text of the *Wealth of Nations*. This might seem slightly odd given the fact that he was clearly aware of the writings of his fellow Scot and how significantly they differed from his own views. In a letter to William Pulteney in 1772, however, Smith explains that Steuart is a silent subject of criticism in the *Wealth of Nations*.[10] Indeed Smith thought that his own theory had completely demolished Steuart's 'false' principles. This may be a reference to Steuart's support for a strong central government that directed the economy of the country, an idea to which Smith is consistently hostile.

It was Smith, and not Steuart, who became recognized as the expert on political economy. Smith's opinion was sought by politicians on issues such as tax and free trade with Ireland. Although he seems to have avoided identifying with any particular party, he advised leading Scottish-born politicians such as Alexander Wedderburn (1733–1805), who served as Lord Chancellor, and Henry Dundas, Viscount Melville (1742–1811), who managed Scotland, as well as the Irish-born William Petty, Earl of Shelburne (1737–1805), who became Prime Minister. Smith's biographer also tells of a dinner party where he was fêted by the leading figures in the politics of the day, including William Pitt the Younger, William Grenville (1759–1834), and William Wilberforce (1759–1833). His time in London in the 1780s was spent in conversation with leading politicians like Edmund Burke, and in advising the government. When in Scotland, he continued to advise his former pupil the Duke of Buccleuch on the management of his vast estates. From 1778 to 1790, Smith served as one of the Commissioners of Customs for Scotland and from his home at Panmure House in Edinburgh he sat at the heart of Scotland's intellectual and political establishment. His dinner parties were attended by a group of close friends supplemented by noted visitors to the Scottish capital.

It is difficult to assess the precise nature of Smith's advice to the British politicians of his day, more difficult still to discern how much of it they took on board.[11] In some very obvious areas, his advice was not followed. In the eighteenth century, his attack on the Corn Laws failed to persuade in the face of vested interests and his ideas had to await the nineteenth-century popular campaign led by Richard Cobden MP (1804–65) and the Anti-Corn Law League's success in 1846–9. As we noted above, this would not have been much of a surprise to Smith, who accepted that his 'very violent attack on the whole commercial system of Great Britain'[12] was unlikely to be able to overcome vested interests. His suggestion for policy towards Britain's American colonies was similarly ignored.

The Scottish Enlightenment was divided on the American Crisis. The historian William Robertson criticized the colonists, and the philosopher Adam Ferguson was part of the Earl of Carlisle's Commission sent to negotiate with them. Ferguson, who was famously hot tempered, had little time for the colonists' complaints and may even have played a role in the failure of the negotiations. Smith, however, was well regarded in the American colonies. Both of his books were widely read and discussed among the Founding Fathers. Thomas Paine (1737–1809) cites Smith in several places. Smith was also personally acquainted with Benjamin Franklin and socialized with him in London and Edinburgh. James Wilson (1742–98), the Scot who served on the first Supreme Court, was a former student of Smith's at Glasgow. John Witherspoon (1723–94), who headed the evangelical party in the Church of Scotland that clashed with Smith's friends in the Moderate clergy, left Scotland to become President of the College of New Jersey (Princeton). Once there, he developed a moral philosophy and rhetoric curriculum that would prove hugely influential on the course of American education – central to his lectures were ideas drawn from Smith.

Smith's death in 1790 produced a few polite notices and a respectful 'Life' written by his friend Dugald Stewart. This was the height of the revolutionary panic in Britain and Emma Rothschild has suggested that the radical nature of some of Smith's ideas was deliberately played down by his more conservative friends like Stewart to protect his reputation.[13] In the nineteenth century, he became the 'founding father of economics', and most of the major thinkers in the newly emerging discipline felt the need to acknowledge and criticize his work in their own writings.

Classical Political Economy

In the nineteenth century, a school of political economists arose who developed Smith's ideas. Smith wrote at the very beginning of the Industrial Revolution and sought to apply science to understand the newly emerging type of society. In the nineteenth century, the process of industrialization accelerated and political economy began to be formalized into a science with 'Laws' and 'Principles'. Thinkers like David Ricardo (1772–1823) built on Smith's ideas, but at the same time acknowledged the problems with them. For example, in Ricardo's *Principles of Political Economy and Taxation* (1817) he moves beyond the account of absolute advantage in international trade that we see in Smith and develops the idea of comparative advantage. Ricardo also criticizes and reformulates Smith's idea that there are three types of economy: growing, stagnant, and declining.

Ricardo was troubled by Smith's faith that growing economies combined rising wages and a greater profusion of affordable goods for the ordinary workers. In his view, a lower cost of living created incentives for employers to lower wages in order to secure higher profits. The problem appears to be compounded by the growth of population that Smith saw as a side-effect of a growing economy. Ricardo's picture of the relationship between growth, population, and wages was altogether more pessimistic than Smith's. If Ricardo was more pessimistic than Smith, however, Thomas Malthus (1766–1834) pushed things in an even darker direction. Malthus was an Anglican clergyman, a fellow of Jesus College, Cambridge, and the first Professor of Political Economy in Britain (at the East India Company's college, Haileybury). His famous *An Essay on the Principle of Population* (1798/1803) includes several detailed engagements with Smith's views on population. Malthus's pessimism about the future prospects of commercial society is based on his theory of population. The basic observation is that food supply increases arithmetically while population increases geometrically, meaning that unless there are 'checks' such as abstinence, or disease and war, population will outstrip food supply.

As Smith observed, a country will 'people up' to its resources. As resources increase, population increases, but if resources then become scarce, or unable to keep up, the population will fall. Malthus's concern was that economic growth changes the incentives for the poor. As the economy grows, the incentives against having children fall and population rises; in turn, as Ricardo had observed, a large population drives down wages. And worse still, when the population outstrips the food supply, then the meagre wages of the poor will leave them to starve. For Malthus, it is only when economic growth exceeds the rise in population that the standard of living rises. Commercial societies would become the victims of their own success by unwittingly supporting more and more people living in increasingly precarious circumstances.

One of the policy consequences of this for Malthus was that we had to be very aware of the changes in incentives created by commercial society. While he supported the provision of aid to the poor, he worried about the negative effects that this might have. As we saw in chapter 7, Smith had observed that the Poor Laws ought to be reformed to allow workers to move from parishes where there was no work to those where employment opportunities existed. For Malthus, the Poor Laws alter incentives, but do not change the underlying relationship between population and food. Redistribution raises prices without removing scarcity. The Poor Laws are parish-based, so raise prices in localities which are suffering economically. This in turn raises the real price of labour there and prevents the growth of employment. Monetary transfers to the poor create inflationary pressures in the economy more generally. This means that the unintended consequence is that they harm the working poor by reducing independence. Redistribution moves capital from productive to unproductive uses, thus decreasing the rate of growth that might raise the poor out of poverty. Malthus seems to be suggesting that economic growth will always bring the prospect of human misery with it. He criticizes the unintended consequences of the Poor Laws. However, he does not say that we should stop trying to help the poor, merely that we may have to accept that the tragedy of poverty will always be with us.

Smith is also subject to praise and criticism by John Stuart Mill (1806–73), whose *Principles of Political Economy* (1848) became a standard textbook on economic subjects in the second half of the nineteenth century. As the 'founding father of economics', Smith became a target for those who were opposed to commercial society and industrialization. The world in which he wrote was far removed from the developing urban squalor and industrial factories of the nineteenth century. Where Smith saw the growing Glasgow of the late eighteenth century as a positive improvement on the rural deprivation suffered by most of its inhabitants before they moved there, by the middle of the nineteenth century, it was not quite so easy to see the conditions of a rapidly expanding industrial city as an improvement on anything.

The essayist and author Thomas Carlyle (1795–1881), a very popular writer in the nineteenth century, who incidentally spent a brief time as a teacher in Smith's old school in Kirkcaldy, was one such critic of political economy. Carlyle's writing is a stylized mixture of fiction, poetry, prose, and fact. His style of writing has gone out of fashion and his views on race mean that he has largely disappeared from contemporary discussions, but he was among the first to formulate what would become very powerful conservative criticisms of the commercial society associated with Smith. He believed that political economy represented a rejection of spirituality, community, and tradition. Its creed is 'Mammonism', a brutish, laissez-faire, God-forgetting, profit-and-loss philosophy that ignores humanity's spiritual needs in favour of crude material concerns.[14] The loss of community and obsession with wealth as a symbol of success have perverted human values and the 'cash nexus' destroys society by reducing human interaction to crude monetary exchange. Carlyle was dismissive of the campaign to repeal the Corn Laws because he thought that it was beside the point. Even if the Laws were repealed, the culture of commercial society would continue to be based on the basic exploitation of workers by industrialists. Carlyle believed that the view of the world taken by political economists had displaced traditional religion and ethics and that it had allowed Britain to become detached from its history and culture. Only a restoration of older notions of spirituality and national community could save the country from disaster. Carlyle's pessimism about the future of industrial capitalism and the danger of the cash nexus was shared by another, very different, giant of nineteenth-century thought: Karl Marx (1818–83).

Marxism

It might seem odd at first to consider Marx in a chapter on Smith's legacy. Their popular caricatures are as the representatives of two polar opposite economic systems, but Marx was a close reader of Smith and was deeply influenced by his ideas. Marx's thought is characterized by a desire to understand how the material and economic conditions of a society shape everything else about it. Before all else, human beings need to eat, drink, and sleep. This fact shapes everything about us: our ideas, religions, beliefs about art, law, philosophy – all of these are determined by the material conditions of the society that we live in. Historical materialism explains how the economic base of a society shapes its legal and political superstructure. This allowed Marx to undertake an analysis of different 'epochs' of society based on the dominant mode of production: Primitive Communism, Slavery, Feudalism, Capitalism, and Communism.

The similarities with the Scottish method of conjectural history and the Smithian 'four stages' theory are obvious.[15] Marx believed that Smith's analysis of commercial society represented a systematic attempt to understand commercial society, but that it was hampered by the fact that Smith was a product of such a society. Smith's discussion of the 'natural' history of property and markets treats as natural features of society that are superstructural and generated by the economics of a commercial society. The propensity to trade, the idea of private property, and so forth, are generated within a historical context, and as a result Smith's analysis of them is naïve and undertaken within the conceptual universe of one particular type of society. Smith's analysis of commerce was grounded in the point of view of a member of the revolutionary bourgeoisie. As a result, his ideas, though ostensibly scientific, were in fact an ideological servant of the interests of the dominant class in the new commercial society.

Marx did not blame Smith for this. Smith's consciousness was shaped by the society he lived in and that society was only just beginning to become capitalist. Smith's inability to take a step back and adopt the Marxist analysis meant that he was unable to see that capitalism was another temporary stage on the way to the final resolution of the dialectic of history in communism. The crisis of capitalism would be brought about by the increasingly sharp antagonism between two classes, and part of Smith's contribution was to open the way to the identification of these two classes, the capitalists and the proletariat, by showing how society had been transformed from a feudal to a commercial order. Smith could see how commercial society was better than feudal society, but he failed to see how commercial society would drive forward into something even better.[16] He saw that workers were freed from dependence on feudal lords, but could not yet grasp how they had become dependent on capitalists.

That said, Marx takes Smith's ideas seriously and devotes considerable energy to criticizing his attempts to find a labour theory of value. Capitalism has simplified the antagonisms of history by producing a stark divide into two classes: capitalists, as owners of the means of production, and the proletariat, who must sell their labour to survive. Marx believed that capitalism was a contradiction because it depended on a faulty notion of value – exchange value or price. This was a chimera that led capitalists to pursue activities that would bring about the fall of the system. In Marx's view, the capitalist operates by extracting surplus value from the productive process. Smith's failure to identify the true nature of the operation of capital meant that he was unable to see that capitalist accumulation is driven by the extraction of the surplus value added by the workers whom capitalists employ. Surplus value exists when the exchange value of a product is greater than the value of the capital and labour involved in the production. The logic of capitalism leads the owners of production to attempt to wring as much value from production as possible. As a result, Smith's analysis of wages and prices failed to capture what Marx thought to be the central feature of an exchange-based economy.

Marx theorized that this would eventually lead to the increasing misery of the proletariat as the capitalists sought to extract more and more surplus value by reducing wages and increasing the use of machines. The eventual result would be a growing awareness of the nature of the class basis of society, what Marx called class consciousness. Marx credits Smith with being partially aware of this in his observation of the effect of the division of labour on the character of the workers. Indeed a number of Smith scholars have suggested that Marx's concept of alienation exists in a nascent form in Smith's discussion of the division of labour.[17] Nevertheless, Marx believes that Smith's proposed solution in education was a panacea that did not address the real problem.[18]

Economists in the Marxist tradition continued to study Smith as a way of understanding the development of Marx's thinking, particularly with regard to the problem of finding a reliable measure of labour value.[19] In more mainstream economics, the so-called 'marginal revolution' of the late nineteenth century led most economists to abandon the search for an objective measure of value and instead develop an understanding of value that was intersubjective and found in the operation of market. The increasing use of mathematics and equations as a way of formalizing economics took the discipline away from the Smithian interest in empirical data and observation of real-world conditions. When such thinkers did return to Smith, they did so to other areas of his thought and he became a sort of honoured ancestor who was name-checked in the classroom rather than taken seriously as a thinker with something to say to contemporary students of economics. Perhaps the clearest example of this was the cursory, and misleading, discussion of Smith in Paul Samuelson's *Economics: An Introductory Analysis* (1948), which became the most popular economics textbook in universities. The caricature of Smith led the economist George Stigler to claim that he was the 'high-priest' of self-interest.[20]

The New Right

It is a sign of how totemic Smith has become as a world historical figure that Marxism's greatest twentieth-century critics, the thinkers of the neo-liberal revival of the 1970s and 1980s, also claimed to be influenced by his thinking. Nobel Prize-winning Classical Liberal economists such as James Buchanan (1919–2013), Milton Friedman (1912–2006), and F. A. Hayek (1899–1992) all claimed to be directly influenced by Smith. Buchanan was a founder of the Virginia or Public Choice School of economics, which sought to develop a model for understanding the incentives created within institutions. The inspiration came from passages in Smith, such as the discussion of education, which analysed policy in terms of the incentive structures created by the rules and institutions. Buchanan applied this approach to the study of politics and constitutional structures, creating a hugely influential field of study in the economics of politics or constitutional political economy.

Milton Friedman's technical economic work in monetary theory appears to be less indebted to Smith's influence than his more popular journalistic writings. Friedman was a highly effective popularizer of free market economics and he often invoked Smith's name in his discussion of the superiority of market mechanisms. This usually took the form of adopting Smith's metaphor of the invisible hand as synonymous with successful markets (a point we will return to below). Of the three, Friedrich Hayek was by far the most careful reader of Smith. Hayek saw Smith as standing at the head of a tradition of social and political thought with which he identified. Hayek distinguishes between the French and the British Enlightenment. The French Enlightenment is guilty of constructivist rationalism and it tends to favour revolution to redesign society along utopian lines. For Hayek, this results in what he calls scientism: the worship of science and the belief that societies' problems can be solved by social engineering. The problem with this is that it suggests that deliberately planned societies are superior to social features that evolve gradually, and that unless an institution is designed by humans to serve a purpose, it is worthless. This is a fatal flaw, in Hayek's view, because it leads not only to intellectual problems, but also to tyranny. In contrast to this, Hayek places himself in a British tradition of liberalism running from Hume and Smith onwards. This tradition is aware of the danger of constructivist rationalism and does not fall into the error of believing that society can be radically redesigned. Instead the focus here is on gradual reform and evolutionary change in pursuit of greater freedom and prosperity. This is not anti-rationalist, like some conservative approaches, but rather it is based on a desire to recognize the limits of reason in order to use it effectively.

As part of his analysis of scientism, Hayek develops an interest in what he calls spontaneous order: an idea that he traces to the work of Smith and the Scottish Enlightenment. Hayek suggests that constructivist rationalists have misunderstood the nature of social order. Societies are not made orders which are deliberately directed by politicians. Instead they are orders which arise by individuals adjusting to each other and to the rules of the society. Hayek believes that humans have evolved a form of association (civilization) that is governed by rules of just conduct rather than deliberate commands. The success of this kind of order arises from the fact that rather than being directed by a few minds it is able to rely on the whole of society adjusting to their local circumstances. This, in Hayek's view, provides an instrumental justification of individual liberty and the market, and he directly associates it with Smith's observations in the *Wealth of Nations*.

Hayek's most famous observation concerns the role of knowledge in society and how we each of us make use of far more knowledge than we possess. The division of labour is based on dispersed knowledge. Interdependence allows us to rely on the knowledge of others and make use of dispersed knowledge without having to gather it into one place or even be conscious of its existence. The more knowledge exists in a society, the smaller the portion of it that any one person can be aware of. As a result, civilization advances by increasing the amount of things we can do without thinking.

In Hayek's hands, this becomes a critique of socialism. Socialists suffer from what he calls the synoptic delusion: the belief that it is possible to plan an economy by centralizing all of the necessary information in the hands of an expert planning board. This will never be as efficient as the free interaction of individuals adjusting to their own conditions. Hayek believes that the free operation of the price mechanism in a market order that respects property rights is the only way to secure both freedom and economic prosperity. Competition and prices are a discovery procedure that allows the efficient communication of information about resources and preferences. The pursuit of socialism will lead to tyranny and poverty, the very opposite of the ideals that inspire it. In Hayek's memorable phrase, it is a road to serfdom.[21] His argument for liberalism is based on the fact that it is the only social system that allows us to make efficient use of dispersed knowledge, and he credits his reading of Smith as one of the inspirations for this view.[22]

Contemporary Political Economy

Smith's impact on contemporary economic thinking can be traced in the writings of another two Nobel Laureates in Economics. Both Amartya Sen and Vernon Smith draw widely on Smith in their work. Indeed both of them seem to be attracted to Smith as the result of their dissatisfaction with the excessive formalism of mainstream economics. In particular, both of them turn to Smith for alternatives to the dominant model of *homo economicus*, or rational economic man. Sen's dissatisfaction with this model led him to look to development and welfare economics to develop a model of economic action that moved beyond crude utility maximization. In Sen's work, understanding economic development as a form of freedom through an increased ability to realize individual human capabilities is combined with a deep appreciation of the importance of cultural and institutional context. In his later work, notably *The Idea of Justice* (2009), Sen finds inspiration in the *Moral Sentiments* and develops a theory of justice that brings together Smithian ideas of impartiality with the work of the twentieth-century theorist of social justice John Rawls. Sen's idea of an open impartiality where we scrutinize our own motivations and the structure of our society through notions of fairness and justice forms the basis of a theory of distributive justice that he thinks is directly inspired by the spirit of Smith's work.

Vernon Smith is similarly dissatisfied with the sorts of models and assumptions made by many mainstream economists. In his work, this is combined with a fascination with modelling human behaviour and designing experiments which test assumptions about motivation and rational strategy. In this new discipline, which he terms humanomics, Smith finds that many of the assumptions from Adam Smith's work are confirmed by experiments.[23] Moreover, his reading of Smith draws as much on the *Moral Sentiments* as it does on the *Wealth of Nations* and demonstrates that social science has much still to learn from Smith's writing. If Adam Smith's thinking about human behaviour can be reproduced and confirmed in contemporary experiments, then the discipline of economics might actually be able to move forward by returning to the ideas of its 'founding father'.

The tendency to revisit Smith's thinking from the *Moral Sentiments* has also found adherents in the hard sciences, particularly in neuropsychology. The development of brain scan technology allowed the exploration of brain function, and a major feature of this is the development of a theory of mirror neurons. Several of the psychologists working in this field have sought inspiration in Smith's thinking on sympathy and spectatorship as a way of trying to understand how this aspect of the human brain operates. Smith's ideas on sympathy, imagination, and 'mirroring' behaviour have been adopted as a framework for the study of mirror neurons.[24]

Smith Studies

In 1976, Oxford University Press began publication of a scholarly edition of Smith's work known as the Glasgow Edition. The project marked the two hundredth anniversary of the publication of the *Wealth of Nations* and, together with a series of academic conferences to celebrate the anniversary, it kicked off a renewed academic interest in Smith's ideas. Over the last forty years, this has expanded into an international community of scholars with their own society, the International Adam Smith Society, and journal, *The Adam Smith Review*.[25] Scholars from a range of academic disciplines have built up an impressive and growing array of work on Smith. This has included work on his previously ignored ideas on science and rhetoric and, most importantly, a revived interest in his moral philosophy.[26]

The reading offered in this book is one that has been most obviously influenced by the development of interest in Smith's *Essays on Philosophical Subjects*. From the late 1960s onwards, Smith scholars such as Andrew Skinner and Christopher J. Berry have explored an interpretation of Smith as developing a self-consciously scientific approach to social phenomena. As the previous chapters demonstrate, this reading allows us to understand the scope and coherence of his intellectual project. But there are other significant studies of Smith's work that emphasize their own interpretations. What follows is a necessarily brief survey of some of the most significant interpretations of Smith with suggestions of how they relate to the reading offered in this book.

In the 1970s, the editors of the *Moral Sentiments*, D. D. Raphael and A. L. Macfie, used their editorial work to popularize a reading of Smith that stressed his indebtedness to the ancient school of

Stoic philosophy. Their argument was based on his interest in unintended order and the account of the virtues, particularly that of self-command, that we discussed in chapter 4. This reading was opposed by T. D. Campbell and others who stressed Smith's commitment to the modern project of a scientific approach to morals and instead saw him as providing a naturalistic account of the development of the moral sentiments to which he attached a form of 'contemplative utilitarianism' in his policy advice. This reading was soon followed by that of Knud Haakonssen, whose work on the *Lectures on Jurisprudence* highlighted Smith's debt to the long-standing tradition of natural jurisprudence and the impact on his thinking of Francis Hutcheson's reading of Pufendorf. More recently, Smith has been read as a virtue theorist by Ryan Hanley and others. Hanley focuses on the practical ethics of Part VI of the *Moral Sentiments*. For Hanley, this is the heart of Smith's pedagogy and normative ethics, and its addition to the final edition published in Smith's lifetime invites us to read it as the completion of his argument on morality. In this reading, Smith is providing an updated version of the ancient and Christian virtues that was better suited to a commercial society.

All of these readings have merit and have shed light on elements of Smith's thinking. But it seems clear that none of them capture Smith's entire project in the *Moral Sentiments*. This should not surprise us, as part of the argument of this book has been that he was hostile to single-principle philosophies and to schools more generally. This has led some Smith scholars to the view that he is an eclectic, someone who mixes and matches from different schools of philosophy as he sees fit. But this would also be a mistake. Smith does not begin from the schools and then create a compound position. Instead he starts from the evidence and builds generalizations which, though they may resemble parts of the various different schools of moral philosophy, owe their authority to none of them.[27] The reality is that Smith recognized the empirical fact that human morality combines elements recognized by Stoicism, utilitarianism, law-governed behaviour, and the virtues. His achievement was to identify each of these elements and bring them together in a single theory of moral experience.

When it comes to the *Wealth of Nations*, Smith scholars have largely been engaged in a project of historical recovery. In the nineteenth and twentieth centuries, Smith's reputation as the 'father of economics' led to him being read as one of the founding fathers of liberalism. The problem with this as a historical reading was that it tended to lead to Smith being read in the light of ideas and political positions that only really developed after his lifetime. Reading him as an early liberal, however, obscures the context in which he actually lived and wrote. As a result, scholars have spent considerable energy trying to place the *Wealth of Nations* in the context of developments in mercantilist and Physiocratic economic thinking. This has allowed us to better appreciate the debates that Smith saw himself as taking part in.

One particular development in this scholarship is worth exploring in some detail. In the twenty-first century, economics has developed into a specialized and highly mathematized discipline based on assumptions about rationality and market behaviour. This is some way from Smith's more empirical work with its stress on the relationship between economic phenomena and other moral and social phenomena. The recovery of a notion of political economy, of a subject matter where economics, politics, and law are intimately intertwined, has allowed us a richer appreciation of Smith's own project.

Contemporary intellectual historians, many of them associated with the Cambridge School in the history of political thought, have sought to understand Smith's political economy in terms of the political debates and issues of his own time.[28] For some of them, such as J. G. A. Pocock, John Robertson, and Nicholas Phillipson, this has involved trying to understand where Smith stands in the complex mix of ideas drawn from traditions of classical republicanism and civic humanism which were still very much alive in his time. Almost all of these discussions end with the view that Smith somehow stands on the edge of these traditions, or at the end of their historical relevance. The project of reclaiming the real Smith from the anachronistic liberal Smith takes on a particular focus in the work of Donald Winch and Istvan Hont. Both Winch and Hont adopt an approach that attempts to read Smith in terms of the intellectual context of his time. But both of them, in their own way, see the main feature of his work as his development of a political economy that attempted to understand the new nature of commercial society. For Winch, this led to a focus on the idea of a 'science of a legislator', which reclaimed Smith as a political thinker from the nineteenth-century liberals who stressed his aversion to politics.[29] Hont, on the other hand, places Smith in the context of a complex set of arguments between Rousseau, Mandeville, and Hume about the nature of the new commercial society that they saw developing around them.[30] For Hont, the defining feature of

Smith's achievement was that he developed a complex political theory that used a historical explanation of the rise of the modern state to reach a position where he was able to offer policy advice that was appropriate for the new challenges faced by his society. On this reading, Smith was not nostalgic for the ancient republics of equal and active citizens. Instead he was someone who realized that that world was gone and that the challenge was to understand what that meant for the economic, political, and moral lives of the modern world.

Smith's work involves an attempt to understand the nature of modern commercial life and to explore the notion of modern liberty, understood as security of person and property. Modern versions of natural jurisprudence, a modern virtue theory, and a new form of political economy were all required to navigate the very new form of society that had evolved in Europe in the eighteenth century. As Duncan Forbes has observed, Smith, like his friend David Hume, was a 'sceptical Whig'.[31] He broadly supported the institutions of British commercial society, but he wanted to avoid the sort of ill-informed political and historical arguments that had been used to defend them. The British system was not perfect; it was not the result of an idealized social contract; and if it were to be defended, it needed to be understood. Smith, then, to use another phrase of Forbes, was a 'scientific Whig':[32] someone who wanted to develop a social theory grounded in the historical evidence that would allow him to understand the operation of commercial society and so be able to offer reliable policy advice to politicians.

Adam Smith Problems

With the dismissal of the crude version of the Adam Smith Problem, Smith scholars were free to explore the other tensions that exist in his thought.[33] One of the issues dividing Smith scholars is the extent to which their research can reconstruct the 'real' Adam Smith and save him from the popular caricature we have noted throughout this book. Many people have claimed to be the heir to Adam Smith or have attempted to associate Smith with their own political and economic ideas. This could lead to an exercise in trying to identify legitimate and illegitimate 'legatees' with contemporary political ideologies squabbling over ownership of Smith's legacy.[34] From the 1980s onwards, a series of Smith scholars have sought to debunk the idea that Smith has anything to do with laissez-faire capitalism or with the libertarian right of the political spectrum. The aim here was a project of reclamation, an attempt to make sure that an accurate portrait of Smith indicated those areas where, to quote the title of Iain McLean's book, Smith was radical and egalitarian.[35] The use of the terminology of left and right is anachronistic when applied to Smith as it refers to political positions that developed after he died, but the central question of whether he would lean to the contemporary left or right were he alive today has opened a debate about the egalitarian and libertarian ideas in his work.

Perhaps the most prominent defender of the egalitarian interpretation of Smith has been Samuel Fleischacker.[36] Fleischacker's case for reading Smith as an egalitarian is based on a series of recurring ideas that we have seen throughout this book. In his view, Smith was among the first to combine ideas that suggested a shift in attitudes to the poor: he was in favour of equality before the law; he was concerned for the poor and wanted to improve their lives; he supported taxation that impacted more heavily on the rich; he supported public education; and he was worried that rank and ambition corrupted the moral sentiments.

The case against Smith as egalitarian has been made by a number of authors, perhaps most prominently by James Otteson.[37] Otteson points out that Smith's defence of markets and individual liberty does indeed imply a role for the government, but that his focus is always on the decentralization of government and the impact of the unintended consequences of government intervention. Smith was suspicious of government, and even where he does support public provision, he generally does so through policies designed to take advantage of market forces – such as his policy for the fee funding of teacher's salaries – and to avoid the capture of the state by vested interests like the merchants.

One particular dispute in the left versus right debate has been the extent to which Smith can be read as having a theory of justice in the modern sense. As we noted in chapter 4, Smith's discussion of justice largely follows the natural jurisprudence tradition of distinguishing between commutative justice (the protection of person and property) and distributive justice (proper beneficence and redistribution of wealth). This reading has been challenged by a number of contemporary Smith scholars. Samuel Fleischacker has made the case for reading Smith as anticipating contemporary notions of social justice, while Amos Witzum and Rudi Verburg have gone further and argued that Smith has a theory of distributive or social justice, and Amartya Sen has built elements of Smith's thought into his own theory of justice.[38] I have argued elsewhere that we should be careful about how we read modern notions of justice back into Smith's theory.[39] The main issue with attempts to read a theory of distributive justice in his work is that, while the various policies that he supports have distributive impacts, it is not clear that he has a 'theory' of distribution in any developed sense.[40] Moreover, his defence of commerce is grounded precisely on the idea that it benefits the ordinary workers without the deliberate intervention of the government.

Like all complex thinkers, Smith's work includes ideas that could lend themselves to either left- or right-wing readings. The redistributive state post-dates Smith, and the idea of directing government action in pursuit of some plan of social justice seems completely at odds with his criticism of the man of system. Similarly, his insistence on the benefits of commerce and the ubiquity of rank to ensure social stability challenge the reading of him as an egalitarian. Smith's interest in helping the poor is perfectly compatible with a realization that the gap between the rich and poor is a necessary feature of commercial society.[41] Indeed one might go further and suggest that Smith's concern for the poor means that he is willing to countenance inequality if the result is a rising living standard for the poorest in society. However, he clearly did think that the government has a role to play in the economy and that considering what that role should be should be undertaken with a presumption against government action and a demand that the evidence show that the policy was necessary, would succeed, and would not lead to negative unintended consequences.[42]

As Gavin Kennedy has pointed out, Smith was not an anarcho-capitalist.[43] The term 'laissez-faire' appears nowhere in his work and fails to capture the cautious and pragmatic assessment of state action that is a particular feature of Book V of the *Wealth of Nations*. This leads Kennedy to cast doubt on the significance of the term 'invisible hand' for understanding Smith's thinking. In previous chapters, we have examined the passages where the metaphor appears in the *Wealth of Nations* and the *Moral Sentiments*, and we have also seen how Smith's interest in evolutionary and unintended consequence explanations is a key feature of his social science. It seems churlish, then, to dispose too hastily of such an elegant term.[44] Smith clearly did think that some social processes produced beneficial unintended consequences, but equally that some others produced socially negative unintended consequences. The invisible hand is not a form of providential explanation for Smith: as we saw, in the two cases where he applies the metaphor he explains the situation and the reasons why the particular outcome is brought about. No one is directing this outcome; it is just that the actors involved do not see it as part of their reasoning for acting. Smith, as social scientist, is able to take a step back and explain the fall of feudalism and the operation of domestic investment. In both those cases, the historical reconstruction explains where the beneficial consequences come from and the invisible hand metaphor captures the fact that the pattern emerges from the complex interaction of individuals pursuing their own goals. There is nothing inevitable in Smith's application of the invisible hand. He does not apply it to the outcome of all market exchanges in all circumstances, still less to the idea that self-interest always issues in the social good. Instead he is saying that if we understand how human beings come together to produce outcomes which none of them intend, then we will see that social change is often brought about without deliberate design. Smith's moral philosophy tells us that he firmly believed in human benevolence and that we had a duty to our fellow humans, but good intentions are not enough if the outcome of social processes turns them into negative results.[45]

We see cases of positive unintended consequences in the story of the fall of feudalism and the tendency to invest in the home market, just as we see negative unintended consequences in the impact of the well-intentioned Poor Law and Corn Laws. The 'science of human nature'[46] helps us to understand why this is the case. Smith's defence of what he calls the 'liberal plan of equality, liberty and justice'[47] is always based on the evidence and is always open to pragmatic responses to changes in circumstances. His aim is to ensure that policy is informed by science and, at the same time, that we are modest about the ability of science to answer all questions at once. This portrayal of Smith as systematic thinker and pragmatic policy adviser is gaining popularity among Smith scholars and can be seen in the recent books by Eric Schliesser and Jesse Norman.[48]

Conclusion

The aim of this book has been to show the reader that there is more to Smith than the caricature of the 'father of economics'. In doing so, I have made the case for reading him as a systematic thinker whose thought fits together in ways that make contributions to a whole range of academic disciplines. Far from there being an Adam

Smith Problem in contrasting his two great books, there are instead a series of Adam Smith challenges to the way we think about moral philosophy, science, literary criticism, politics, and economics. Although there is a growing body of Adam Smith scholars, Smith is still not read as much as he should be. The caricature of Smith has been allowed to continue in the popular imagination precisely because most of those who contribute to it do not read beyond the first few chapters of the *Wealth of Nations* and the *Moral Sentiments*. The Smith we have seen in this book is a philosophical and systematic thinker, but also a practical and modest thinker whose ideas serve a pragmatic and gradualist policy agenda. Smith thought that life in commercial society was better than in earlier societies. He thought that this was particularly the case for the poor, who were richer and freer than they had ever been. But he did not think that commercial societies were perfect. Indeed many of the imperfections of commercial society were the result of the behaviour of merchants and businessmen. These groups had their own partial interests and were seldom friends of the sort of free markets that Smith advocated.

The task that Smith set himself was to understand the society that was developing around about him: to see how undeveloped societies like early eighteenth-century Scotland could become richer and freer by adopting the commercial way of life. At bottom, Smith is a thinker who cared about the standard of living of all people, and saw commerce as a way of putting an end to the horror of watching your own children starve to death through hunger. As he would have it: '[O]pulence and freedom are the two greatest blessings man can possess.'[49]

Notes

Chapter 1 Smith and the Scottish Enlightenment

1 For details on Smith's time at Glasgow, see Scott, *Adam Smith as Student and Professor*.
2 For a contemporary biography, see Stewart, 'Account of the Life and Writings of Adam Smith'. The best source for biographical details on Smith is Ross's *The Life of Adam Smith*. Phillipson's *Adam Smith* is the best intellectual biography, whilst Kennedy's *Adam Smith* is the most rounded introduction to his economics and moral philosophy. Other general overviews include Lindgren's *Social Philosophy of Adam Smith* and Muller's *Adam Smith in His Time and Ours*.
3 The clearest introduction to the subject is Broadie's *The Scottish Enlightenment*. The most comprehensive account of the social and political thought of the period is Berry's *Social Theory of the Scottish Enlightenment*.
4 See Montes, 'Newtonianism and Adam Smith'.
5 Hume, *Treatise*, 273.
6 Phillipson, *Adam Smith*, 71. Rasmussen's *The Infidel and the Professor* is the best discussion of the close intellectual friendship between Hume and Smith.

Chapter 2 Science and System

1 The general consensus among contemporary Smith scholars is that the Problem is a non-problem and based on a faulty reading by the German historical school.
2 *Moral Sentiments*, 287.

3 Also included in this volume is Smith's short essay on the *External Senses*. This represents an engagement with the ideas of Berkeley and Locke on the nature of the relationship between our perception of external objects and the sensory organs of the body.

4 *Astronomy*, 33.

5 *Astronomy*, 41.

6 It is worth noting that this passage also marks the first of three appearances of the phrase 'invisible hand' in Smith's works. Here the invisible hand is that of the Roman God Jupiter, marking the usage as distinct from the two later appearances of the term, which we will examine in subsequent chapters.

7 *Astronomy*, 50.

8 *Astronomy*, 45.

9 *Astronomy*, 96.

10 *Astronomy*, 46.

11 *Astronomy*, 66.

12 *Astronomy*, 45.

13 For a discussion of Smith on system, see Skinner, *A System of Social Science*; Phillipson, *Adam Smith*; and Schliesser, *Adam Smith*.

14 *Astronomy*, 42.

15 *Astronomy*, 74.

16 *Astronomy*, 59.

17 *Ancient Physics*, 107–8.

18 Hutcheson, *Inquiry*, 39–40.

19 *Astronomy*, 71.

20 *Astronomy*, 89.

21 The similarities between Smith's theory and that of the twentieth-century philosopher of science Thomas Kuhn, with its division between normal science and paradigm shifts, has been widely noted, though it seems Kuhn was not aware of Smith's essay as he developed his view.

22 For a discussion of Smith's relationship to Newtonianism see Montes, 'Newtonianism and Smith'.

23 The best short account of Smith's theory of science is Berry, 'Smith and Science'.

24 Smith makes almost exactly the same observation in the *Wealth of Nations* when he points to 'the beauty of systematical arrangement of different observations connected by a few common principles' (*Wealth of Nations*, 768–9), and in his essay on the *Imitative Arts* published in the *Essays on Philosophical Subjects* showing how key it was to his conception of proper philosophy.

25 See Berry, 'Smith and Science', for Smith as social scientist.

26 Phillipson, *Adam Smith*, 92.

27 The *Essays on Philosophical Subjects* also includes two short essays on 'Of the Affinity between Music, Dancing, and Poetry and Of the

Affinity between certain English and Italian Verses', which may have formed part of Smith's unrealized book on art and literature. For discussions of Smith's aesthetics, see Labio, 'Adam Smith's Aesthetics' and McKenna, *Adam Smith*.

28 See de Marchi, 'Smith on Ingenuity'.
29 *Imitative Arts*, 183.
30 *Imitative Arts*, 185.
31 *Rhetoric*, 6.
32 *Rhetoric*, 25–6.
33 *Rhetoric*, 43.
34 *Rhetoric*, 136.
35 *Rhetoric*, 137. Smith also suggests that there is a difference in literary taste between the 'ignorant' and the 'enlightened' (*Rhetoric*, 111). The 'vulgar' are amused by fabulous tales of supernatural phenomena, while the refined prefer recognizable tales of human emotions.
36 *Rhetoric*, 98.
37 *Rhetoric*, 146.
38 On Smith's character sketches, see Heydt, '"A Delicate and an Accurate Pencil"'.
39 For the classic statement on this, see Forbes, 'Scientific Whiggism'.
40 See David Hume's argument in 'Of the Original Contract', Hume, *Essays*, 465–87.
41 Ferguson, *Essay*, 14.
42 Stewart, 'Account of the Life and Writings of Adam Smith', 293.
43 Stewart, 'Account of the Life and Writings of Adam Smith', 293.
44 See Land, 'Adam Smith's "Considerations"' and Otteson, 'Adam Smith's First Market'.
45 The approach is ubiquitous among the Scots and examples can be found in the work of Lord Kames, William Robertson, and a host of minor figures. Adam Ferguson operates with a variant of the approach which has three stages: savage, barbarian, and civilized.
46 For the influence of Rousseau on Smith's thinking see Rasmussen, *The Problems and Promise*.

Chapter 3 Morality and Sympathy

1 The most comprehensive accounts of Smith's moral philosophy are Campbell, *Adam Smith's Science of Morals* and Griswold, *Adam Smith and the Virtues of Enlightenment*. A shorter and clear overview is offered by Raphael, *The Impartial Spectator*.
2 Hume, *Treatise*, 620–1.
3 *Moral Sentiments*, 265.
4 *Wealth of Nations*, 769.
5 *Moral Sentiments*, 139.

6 *Moral Sentiments*, 127.
7 *Moral Sentiments*, 17.
8 *Moral Sentiments*, 9.
9 For the critique of Mandeville, see *Moral Sentiments*, 309; of Hobbes, *Moral Sentiments*, 315–17; and Hutcheson, *Moral Sentiments*, 322–3.
10 *Wealth of Nations*, 769.
11 *Moral Sentiments*, 10.
12 *Moral Sentiments*, 10.
13 *Moral Sentiments*, 116.
14 *Moral Sentiments*, 13.
15 *Moral Sentiments*, 19.
16 *Moral Sentiments*, 17–18.
17 *Moral Sentiments*, 22.
18 See Paganelli, 'The Moralizing Role of Distance'.
19 *Moral Sentiments*, 110.
20 *Moral Sentiments*, 145.
21 *Moral Sentiments*, 27.
22 *Moral Sentiments*, 116.
23 *Moral Sentiments*, 24.
24 *Moral Sentiments*, 76.
25 *Moral Sentiments*, 24.
26 *Moral Sentiments*, 200.
27 See Weinstein, *Adam Smith's Pluralism*.
28 *Moral Sentiments*, 209.
29 *Astronomy*, 41.
30 *Moral Sentiments*, 194.
31 *Moral Sentiments*, 199.
32 *Moral Sentiments*, 199.
33 *Moral Sentiments*, 201.
34 *Moral Sentiments*, 159–60.
35 *Moral Sentiments*, 204.
36 *Moral Sentiments*, 205.
37 *Moral Sentiments*, 208.
38 *Moral Sentiments*, 204.
39 *Wealth of Nations*, 10.
40 *Moral Sentiments*, 210. Smith is also sharply critical of infanticide among the poor in China (*Wealth of Nations*, 89–90).
41 *Moral Sentiments*, 210.
42 *Moral Sentiments*, 210.
43 *Moral Sentiments*, 199.
44 *Moral Sentiments*, 211.
45 *Moral Sentiments*, 209.
46 *Moral Sentiments*, 200.
47 *Moral Sentiments*, 209.
48 *Moral Sentiments*, 208.

49 *Moral Sentiments*, 207.
50 *Jurisprudence*, 112.
51 See Broadie, 'Sympathy and the Impartial Spectator' and Fricke, 'Adam Smith'.
52 *Moral Sentiments*, 113.
53 *Moral Sentiments*, 112.
54 *Moral Sentiments*, 113.
55 *Moral Sentiments*, 115.
56 *Moral Sentiments*, 42.
57 *Moral Sentiments*, 130.
58 *Moral Sentiments*, 160.
59 Griswold, *Adam Smith and the Virtues of Enlightenment*.
60 Though it is worth noting, as Fonna Forman-Barzilai does, that the content of the impartial spectator's judgement is generated within the society in question. Forman-Barzilai, *Adam Smith and the Circles of Sympathy*, 96–104.
61 *Moral Sentiments*, 159. See also *Moral Sentiments*, 135, where Smith says that we have so fully habituated the impartial spectator that we are 'scarce sensible' that we consult it.
62 *Moral Sentiments*, 220.
63 *Moral Sentiments*, 225.
64 *Moral Sentiments*, 237.
65 *Moral Sentiments*, 136–7.
66 *Moral Sentiments*, 25.
67 *Moral Sentiments*, 140.
68 *Moral Sentiments*, 146.
69 *Moral Sentiments*, 249.
70 *Moral Sentiments*, 233–4. As we will see below, this links into Smith's general distrust of innovation in government (*Moral Sentiments*, 231) and political factionalism (*Moral Sentiments*, 232).

Chapter 4 Justice and Virtue

1 See Hanley, *Adam Smith and the Character of Virtue* and Berry, 'Adam Smith and the Virtues of a Modern Economy'.
2 *Moral Sentiments*, 259.
3 *Moral Sentiments*, 26.
4 *Moral Sentiments*, 152.
5 *Moral Sentiments*, 215.
6 *Moral Sentiments*, 216. See the discussion in Clark, 'Conversation and Moderate Virtue'.
7 *Moral Sentiments*, 215. For a discussion of self-interest and prudence in Smith, see Heath, 'Adam Smith and Self-Interest'.
8 *Moral Sentiments*, 215.

9 *Moral Sentiments*, 86.
10 *Moral Sentiments*, 269.
11 *Moral Sentiments*, 269.
12 *Moral Sentiments*, 270.
13 *Jurisprudence*, 9.
14 *Moral Sentiments*, 76.
15 *Moral Sentiments*, 70–1.
16 *Moral Sentiments*, 175–6.
17 *Moral Sentiments*, 80.
18 See Stalley, 'Adam Smith and the Theory of Punishment'.
19 *Moral Sentiments*, 83.
20 Hume, *Treatise*, 499–500.
21 *Moral Sentiments*, 20.
22 *Moral Sentiments*, 262.
23 *Jurisprudence*, 9. See also *Moral Sentiments*, 390.
24 *Rhetoric*, 29.
25 *Moral Sentiments*, 82.
26 *Moral Sentiments*, 86.
27 *Moral Sentiments*, 78.
28 *Moral Sentiments*, 106.
29 *Moral Sentiments*, 190–1.
30 A distinction that Smith underlines in the structure of the book by dividing his discussion of what we owe individuals (VI.ii.i) from that of what we owe to societies (VI.ii.ii).
31 Stewart, 'Account of the Life and Writings of Adam Smith', 275.
32 *Jurisprudence*, 6.
33 *Jurisprudence*, 486.
34 *Jurisprudence*, 5.
35 *Moral Sentiments*, 81.
36 *Moral Sentiments*, 81.
37 Raphael, 'Hume and Adam Smith on Justice'. *Moral Sentiments*, 90–1.
38 *Moral Sentiments*, 91.
39 *Moral Sentiments*, 247.
40 *Moral Sentiments*, 247.
41 See Hanley, *Adam Smith and the Character of Virtue*.
42 *Moral Sentiments*, 168.
43 *Moral Sentiments*, 132.
44 *Moral Sentiments*, 132.
45 See Kennedy, 'The Hidden Adam Smith' for the case against a religious Smith and the papers collected in Oslington, *Adam Smith as Theologian* for those for a religious Smith. The clearest discussion of Smith's descriptive theory of religious belief is Heydt, 'The Problem of Natural Religion'.
46 *Moral Sentiments*, 163–4.
47 See Tegos, 'Adam Smith'.

48 *Moral Sentiments*, 50.
49 *Moral Sentiments*, 226.
50 *Moral Sentiments*, 62.
51 Smith, 'Adam Smith's "Collateral" Inquiry'.
52 *Wealth of Nations*, 190.
53 *Moral Sentiments*, 50.
54 *Moral Sentiments*, 212–13.
55 *Wealth of Nations*, 870.
56 *Wealth of Nations*, 794.
57 *Moral Sentiments*, 57.
58 *Moral Sentiments*, 62.
59 In the *Lectures on Rhetoric*, Smith returns to this theme and discusses the class system in ancient Rome. He suggests that a key role was played by the middle class in constraining the excesses of the nobles and the mob (*Rhetoric*, 156–7).
60 *Moral Sentiments*, 181.
61 *Moral Sentiments*, 181.
62 *Moral Sentiments*, 183. See Fleischacker, 'True to Ourselves?'
63 *Moral Sentiments*, 184–5.
64 *Moral Sentiments*, 185.
65 *Moral Sentiments*, 45.
66 *Moral Sentiments*, 50.
67 *Moral Sentiments*, 55.
68 *Moral Sentiments*, 55.
69 *Moral Sentiments*, 56.
70 *Moral Sentiments*, 55.
71 *Moral Sentiments*, 232–3.
72 *Moral Sentiments*, 234.

Chapter 5 Jurisprudence

1 *Jurisprudence*, 5.
2 *Jurisprudence*, 5.
3 *Jurisprudence*, 338.
4 See Haakonssen, *The Science of a Legislator* and Flanders, 'Adam Smith's Jurisprudence'. Winch, *Adam Smith's Politics* puts the discussion in its eighteenth-century context.
5 Smith was not alone in his praise for the British constitution and its mixed and limited government. Montesquieu discussed it in detail and it was a popular nationalistic trope in British political debate of the time.
6 *Jurisprudence*, 105.
7 *Jurisprudence*, 316, 320. Smith's criticism of social contract theories and his evolutionary account of subordination are deeply indebted

to Hume's essays 'Of the Original Contract' and 'Of the Origin of Government' (*Essays*).

8 *Jurisprudence*, 402–3.
9 *Jurisprudence*, 323.
10 *Jurisprudence*, 14.
11 *Wealth of Nations*, 97.
12 *Jurisprudence*, 13
13 *Jurisprudence*, 129–30.
14 *Jurisprudence*, 39.
15 *Jurisprudence*, 93–4.
16 *Jurisprudence*, 208.
17 *Jurisprudence*, 409.
18 *Jurisprudence*, 408–9, 460.
19 *Jurisprudence*, 7.
20 *Jurisprudence*, 202–3, 433.
21 *Wealth of Nations*, 715.
22 *Wealth of Nations*, 709–10.
23 *Jurisprudence*, 208.
24 *Jurisprudence*, 433.
25 *Rhetoric*, 174.
26 *Rhetoric*, 174.
27 *Rhetoric*, 176.
28 *Jurisprudence*, 338.
29 Sher, 'Adam Ferguson, Adam Smith and the Problem of National Defense'.
30 *Wealth of Nations*, 703.
31 *Jurisprudence*, 265.
32 *Wealth of Nations*, 706–7.
33 See van de Harr, 'Adam Smith on Empire' and Paganelli & Schumacher, 'Do Not Take Peace for Granted'.
34 *Wealth of Nations*, 378.
35 *Wealth of Nations*, 383.
36 *Wealth of Nations*, 386–7.
37 *Wealth of Nations*, 399.
38 *Wealth of Nations*, 401.
39 *Wealth of Nations*, 402.
40 *Wealth of Nations*, 405.
41 *Wealth of Nations*, 405.
42 *Wealth of Nations*, 411.
43 *Wealth of Nations*, 412.
44 *Wealth of Nations*, 416–17.
45 *Wealth of Nations*, 418.
46 *Wealth of Nations*, 419.
47 *Wealth of Nations*, 400.
48 *Wealth of Nations*, 422.

49 *Wealth of Nations*, 422.
50 *Wealth of Nations*, 426.
51 *Wealth of Nations*, 412.
52 See Salter, 'Adam Smith on Feudalism'.
53 *Jurisprudence*, 453.
54 *Wealth of Nations*, 387.
55 *Jurisprudence*, 453.
56 *Jurisprudence*, 192.
57 *Jurisprudence*, 182–7.
58 *Jurisprudence*, 487.
59 *Wealth of Nations*, 392.
60 *Jurisprudence*, 333.
61 *Jurisprudence*, 487.
62 Forbes, 'Scientific Whiggism', 'Sceptical Whiggism'.
63 *Jurisprudence*, 271.
64 *Wealth of Nations*, 256.

Chapter 6 The Nature of Wealth

1 For more detailed overviews of Smith's economics, see Brown, *Adam Smith's Economics*; Evensky, *Adam Smith's Wealth of Nations*; Aspromourgis, *The Science of Wealth*; Young, *Economics as Moral Science*; and Hollander, *The Economics of Adam Smith*. For a shorter summary, see Rothschild and Sen, 'Adam Smith's Economics'.
2 *Wealth of Nations*, 23.
3 *Wealth of Nations*, 25.
4 *Wealth of Nations*, 26.
5 *Wealth of Nations*, 28–9.
6 *Wealth of Nations*, 26.
7 *Wealth of Nations*, 44.
8 *Wealth of Nations*, 47.
9 *Wealth of Nations*, 47.
10 *Wealth of Nations*, 73.
11 *Wealth of Nations*, 73.
12 *Wealth of Nations*, 80.
13 *Wealth of Nations*, 98.
14 *Wealth of Nations*, 95.
15 *Wealth of Nations*, 124.
16 Boucoyannis, 'The Equalizing Hand' develops Smith's argument that a growing economy allowed for overall increases in wealth without steep inequality.
17 *Wealth of Nations*, 99.
18 *Wealth of Nations*, 145.
19 *Wealth of Nations*, 278.

20 *Wealth of Nations*, 341.
21 *Wealth of Nations*, 343.
22 *Wealth of Nations*, 345.
23 *Wealth of Nations*, 346.
24 *Wealth of Nations*, 333.
25 *Wealth of Nations*, 291.
26 *Wealth of Nations*, 316.
27 *Wealth of Nations*, 321.
28 Interestingly, this was the subject of one of the earliest detailed criticisms of Smith's theory. In *A Defence of Usury* (1787), Jeremy Bentham wrote an extensive critique accusing Smith of inconsistency and arguing that he should have left the interest rate to be determined by the market.

Chapter 7 Government and the Market

1 See Coats, 'Adam Smith and the Mercantile System'.
2 *Wealth of Nations*, 439.
3 *Wealth of Nations*, 435. Once again Smith is reacting to and developing ideas first outlined by his friend Hume. In a series of essays on political economy, Hume (*Essays*) undermines the balance of trade argument and casts doubt on the usefulness of restrictions on the transfer of gold and silver: the so-called 'specie-flow mechanism'.
4 *Wealth of Nations*, 452.
5 *Wealth of Nations*, 453.
6 *Wealth of Nations*, 456.
7 Incidentally, in 2018, Smith's proposition found empirical support when the only vineyard in Scotland went out of business (Marc Horne, 'Ex-Winemaker is Not Toasting the Summer', *The Times*, 9 July 2018).
8 *Wealth of Nations*, 488.
9 See van de Haar, 'Adam Smith on Empire'.
10 See Muthu, 'Adam Smith's Critique of International Trading Companies'.
11 *Wealth of Nations*, 660.
12 *Wealth of Nations*, 673.
13 *Wealth of Nations*, 687.
14 *Wealth of Nations*, 705.
15 *Wealth of Nations*, 687.
16 *Wealth of Nations*, 722.
17 *Wealth of Nations*, 719.
18 *Wealth of Nations*, 731.
19 See Campbell and Ross, 'The Utilitarianism of Adam Smith's Policy Advice'; Stigler, 'Smith's Travels on the Ship of State'; and Young, 'Unintended Order and Intervention'.

20 *Wealth of Nations*, 753.
21 *Wealth of Nations*, 769.
22 *Wealth of Nations*, 772.
23 For a discussion of Smith's supposed ambivalence about the division of labour, see Heilbroner, 'The Paradox of Progress'; West, 'Adam Smith's Two Views'; and Rosenberg, 'Adam Smith on the Division of Labour'.
24 *Wealth of Nations*, 788.
25 *Wealth of Nations*, 791.
26 *Wealth of Nations*, 793.
27 *Wealth of Nations*, 861.
28 *Wealth of Nations*, 825.
29 *Wealth of Nations*, 69.
30 *Jurisprudence*, 324.
31 *Wealth of Nations*, 884.
32 *Wealth of Nations*, 456.

Chapter 8 Legacy and Influence

1 Oncken, 'Das Adam Smith-Problem'.
2 *Correspondence*, 43.
3 Reeder, ed., *On Moral Sentiments*.
4 *Correspondence*, 51–7.
5 See Griswold, *Adam Smith and the Virtues of Enlightenment* and Forman-Barzilai, *Adam Smith and the Circles of Sympathy*.
6 See Weinstein, *Adam Smith's Pluralism*.
7 See Smith, *Adam Ferguson*.
8 Wollstonecraft, *Vindication*, 288. As Maureen Harkin notes, Smith does not say much about the position of women, but what he did say on other matters seems to have made a significant impact on early feminist thinkers (Harkin, 'Adam Smith').
9 Wollstonecraft, *Vindication*, 294.
10 *Correspondence*, 164.
11 Ross, ed., *On the Wealth of Nations* and Stigler, 'Smith's Travels on the Ship of State'.
12 *Correspondence*, 208.
13 Rothschild, 'Adam Smith and the Invisible Hand'.
14 Carlyle, *Past and Present*, 152–3.
15 See Meek, 'The Scottish Contribution to Marxist Sociology' and *Smith, Marx, and After*.
16 See Pack, 'Adam Smith and Marx'.
17 See the debate between Lamb, 'Adam Smith's Concept of Alienation', Rosenberg, 'Adam Smith on the Division of Labour', and West, 'Adam Smith's Two Views'.

18 Indeed in *Capital*, Vol. 1, Ch. 14, Sect. 4, Marx suggests that Ferguson's more sceptical analysis of alienation was better than Smith's.

19 This was particularly true in China, where the *Wealth of Nations* was translated and read widely in the twentieth century as part of Marxism studies. See Luo Wei-Dong, 'Adam Smith in China', who notes three waves of reading Smith in China: the end of the imperial period, the period of high Marxism, and the post-1979 reform period.

20 Stigler, 'Smith's Travels on the Ship of State', 246.

21 Hayek, *Road to Serfdom.*

22 Hayek, 'Adam Smith'.

23 Smith and Wilson, *Humanomics.*

24 Kiesling, 'Mirror Neuron Research'.

25 For a sense of the current debates on Smith, see the chapters collected in Berry et al., eds, *The Oxford Handbook of Adam Smith* and Haakonssen, *The Cambridge Companion to Adam Smith.*

26 Darwall, *The Second-Person Standpoint.*

27 See Garret and Hanley, 'Adam Smith'.

28 For attempts to read Smith and the Scottish Enlightenment in this context, see Pocock, *Machiavellian Moment*; Phillipson, 'Adam Smith as Civic Moralist'; and Robertson, 'Scottish Political Economy'. For a critical response, see Harpham, 'Liberalism, Civic Humanism and the Case of Adam Smith'.

29 Winch, *Adam Smith's Politics.*

30 See Hont, 'Adam Smith's History' and *Jealousy of Trade.*

31 Forbes, 'Sceptical Whiggism'.

32 Forbes, 'Scientific Whiggism'.

33 See, for example, Alvey, *Adam Smith: Optimist or Pessimist?*

34 See Haakonssen and Winch, 'The Legacy of Adam Smith', 367. See also Sen, 'The Uses and Abuses of Adam Smith'.

35 McLean, *Adam Smith, Radical and Egalitarian.*

36 Fleischacker, 'Adam Smith on Equality'. See also Debes, 'Adam Smith on Dignity and Equality'.

37 Otteson, *Adam Smith's Marketplace of Life.*

38 Fleischacker, *On Adam Smith's Wealth of Nations*; Witzum, 'Distributive Considerations'; Verburg, 'Adam Smith's Growing Concern'; Sen, *The Idea of Justice.*

39 Smith, 'Adam Smith: Left or Right?' and 'Smith, Justice and the Scope'.

40 See Vivenza, 'Justice as a Virtue' for a similar view.

41 Though, as Boucoyannis, points out, he also thought that this would not be the case in a growing economy where competition would drive down the returns to capital and drive up wages. Boucoyannis, 'The Equalizing Hand'.

42 A point stressed by Stigler and accepted by Fleischacker and Griswold.

43 Kennedy, *Adam Smith.*

44 For the history of the term, see Harrison, 'Adam Smith and the

History of the Invisible Hand'. For a criticism of it as un-Smithian, see Rothschild, 'Adam Smith and the Invisible Hand'. For sustained engagement, see Samuels, *Erasing the Invisible Hand*.

45 Smith, *Adam Smith's Political Philosophy*.
46 *Moral Sentiments*, 319.
47 *Wealth of Nations*, 664.
48 See Schliesser, *Adam Smith* and Norman, *Adam Smith*.
49 *Jurisprudence*, 185.

Bibliography

Alvey, James E., *Adam Smith: Optimist or Pessimist? A New Problem Concerning the Teleological Basis of Commercial Society*. Aldershot: Ashgate, 2003.

Aspromourgos, Tony, *The Science of Wealth: Adam Smith and the Framing of Political Economy*. London: Routledge, 2009.

Bentham, Jeremy, *A Defence of Usury: Showing the Impolicy of the Present Legal Restraints on the Terms of Pecuniary Bargains, in a Series of Letters to a Friend*. Cambridge: Cambridge University Press, 2014 [1787].

Berry, Christopher J., 'Adam Smith and the Virtues of a Modern Economy', in Christopher J. Berry (ed.), *Essays on Hume, Smith and the Scottish Enlightenment*. Edinburgh: Edinburgh University Press, 2018, pp. 347–63.

Berry, Christopher J., 'Smith and Science', in Knud Haakonssen (ed.), *The Cambridge Companion to Adam Smith*. Cambridge: Cambridge University Press, 2006, pp. 112–35.

Berry, Christopher J., *Social Theory of the Scottish Enlightenment*. Edinburgh: Edinburgh University Press, 1997.

Berry, Christopher J., Paganelli, Maria Pia, & Smith, Craig (eds), *The Oxford Handbook of Adam Smith*. Oxford: Oxford University Press, 2013.

Boucoyannis, Deborah, 'The Equalizing Hand: Why Adam Smith Thought the Market Should Produce Wealth Without Steep Inequality', *Perspectives on Politics* 11 (4), 2013, pp. 1051–70.

Broadie, Alexander, *The Scottish Enlightenment: The Historical Age of the Historical Nation*. Edinburgh: Birlinn, 2007.

Broadie, Alexander, 'Sympathy and the Impartial Spectator', in Knud Haakonssen (ed.), *The Cambridge Companion to Adam Smith*. Cambridge: Cambridge University Press, 2006, pp. 158–88.

Brown, Maurice, *Adam Smith's Economics: Its Place in the Development of Economic Thought*. London: Croom Helm, 1988.

Campbell, T. D., *Adam Smith's Science of Morals*. London: George Allen & Unwin, 1971.

Campbell, T. D. & Ross, I. S., 'The Utilitarianism of Adam Smith's Policy Advice', *Journal of the History of Ideas* 42 (1), 1981, pp. 73–92.

Carlyle, Thomas, *Past and Present*. Oxford: Oxford University Press, 1938 [1843].

Clark, H. C., 'Conversation and Moderate Virtue in Adam Smith's Theory of Moral Sentiments', *Review of Politics* 54, 1992, pp. 185–201.

Coats, A. W., 'Adam Smith and the Mercantile System', in Andrew S. Skinner and Thomas Wilson (eds), *Essays on Adam Smith*. Oxford: Clarendon Press, 1975, pp. 219–36.

Darwall, Stephen, *The Second-Person Standpoint: Morality, Respect, and Accountability*. Cambridge, MA: Harvard University Press, 2006.

de Marchi, Neil, 'Smith on Ingenuity, Pleasure, and the Imitative Arts', in Knud Haakonssen (ed.), *The Cambridge Companion to Adam Smith*. Cambridge: Cambridge University Press, 2006, pp. 136–57.

Debes, Remy, 'Adam Smith on Dignity and Equality', *British Journal for the History of Philosophy* 20, 2012, pp. 109–40.

Evensky, Jerry, *Adam Smith's Wealth of Nations: A Reader's Guide*. Cambridge: Cambridge University Press, 2015.

Ferguson, Adam, *An Essay on the History of Civil Society*, ed. Fania Oz-Salzberger. Cambridge: Cambridge University Press, 1994 [1767].

Ferguson, Adam, *The History of the Progress and Termination of the Roman Republic*. New York: J. C. Derby, 1856 [1783].

Flanders, Chad, 'Adam Smith's Jurisprudence: Resentment, Punishment, Justice', in Ryan Patrick Hanley (ed.), *Adam Smith: His Life, Thought, and Legacy*. Princeton: Princeton University Press, 2016, pp. 371–86.

Fleischacker, Samuel, 'Adam Smith on Equality', in Christopher J. Berry, Maria Pia Paganelli, & Craig Smith (eds), *The Oxford Handbook of Adam Smith*. Oxford: Oxford University Press, 2013, pp. 485–500.

Fleischacker, Samuel, *On Adam Smith's Wealth of Nations: A Philosophical Companion*. Princeton: Princeton University Press, 2004.

Fleischacker, Samuel, 'True to Ourselves? Adam Smith on Self-Deceit', *The Adam Smith Review* 6, pp. 75–92.

Forbes, Duncan, 'Sceptical Whiggism, Commerce and Liberty', in Andrew S. Skinner & Thomas Wilson (eds), *Essays on Adam Smith*. Oxford: Clarendon Press, 1975, pp. 179–95.

Forbes, Duncan, 'Scientific Whiggism: Adam Smith and John Millar', *Cambridge Journal* 7, 1954, pp. 643–70.

Forman-Barzilai, Fonna, *Adam Smith and the Circles of Sympathy: Cosmopolitanism and Moral Theory*. Cambridge: Cambridge University Press, 2010.

Fricke, Christel, 'Adam Smith: The Sympathetic Process and the Origin and Function of Conscience', in Christopher J. Berry, Maria Pia Paganelli, & Craig Smith (eds), *The Oxford Handbook of Adam Smith*. Oxford: Oxford University Press, 2013, pp. 177–200.

Garrett, Aaron & Hanley, Ryan Patrick, 'Adam Smith: History and Impartiality', in Aaron Garrett & James A. Harris (eds), *Scottish Philosophy in the Eighteenth Century, Vol. 1: Morals, Politics, Art, Religion*. Oxford: Oxford University Press, 2015, pp. 239–82.

Griswold, Charles L., *Adam Smith and the Virtues of Enlightenment*. Cambridge: Cambridge University Press, 1999.

Haakonssen, Knud (ed.), *The Cambridge Companion to Adam Smith*. Cambridge: Cambridge University Press, 2006.

Haakonssen, Knud, *The Science of a Legislator: The Natural Jurisprudence of David Hume and Adam Smith*. Cambridge: Cambridge University Press, 1989.

Haakonssen, Knud & Winch, Donald, 'The Legacy of Adam Smith', in Knud Haakonssen (ed.), *The Cambridge Companion to Adam Smith*. Cambridge: Cambridge University Press, 2006, pp. 366–94.

Hanley, Ryan Patrick, *Adam Smith and the Character of Virtue*. Cambridge: Cambridge University Press, 2009.

Harkin, Maureen, 'Adam Smith on Women', in Christopher J. Berry, Maria Pia Paganelli, & Craig Smith (eds), *The Oxford Handbook of Adam Smith*. Oxford: Oxford University Press, 2013, pp. 501–20.

Harpham, Edward J., 'Liberalism, Civic Humanism and the Case of Adam Smith', *American Political Science Review* 78, 1984, pp. 764–74.

Harrison, Peter, 'Adam Smith and the History of the Invisible Hand', *Journal of the History of Ideas* 72 (1), 2011, pp. 29–49.

Hayek, F. A., 'Adam Smith (1723–1790): His Message in Today's Language', in *The Collected Works of F. A. Hayek, Vol. 3: The Trend of Economic Thinking: Essays on Political Economists and Economic History*, eds W. W. Bartley III & Stephen Kresge. Indianapolis: Liberty Fund, 1991, pp. 119–24.

Hayek, F. A., *The Road to Serfdom*. London: Routledge, 2001 [1944].

Heath, Eugene, 'Adam Smith and Self-Interest', in Christopher J. Berry, Maria Pia Paganelli, & Craig Smith (eds), *The Oxford Handbook of Adam Smith*. Oxford: Oxford University Press, 2013, pp. 241–64.

Heilbroner, Robert L., 'The Paradox of Progress: Decline and Decay in *The Wealth of Nations*', in Andrew S. Skinner & Thomas Wilson (eds), *Essays on Adam Smith*. Oxford: Clarendon Press, 1975, pp. 524–39.

Heydt, Colin, '"A Delicate and an Accurate Pencil": Adam Smith, Description, and Philosophy as Moral Education', *History of Philosophy Quarterly* 25, 2008, pp. 57–74.

Heydt, Colin, 'The Problem of Natural Religion in Smith's Moral Thought', *Journal of the History of Ideas* 78 (1), 2017, pp. 73–94.

Hollander, Samuel, *The Economics of Adam Smith*. Toronto: University of Toronto Press, 1973.

Home, Henry, Lord Kames, *The Gentleman Farmer*. Edinburgh: W. Creech and T. Cadell, 1776.

Hont, Istvan, 'Adam Smith's History of Law and Government as Political Theory', in Richard Bourke & Raymond Geuss (eds), *Political Judgement:*

Essays for John Dunn. Cambridge: Cambridge University Press, 2009, pp. 131–71.

Hont, Istvan, *Jealousy of Trade: International Competition and the Nation-State in Historical Perspective*. Cambridge, MA: Belknap Press, 2005.

Hume, David, *Dialogues concerning Natural Religion*, ed. J. C. A. Gaskin. Oxford: Oxford University Press, 2008 [1779].

Hume, David, *Essays Moral, Political, and Literary*, ed. Eugene F. Miller, Indianapolis: Liberty Fund, 1985 [1777].

Hume, David, *The History of England*, ed. W. B. Todd, 6 vols. Indianapolis: Liberty Fund, 1985 [1778].

Hume, David, *A Treatise of Human Nature*, ed. L. A. Selby-Bigge, revised P. H. Nidditch, Oxford: Clarendon, 1976 [1739–40].

Hutcheson, Francis, *An Inquiry into the Original of Our Ideas of Beauty and Virtue*, ed. Wolfgang Leidhold. Indianapolis: Liberty Fund, 2004 [1725].

Hutton, James, *Theory of the Earth*. London and Edinburgh: T. Cadell and W. Creech, 1795.

Kennedy, Gavin, *Adam Smith: A Moral Philosopher and His Political Economy*. Basingstoke: Palgrave Macmillan, 2008.

Kennedy, Gavin, 'The Hidden Adam Smith in his Alleged Theology', *Journal of the History of Economic Thought* 33 (3), 2011, pp. 385–402.

Kiesling, L. Lynne, 'Mirror Neuron Research and Adam Smith's Concept of Sympathy: Three Points of Convergence', *Review of Austrian Economics* 25 (4), 2012, pp. 299–313.

Labio, Catherine, 'Adam Smith's Aesthetics', in Christopher J. Berry, Maria Pia Paganelli, & Craig Smith (eds), *The Oxford Handbook of Adam Smith*. Oxford: Oxford University Press, 2013, pp. 105–25.

Lamb, Robert, 'Adam Smith's Concept of Alienation', *Oxford Economic Papers* 25, 1973, pp. 275–85.

Land, Stephen K., 'Adam Smith's "Considerations Concerning the First Formation of Languages"', *Journal of the History of Ideas* 38, 1977, pp. 677–90.

Lindgren, J. Ralph, *The Social Philosophy of Adam Smith*. The Hague: Martinus Nijhoff, 1973.

Locke, John, *Two Treatises of Government*, ed. Peter Lasslett. Cambridge: Cambridge University Press, 2008 [1689].

Luo Wei-Dong, 'Adam Smith in China: From Ideology to Academia', in Ryan Patrick Hanley (ed.), *Adam Smith: His Life, Thought, and Legacy*. Princeton: Princeton University Press, 2016, pp. 512–24.

Malthus, Thomas, *An Essay on the Principles of Population and a Summary View of the Principle of Population*, ed. Antony Flew. London: Penguin Books, 1982 [1803].

Mandeville, Bernard, *The Fable of the Bees: Or Private Vices, Publick Benefits*, ed. Frederick Benjamin Kaye, 2 vols. Indianapolis: Liberty Fund, 1988 [1732].

Marx, Karl, *Capital*, ed. Ernest Mandel, trans. Ben Fowkes, 3 vols. London: Penguin Classics, 1990 [1867, 1884, 1894].

McKenna, Stephen J., *Adam Smith: The Rhetoric of Propriety*. Albany: State University of New York Press, 2006.

McLean, Iain, *Adam Smith, Radical and Egalitarian: An Interpretation for the Twenty-First Century*. Edinburgh: Edinburgh University Press, 2006.

Meek, Ronald L., 'The Scottish Contribution to Marxist Sociology', in Ronald L. Meek (ed.), *Economics and Ideology and Other Essays: Studies in the Development of Economic Thought*. London: Chapman and Hall, 1967, pp. 34–50.

Meek, Ronald L. *Smith, Marx and After*. London: Chapman and Hall, 1977.

Mill, John Stuart, *Principles of Political Economy and Chapters on Socialism*, ed. Jonathan Riley. Oxford: Oxford University Press, 1994 [1848].

Millar, John, *The Origin of the Distinction of Ranks*, ed. Aaron Garrett. Indianapolis: Liberty Fund, 2006 [1771].

Montes, Leonidas, 'Newtonianism and Adam Smith', in Christopher J. Berry, Maria Pia Paganelli, & Craig Smith (eds), *The Oxford Handbook of Adam Smith*. Oxford: Oxford University Press, 2013, pp. 36–53.

Montesquieu, Charles Louis de Secondat Baron de, *The Spirit of the Laws*, eds Anne M. Cohler, Basia Carolyn Miller, & Harold Samuel Stone. Cambridge: Cambridge University Press, 1989 [1748].

Muller, Jerry, *Adam Smith in His Time and Ours: Designing the Decent Society*. Princeton: Princeton University Press, 1993.

Munn, Thomas, *England's Treasure by Forraign Trade*. London, 1664.

Muthu, Sankar, 'Adam Smith's Critique of International Trading Companies: Theorizing "Globalization" in the Age of Enlightenment', *Political Theory* 36, 2008, pp. 185–212.

Newton, Isaac, *The Principia: Mathematical Principles of Natural Philosophy*, trans. I. Bernard Cohen & Ann Whitman. Berkeley: University of California Press, 1999 [1687].

Norman, Jesse, *Adam Smith: What He Thought, and Why It Matters*. London: Allen Lane, 2018.

Oncken, August, 'Das Adam Smith-Problem', *Zeitschrift für Socialwissenschaft* I, 1898, pp. 25–33.

Oslington, Paul (ed.), *Adam Smith as Theologian*. London: Routledge, 2011.

Otteson, James R., 'Adam Smith's First Market: The Development of Language', *History of Philosophy Quarterly* 19, 2002, pp. 65–86.

Otteson, James R., *Adam Smith's Marketplace of Life*. Cambridge: Cambridge University Press, 2002.

Pack, Spencer, 'Adam Smith and Marx', in Christopher J. Berry, Maria Pia Paganelli, & Craig Smith (eds), *The Oxford Handbook of Adam Smith*. Oxford: Oxford University Press, 2013, pp. 523–38.

Paganelli, Maria Pia, 'The Moralizing Role of Distance in Adam Smith: *The Theory of Moral Sentiments* as Possible Praise of Commerce', *History of Political Economy* 42, 2010, pp. 425–41.

Paganelli, Maria Pia & Schumacher, Reinhard, 'Do Not Take Peace for Granted: Adam Smith's Warning on the Relation between Commerce and Wealth', *Cambridge Journal of Economics* 43 (4), 2019, pp. 785–97.

Phillipson, Nicholas, *Adam Smith: An Enlightened Life*. London: Allen Lane, 2010.

Phillipson, Nicholas, 'Adam Smith as Civic Moralist', in Istvan Hont & Michael Ignatieff (eds), *Wealth and Virtue: The Shaping of Political Economy in the Scottish Enlightenment*. Cambridge: Cambridge University Press, 1985, pp. 179–202.

Pocock, J. G. A., *The Machiavellian Moment: Florentine Political Thought and the Atlantic Republican Tradition*. Princeton: Princeton University Press, 1975.

Raphael, D. D., 'Hume and Adam Smith on Justice and Utility', *Proceedings of the Aristotelian Society* 73, 1973, pp. 87–103.

Raphael, D. D., *The Impartial Spectator: Adam Smith's Moral Philosophy*. Oxford: Clarendon Press, 2007.

Rasmussen, Dennis C., *The Infidel and the Professor: David Hume, Adam Smith, and the Friendship That Shaped Modern Thought*. Princeton: Princeton University Press, 2017.

Rasmussen, Dennis C., *The Problems and Promise of Commercial Society: Adam Smith's Response to Rousseau*. University Park: Pennsylvania State University Press, 2008.

Reeder, John (ed.), *On Moral Sentiments: Contemporary Responses to Adam Smith*. Bristol: Thoemmes Press, 1997.

Ricardo, David, *Principles of Political Economy and Taxation*. New York: Dover, 2004 [1817].

Robertson, John, 'Scottish Political Economy beyond the Civic Tradition: Government and Economic Development in the *Wealth of Nations*', *History of Political Thought* 4, 1983, pp. 451–82.

Rosenberg, Nathan, 'Adam Smith on the Division of Labour: Two Views or One?' *Economica* 32, 1965, pp. 127–39.

Ross, Ian S., *The Life of Adam Smith*, 2nd edn. Oxford: Oxford University Press, 2010.

Ross, Ian S. (ed.), *On the Wealth of Nations: Contemporary Responses to Adam Smith*. Bristol: Thoemmes Press, 1998.

Rothschild, Emma, 'Adam Smith and the Invisible Hand', *American Economic Association Papers and Proceedings*, May 1994, pp. 319–22.

Rothschild, Emma & Sen, Amartya, 'Adam Smith's Economics', in Knud Haakonssen (ed.), *The Cambridge Companion to Adam Smith*. Cambridge: Cambridge University Press, 2006, pp. 319–65.

Rousseau, Jean-Jacques, *The Major Political Writings of Jean-Jacques Rousseau: The Two Discourses and The Social Contract*, ed. J. T. Scott. Chicago: University of Chicago Press, 2012.

Salter, John, 'Adam Smith on Feudalism, Commerce and Slavery', *History of Political Thought* XIII (2), 1989, pp. 219–41.

Salter, John, 'Adam Smith on Justice and the Needs of the Poor', *Journal of the History of Economic Thought* 34 (4), 2012, pp. 559–75.

Samuels, Warren J., *Erasing the Invisible Hand: Essays on an Elusive and Misused Concept in Economics*. Cambridge: Cambridge University Press, 2011.

Samuelson, Paul A., *Economics: An Introductory Analysis*. New York: McGraw-Hill, 1948.

Schliesser, Eric, *Adam Smith: Systematic Philosopher and Public Thinker*. Oxford: Oxford University Press, 2017.

Scott, W. R., *Adam Smith as Student and Professor*. Glasgow: Jackson, 1937.

Sen, Amartya, *The Idea of Justice*. London: Penguin Books, 2009.

Sen, Amartya, 'The Uses and Abuses of Adam Smith', *History of Political Economy* 43, 2011, pp. 257–71.

Sher, R. B., 'Adam Ferguson, Adam Smith and the Problem of National Defense', *The Journal of Modern History* 61 (2), 1989, pp. 240–68.

Skinner, Andrew S., *A System of Social Science: Papers Relating to Adam Smith*, 2nd edn. Oxford: Clarendon Press, 1996.

Skinner, Andrew S. & Wilson, Thomas (eds), *Essays on Adam Smith*. Oxford: Clarendon Press, 1975.

Smith, Craig, *Adam Ferguson and the Idea of Civil Society: Moral Science in the Scottish Enlightenment*. Edinburgh: Edinburgh University Press, 2019.

Smith, Craig, 'Adam Smith: Left or Right?' *Political Studies* 61 (4), 2013, pp. 784–98.

Smith, Craig, 'Adam Smith's "Collateral" Inquiry: Fashion and Morality in the Theory of Moral Sentiments and the Wealth of Nations', *History of Political Economy* 45 (3), 2013, pp. 505–22.

Smith, Craig, *Adam Smith's Political Philosophy: The Invisible Hand and Spontaneous Order*. London: Routledge, 2006.

Smith, Craig, 'Smith, Justice and the Scope of the Political', in David F. Hardwick & Leslie March (eds), *Propriety and Prosperity: New Studies on the Philosophy of Adam Smith*. London: Palgrave Macmillan, 2014, pp. 254–74.

Smith, Vernon & Wilson, Bart J., *Humanomics: Moral Sentiments and the Wealth of Nations for the Twenty-First Century*. Cambridge: Cambridge University Press, 2018.

Stalley, Richard, 'Adam Smith and the Theory of Punishment', *Journal of Scottish Philosophy* 10, 2012, pp. 69–89.

Steuart, James, *An Inquiry into the Principles of Political Oeconomy*. London: A. Miller and T. Cadell, 1767.

Stewart, Dugald, 'Account of the Life and Writings of Adam Smith', in W. P. D. Wightman (ed.), *Essays on Philosophical Subjects*. Oxford: Oxford University Press, 1980 [1795], pp. 263–351.

Stigler, George J., 'Smith's Travels on the Ship of State', in Andrew S. Skinner & Thomas Wilson (eds), *Essays on Adam Smith*. Oxford: Clarendon, 1975, pp. 237–46.

Tegos, Spiros, 'Adam Smith: Theorist of Corruption', in Christopher J. Berry, Maria Pia Paganelli, & Craig Smith (eds), *The Oxford Handbook of Adam Smith*. Oxford: Oxford University Press, 2013, pp. 353–71.

van de Haar, Edwin, 'Adam Smith on Empire and International Relations', in Christopher J. Berry, Maria Pia Paganelli, & Craig Smith (eds), *The Oxford Handbook of Adam Smith*. Oxford: Oxford University Press, 2013, pp. 417–39.

Verburg, Rudi, 'Adam Smith's Growing Concern on the Issue of Distributive Justice', *The European Journal of the History of Economic Thought* 7 (1), 2000, pp. 23–44.

Vivenza, Gloria, 'Justice as a Virtue – Justice as a Principle in Adam Smith's Thought', *Revista Empresa y Humanismo* XIII (1/10), pp. 297–332.

Weinstein, Jack Russell, *Adam Smith's Pluralism: Rationality, Education, and the Moral Sentiments*. New Haven: Yale University Press, 2013.

West, E. G., 'Adam Smith's Two Views on the Division of Labour', *Economica* 31, 1964, pp. 23–32.

Winch, Donald, *Adam Smith's Politics: An Essay in Historiographic Revision*. Cambridge: Cambridge University Press, 1978.

Witzum, Amos, 'Distributive Considerations in Smith's Conception of Economic Justice', *Economics and Philosophy*, 13, 1997, pp. 241–59.

Wollstonecraft, Mary, *A Vindication of the Rights of Men and A Vindication of the Rights of Woman*, ed. Sylvana Tomaselli. Cambridge: Cambridge University Press, 2007 [1790, 1792].

Young, Jeffrey T., *Economics as Moral Science: The Political Economy of Adam Smith*. Cheltenham: Edward Elgar, 1997.

Young, Jeffrey T., 'Unintended Order and Intervention: Adam Smith's Theory of the Role of the State', *History of Political Economy*, 37, 2005, pp. 91–119.

Index

absolute advantage, 133, 163
Adam, Robert, 15
Adam Smith Problems, 2, 21, 156, 174–7
Adam Smith Review, 171
Addison, Joseph, 3, 31, 44
agriculture
  agricultural societies, 36, 91, 92, 94, 96–7, 98–9
  division of labour and, 109
  improvement, 13, 103, 106
  investment in, 127
  Physiocrats and, 123, 139–40
  tenant farmers, 105, 106, 150
Aikenhead, Thomas, 10
alienation, 167
anger, 49
apprenticeships, 119
architecture, 15
Aristotle, 32
artists, 15
astronomy, 22–3, 26, 27–8
Ayr Bank, 125–6

Bacon, Francis, 16, 23
Bank of England, 125
banking, 124–6, 145
barbarians *see* savages
beggars, 44, 72, 84, 111

benevolence
  justice and, 72–4, 175
  morality and, 39, 42–3, 44, 62–4, 177
Berry, Christopher, 171
Black, Joseph, 8, 14, 22
Blair, Hugh, 13–14
Boswell, James, 6
Buccleuch, Henry Scott, 3rd Duke of, 6, 106, 125–6, 146, 161
Buchanan, James, 168
Burke, Edmund, 8, 16, 161
Burns, Robert, 15
Butler, Joseph, 39

Calvinism, 10, 14
Cambridge School, 173
Cameron of Lochiel, Donald, 103
Campbell, T. D., 172
canals, 15, 143, 145
capital
  banking, 124–6
  circulating capital, 120–1
  division of labour and, 120–1
  fixed capital, 120
  saving, 121–3
  Wealth of Nations, 120–7
capitalism, 1, 155, 165–7, 174–5, 176–7

Carlisle Commission, 162
Carlyle, Thomas, 164–5
Carmichael, Gershom, 89
character sketches, 32
chemistry, 14
China, 57, 184n19
Christianity, 64, 172
Church of Scotland, 9–10, 14, 148, 162
civic humanism, 173
civilization *see* savages
clans, 4, 9, 11, 21
clubs, 7, 15, 16
Cobden, Richard, 161
colonialism
    American colonies, 137, 153, 162
    British colonies, 137
    Glasgow tobacco trade, 10
    mercantilism and, 129–31, 136–9
    slavery, 105, 137
    Smith's critique of, 100
commercial societies
    case for, 127
    critiques, 163–4, 165
    development, 91, 94, 100–4, 173–4
    division of labour, 99, 110
    government role, 141
    markets, 113–16
    Marx, 166
    trade, 111–13
    warfare and, 99–100
    see also trade
communism, 165, 166
commutative justice, 69, 70, 71, 175
competition
    banking and, 126
    centrality, 116
    company structures and, 144
    efficiency, 169
    Hayek on, 169
    justice and, 71
    profits and, 116, 118
    public interest and, 120
    shipping, 137
    Smith lectures on, 5
    wages and, 117, 119
Condorcet, Nicolas de, 159

conjectural history, 33–7, 89, 113, 166
constructivism, 168–9
Copernicus, 28
Corn Laws, 161–2, 165, 177
corn market, 135–6
corporations, 119
corruption
    financial schemes, 151
    local government, 143
    moral corruption, 13, 65, 78–83, 86, 97, 143
    Rousseau on, 38
Cullen, William, 14
Culloden, battle of (1746), 4, 99
Cunninghame, William, 10
custom, moral philosophy and, 54–9

Darien colony, 10
Darwin, Charles, 155
De Origine Idearum, 5
defence, 140–1
demagogues, 65, 86, 147
demography, 163–4
Descartes, René, 16, 28
distributive justice, 69, 88–9, 170, 175
division of labour
    capital and, 120–1
    effect on workers, 146–7, 167
    government functions, 141
    Hayek on, 169
    preconditions, 120–1
    professional army, 140
    scientific development and, 25
    social paths and, 112
    trade and, 111–13
    wages and, 118
    Wealth of Nations, 29, 109–10
Douglas, Heron and Co., 125–6
Douglas, David, Lord Reston, 6, 8, 146
Douglas, Janet, 7, 8
Dundas, Henry, Viscount Melville, 161

East India Company, 129, 138, 143, 144, 145, 163

economy *see* political economy
education
  curriculum, 147
  importance, 112, 167, 175
  Marxist critique, 167
  religious instruction, 147
  Scottish system, 10–11, 145–50
  Smith proposals, 145–9
  universities, 145–6
  Wealth of Nations, 67–8, 145–9
egalitarianism, 175, 176, 177
Elliot of Minto, Gilbert, 157
emotions
  management, 42
  moral philosophy and, 43, 44–7
  science and, 23–6, 28
  self-command, 42, 52, 63–6
empire *see* colonialism
empirical evidence, 17, 42, 108, 136,
    151
engineering, 15
entails, 101, 105, 107
Epicureanism, 41, 43
Essays on Philosophical Subjects
  new interest in, 171
  publication, 21, 22
  science, 22–30

famines, 10, 24, 127, 136
farming *see* agriculture
Ferguson, Adam, 13, 33, 98, 99, 158,
    162
Fergusson, Robert, 15
feudalism, 100–4, 106, 121, 124, 139,
    165, 166, 177
Fleischacker, Samuel, 175
food, 91–2
foot binding, 57
Forbes, Duncan, 107, 174
Forman-Barzilai, Fonna, 157–8
Foulis brothers, 15
four stages theory, 36–7, 91–2, 95,
    98, 100, 140, 166
France
  Enlightenment, 6, 9, 168
  expeditions, 16
  John Law and, 151
  Physiocrats, 123, 139–40

Smith's life in, 6
Smith scholarship, 159
wars with Britain, 131
wine, 134
Franklin, Benjamin, 16, 162
freedom *see* liberty
Friedman, Milton, 168
frugality, 121, 123

geology, 14
geometry, 3, 4, 29, 147
Germany, Adam Smith Problem,
    2, 156
Glasgow University, 3–4, 5, 8, 12,
    15, 21, 145–6, 155
Glassford, John, 10
Godwin, William, 159
gold, 129, 130–1, 137
government
  administration of justice, 141–2
  consent, 91
  corruption, 143
  defence, 140–1
  division of labour, 97
  East India Company and, 138–9
  functions, 140–5, 150
  growth, 106
  historical development, 94–7
  public services, 142–5, 150
  role, 153–4
  shepherding societies and, 95
  Smith scholarship, 175, 176
  taxation *see* taxation
  towns and, 102
  trade regulation, 104–5, 142–3
  warfare, 98–100
  Wealth of Nations, 140–5, 176
Grand Tours, 146
Gregory, John, 14
Grenville, William, 161
Griswold, Charles, 157
Grotius, Hugo, 89
Grouchy, Sophie de, 159
guilds, 101, 105, 119, 144

Haakonssen, Knud, 172
habits, 54–9
Halley's Comet, 16

Hamilton, Gavin, 15
Hanley, Ryan, 172
Hanseatic League, 102
Hayek, Friedrich, 168–9
history
    conjectural history, 33–7, 89, 113,
        166
    four stages theory, 36–7, 91–2, 95,
        98, 100, 140, 166
    historical materialism, 165
    Marx, 165–6
    social change, 37–9
    writing styles, 31–2
Hobbes, Thomas, 39, 42–3
Hont, Istvan, 173–4
Hume, David
    on beauty, 53
    on British constitutional order,
        106–7
    death, 7
    *Dialogues concerning Natural
        Religion*, 7
    Glasgow University and, 5
    History of England, 90, 148
    ideas and experience, 18, 23
    influence on Smith, 19, 20
    on justice, 71–2, 75
    on metaphysics, 19
    moral philosophy, 41
    Moral Sentiments and, 157
    'Of National Characters', 37
    politics and, 33
    religion and, 14, 147–8, 149
    Scottish Enlightenment and,
        17–19, 168
    Smith scholarship and, 173
    social contract and, 33
    Treatise of Human Nature, 4,
        17–19, 23–4
Hunter, John, 14
Hunter, William, 14
hunting societies, 36, 91, 93, 95, 98
Hutcheson, Francis
    on beauty, 27, 53
    benevolence and moral
        philosophy, 39, 43, 62, 73
    *Essay on the History of Civil
        Society*, 13

    Glasgow University professor,
        4, 12
    on law, 33, 89
    moral sentiments, on 44
    Pufendorf and, 33, 172
Hutton, James, 8, 14, 22

imagination, 48, 49, 50, 70
Imitative Arts, 29–30
impartial spectator, 51, 59–62, 86,
    149, 157–8, 158–9, 170
imperialism *see* colonialism
incentives, 102–3
independence, 105–7, 164
Industrial Revolution, 15, 162–3
inequality *see* social inequality
infanticide, 56–8, 93, 117
*Inquiry into the Nature and Causes
    of the Wealth of Nations see
    Wealth of Nations*
insurance companies, 145
interdependence, 110, 120, 169
interest rates, 126
International Adam Smith Society,
    171
international relations, 100
invisible hand, 1, 83–5, 132, 155,
    168, 176–7
Italy, cities, 102

Jacobite rising (1715), 3
Jacobite rising (1745), 4, 10, 11, 103
James VII/II, 33
joint stock companies, 144, 145
judiciary, independence, 142
Jurisprudence
    conjectural history, 35
    contemporary scholarship, 172
    discovery, 21, 156
    four stages theory, 36
    justice, 69–70
    liberty, 104–7
    overview, 88–97
    police, 74
    structure, 88–9
    see also law
justice
    administration of, 141–2

justice (*cont.*)
  benevolence and, 72–4
  commutative justice, 69, 70, 71,
    88–9, 175
  contemporary thought, 170
  distributive justice, 69, 88–9, 170,
    175
  government and, 96, 141–2
  moral corruption, 78–83
  natural justice, 90
  perfect justice, 69, 75–6
  Plato, 69, 75–6, 88–9
  police and, 74–6
  primary virtue, 69–72, 76, 177
  public utility and, 75
  Smith scholarship, 175–6
  social inequality, 79–83, 175
    implications, 85–6
    invisible hand, 83–5

Kames, Henry Home, Lord, 5, 12–13
Kant, Immanuel, 9, 160
Kay, John, 7, 15
Kennedy, Gavin, 176
Kepler, Johannes, 28
Kirk *see* Church of Scotland
Kirkcaldy, 3, 15

labour
  immigration, 117
  industrial relations, 116–17
  productive and unproductive
    labour, 123–4
  scarcity, 117
  source of value, 113–14
  wages, 114–15, 116–20
  see also division of labour
laissez-faire, 153, 155, 165, 174–5,
  176–7
language theory, 34–5
law
  administration of justice, 141–2
  commutative justice, 88, 89
  Enlightenment, 32–3
  government *see* government
  Lectures on Jurisprudence, 88–97
  methodological principles, 89–91
  natural law, 89, 91

property, 92–4
punishment, 93
rule of law, 94, 104, 106, 128
Law, John, 151
Lectures on Jurisprudence see
  Jurisprudence
Lectures on Rhetoric and Belles Lettres
  see Rhetoric
legacy
  Adam Smith Problems, 2, 21,
    156, 174–7
  classical political economy,
    162–5
  contemporary political economy,
    170–1
  Marxism, 165–7
  moral philosophy, 157–60
  New Right, 168–70
  overview, 155–72
  popular caricature, 1–2, 120, 130,
    155, 165, 167, 178
  Smith scholarship, 171–4
  Wealth of Nations, 160–7
liberalism, 168–70, 172–3
liberty
  centrality, 177, 178
  Hayek, 169
  justified restrictions, 133–4
  modern concept, 89–90, 104–7,
    155–6
  natural liberty, 128, 131, 139
  perfect liberty, 119
  restrictions, 126
  Smith scholarship, 175
  spontaneous order and, 169
  wages and, 119
Locke, John, 17, 18, 33
Loudon, Earl of, 3
love, 46

Macfie, A. L., 171–2
machines, 109–10
MacKenzie, Henry, 15
Maclaurin, Colin, 16
magnanimity, 71, 76
Malthus, Thomas, 163–4
Mandeville, Bernard, 38, 39, 42–3,
  51, 82, 84, 121, 173

markets
  invisible hand, 1, 132, 155, 168,
    176–7
  measuring value, 113–14
  mercantilism, 100, 128–39
  prices, 113, 114, 115
  Smith scholarship, 175
  Wealth of Nations, 113–16, 128–54
Marx, Karl, 91, 155, 165–7
McLean, Iain, 175
medicine, 14
mercantilism
  empire, 129–31, 136–9
  policies, 131–6
  Smith's critique of, 100, 128–39
  system, 128–31
  Wealth of Nations and, 173
merchants
  agricultural improvements and,
    102–3
  colonies, 129
  corn dealers, 136
  economic function, 103–4, 127
  Glasgow, 11
  monopolies and, 131
  politics, 135, 144–5
  Smith's distrust of, 120, 130, 139
  Tobacco Lords, 10, 135
  unproductive labour, 124
  urban centres, 101
metaphysics, 19, 22, 28
migration, 117, 134
militias, 98–100, 140
Mill, John Stuart, 164
Millar, John, 6, 36
Miller, David, 3
monarchy, 79, 149–50
money
  circulating capital, 125
  conjectural history, 113
  neo-liberal monetary theory, 168
  value and, 114
  wealth and, 130
monopolies, 116, 119, 129–33, 138,
  145
Montesquieu, Charles de, 32–3, 37,
  100
moral philosophy

conscience, 60, 61, 159
critiques, 157–60
custom and, 54–9
examples, 41, 44–5, 46, 49, 70
general rules, 52–4, 61
Hume, 41
impartial spectator, 51, 59–62,
  86, 149
  critiques, 157–8, 158–9
  legacy, 170
legacy, 157–60, 170–1, 172, 177
moral change, 56–9
moral corruption, 13, 65, 78–83,
  86, 97, 143
moral sentiments, 44
overview, 40–66
propriety, 50–2, 60, 62, 157–8
reason and, 43
relativism, 157–8
Scottish university teaching, 146
self-command, 42, 52, 63–6
Smith's critique, 40–3
sociability, 47–50
social convention and, 53, 61
sympathy
  central principle, 29, 44–50
  critiques, 156, 157, 158, 159
  legacy, 171
  limits, 62–3
systematic theory, 42–3
universalism, 54
Moral Sentiments
  benevolence, 73–4
  contemporary debate, 39
  critiques, 157–60
  development, 40
  editions, 34, 40, 157, 171–2
  invisible hand, 83–5
  justice, 69–74, 76
  legacy, 157–60, 170–1, 172, 178
  moral corruption, 78–83
  moral system, 40–66
  nature, 78
  police, 75
  publication, 6, 8, 20, 40
  religion, 77–8
  revisions, 156, 157
  scope, 1, 21

Moral Sentiments (cont.)
  social inequality, 79–86, 95–6
  virtues, 67
  Wealth of Nations and, 160
Mun, Thomas, 129–30

natural law, 12, 33, 69, 89, 91, 172,
    174, 175
Navigation Act, 133, 137
neo-liberalism, 168–70, 172–3
Netherlands, trade, 134
Newton, Isaac, 16, 17, 26, 28, 32
Norman, Jesse, 177

Otteson, James, 175
ownership *see* property
Oxford, 4, 145–6
Oyster Club, 7, 15

Paine, Thomas, 162
partnerships, 144–5
Phillipson, Nicholas, 19, 29, 173
philosophy, Smith on, 25
Physiocrats, 6, 123, 139–40, 173
pin factories, 109, 146–7
piracy, 130
Pitt, William the Younger, 8, 161
Plato, 41, 69, 75–6, 88–9
Pocock, J. G. A., 173
poets, 15
police, 74–6, 88
political economy
  agriculture *see* agriculture
  classical economy, 162–5
  contemporary thought, 170–1
  division of labour *see* division of
    labour
  government role, 153–4
  markets *see* markets
  Marx, 165–7
  nature of wealth, 108–27
  New Right, 168–70
  trade *see* trade
  Wealth of Nations, 108–54
    legacy, 172–4
politics
  Smith and, 173–4, 175
  social contract, 33, 90, 93, 107

social philosophies, 33
trade and, 134–5
Whigs, 2, 33, 90–1, 107, 174
poll taxes, 152
poor relief, 134, 164, 177
Pope, Alexander, 16, 54–5
population growth, 163
Portugal
  British trade treaty, 136
  colonialism, 130, 136
  wine, 134
Post Office, 142
Presbyterianism, 2–3, 9–10, 148
prescription, 94
prices
  Hayek on, 169
  measuring value and, 113, 114
  natural v. market prices, 115
  perfect liberty and, 119
  price-fixing, 120
  supply and demand, 115
primogeniture, 101, 105, 107
prodigality, 121–2
production
  costs, 114–15
  division of labour, 109–10
  interdependence, 110
  machines, 109–10
  productive and unproductive
    labour, 123–4
  purpose, 139
profits
  competition and, 116, 118
  concept, 114
  prices and, 115
promissory notes, 125
property
  agricultural societies, 94
  conjectural history, 36
  Hayek on, 169
  hunting societies and, 93, 95
  origins, 92–4
  shepherding societies, 93, 94
  state protection, 141
propriety, moral philosophy and,
    50–2, 60, 62, 157–8
prudent man, 68–9
Ptolemy, 28

public debt, 150–1
public interest, 74, 75, 89, 120
public services, 142–5, 150
Pufendorf, Samuel, 27, 33, 89, 172
Pulteney, William, 161

Quesnay, François, 6

racism, 165
Raeburn, Henry, 15
Ramsay, Allan, 15
Raphael, D. D., 75, 171–2
Rawls, John, 170
reason, moral philosophy and, 43
Reid, Thomas, 13, 159
relativism, 157–8
religion
    monopoly, 148–9
    morality and, 77–8
    national religion, 148–9
    origins, 24–5, 77
    religious instruction, 147
    science and, 26
    systems, 28
    toleration, 148–9
republicanism, 173
rhetoric, 29–32
Rhetoric
benevolence, 72
    development of government, 96
    justice, 72
    overview, 29–32
    rediscovery, 21
Ricardo, David, 163
roads, 143–4
Robertson, John, 173
Robertson, William, 14, 162
Roman Catholicism, 148
Rome, 98, 99, 100, 105
Rothschild, Emma, 162
Rousseau, Jean-Jacques, 38, 51, 82,
        84, 110, 159, 173
Royal Society of Edinburgh, 15
rule of law, 94, 104, 106, 128

Samuelson, Paul, 167
savages, 13, 34, 55, 56, 58
saving, 121–3

Schliesser, Eric, 177
science
    astronomy, 22–3
    emotions and, 23–6, 28
    experience and, 23
    Hume on, 17–18
    Newton, 16
    religion and, 24–5
    Scottish Enlightenment, 11,
        14–15
    Smith's approach, 22–6
    social sciences, 32–3
    systems, 26–9
    wonder, surprise, and
        admiration, 23–6
scientism, 168
Scotland
    banking system, 125
    education system, 10–11, 145–50
    Enlightenment *see* Scottish
        Enlightenment
    famines, 10, 127
    medicine, 14
    seventeenth-century, 9–10
    Union with England (1707), 3,
        10, 106
Scottish Enlightenment
    American colonies and, 162
    conjectural history, 89
    historical writing, 91
    Hume *see* Hume, David
    leading figures, 12–16
    Locke and, 17
    Newton and, 16
    overview, 9–19
    politics, 33
    science, 11, 14–15
    social sciences, 32
    tradition, 168–9
    universal human nature, 37
self-command, 42, 52, 63–6
self-interest
    debate, 39, 177
    Hobbes, 39
    invisible hand and, 132, 177
    moral sentiments and, 44
    morality and, 42, 47
    popular caricature, 167

self-interest (*cont.*)
  sympathy and, 47
  trade and, 111
  virtuous self-interest, 38
  Wealth of Nations, 156
Sen, Amartya, 170, 175–6
servants, 106, 123
Shaftesbury, Lord, 31, 39
Shelburne, William Petty, Earl of, 161
shepherding societies, 36, 91, 92, 93, 94, 95, 98
Simson, Robert, 4
Skinner, Andrew, 171
slavery, 105, 137, 165
Smith, Adam
  banknotes, 155
  biography, 2–8
  caricature of, 1–2, 120, 130, 155, 165, 167, 178
  character, 8
  Commissioner of Customs, 7, 161
  death, 8, 162
  Edinburgh period, 7–8, 161
  education, 3–4
  egalitarianism, 175, 176, 177
  fame, 160–2
  father of economics, 172–3
  legacy *see* legacy
  politics and, 173–4, 175
  portrait, 7
  professional career, 4–6
  statue, 155
  works
    consistency, 1–2, 20–2
    early publications, 5, 38
    methodology, 29
    scholarly editions, 171
  writing style, 29–32
Smith, Adam, Sr, 2–3, 10
Smith, Margaret (Smith's mother), 3, 8
Smith, Vernon, 170
Smollett, Tobias, 15, 16
smuggling, 3, 7, 130
sociability, 47–50
social change, 37–9

social contract, 33, 90, 93, 107
social inequality
  implications, 85–6
  invisible hand, 83–5
  justice and, 79–83
  law, government, and, 95
  necessity, 97
  Smith politics, 175, 176
socialism, 169
Socrates, 32
Spain, colonialism, 130, 136
Spectator, 3, 44
speculators, 122, 126
Spiers, Alexander, 10
spontaneous order, 169
stamp duties, 152
Steele, Richard, 3, 44
Steuart, James, 161
Stewart, Dugald, 22, 34, 37, 74, 88, 159, 162
Stigler, George, 167
Stoicism, 41, 42, 43, 84, 172
Stuart, Charles Edward, 4
subsidies, 133, 135
succession, 94
surplus value, 166–7
sympathy
  extreme sympathy, 64
  habitual sympathy, 62
  imagination and, 48, 49, 50
  joy v. sorrow, 78–9, 157
  limits, 62–3
  meaning, 46–7
  moral philosophy and, 29, 44–50
    critiques, 156, 157, 158, 159
    legacy, 171
  mutual sympathy, 48, 50
  writing style and, 30
systems
  beauty, 29–30
  developing, 25–6
  men of systems, 76
  moral philosophy, 42–3
  theories, 26–9

Tacitus, 31
taxation

American colonies, 153
local taxes, 143
luxury items, 151, 152–3
necessities of life, 133, 152
oppressive taxation, 152
principles, 151
proportionality, 151, 152, 175
public debt, 150–1
retaliation policies, 134
sources of revenue, 150, 151, 152
trade, 132–4
Wealth of Nations, 150–4
Telford, Thomas, 15
tenant farmers, 105, 106, 150
Theory of Moral Sentiments see Moral Sentiments
Thucydides, 31
tobacco trade, 10, 135
tolls, 143–4
towns
commercial societies, 94
countryside and, 100–1, 102–3
government, 102
growth, 94, 101–2, 112
morality and, 149
Physiocrats and, 139
privileges, 105
Townshend, Charles, 6
trade
absolute advantage, 133, 163
balance of trade, 129, 135
barriers, 131–5, 153
benefits, 176
colonies, 7, 137–8
corn, 135–6
division of labour and, 111–13
export policies, 135–6
export subsidies, 135
government regulation, 104–5, 142–3
import policies, 131–5
imports for re-export, 134
interdependence, 110
invisible hand, 132, 155, 168
Ireland, 8
justified restrictions, 133–4
mercantilism *see* mercantilism

origins, 111–12
politics and, 134–5
rule of law and, 94, 104–5
Smith's social context, 166
treaties, 136
war and, 100
wealth and, 112–13
Wealth of Nations, 111–13, 128–54
trading companies, Smith's critique of, 100, 144–5
Turgot, Jacques, 6

unintended consequences, 38, 83, 90, 97, 102, 132, 134, 141, 155, 164, 176–7
Union of Parliaments (1707), 3, 10, 106
United States
British colonialism, 137, 153, 162
neo-liberalism, 168–70
universal human nature, 13, 35, 36–7, 44, 47–8, 54, 58, 91, 158
universities, 145–6
utilitarianism, 23, 160, 172

value, measuring, 113–14, 167
Verburg, Rudi, 175
virtues
contemporary legacy, 172
justice *see* justice
systematic moral theory, 67–9
Voltaire, 6, 16, 148

wages
colonies, 137
division of labour and, 118
industrial relations and, 116–17
measure of labour, 114–15
prices and, 115
rise, 140–1, 163
signalling role, 118
subsistence levels, 117–19
taxation and, 133
Wealth of Nations, 116–20
warfare, 98–100, 131, 140–1

Watt, James, 15
wealth
  Carlyle on, 165
  government and, 95
  nature, 108–27, 129, 130
  slavery and, 105
  trade and, 112–13
Wealth of Nations
  agriculture, 139–40
  capital, 120–7
  commercial societies, 100–4
  division of labour, 29, 109–10
  editions, 156, 160–1
  education, 67–8, 145–9
  government, 140–5, 176
  historical context, 153
  legacy, 160–7
  liberty, 104–7
  markets, 113–16, 128–54
  Moral Sentiments and, 160
  nature of wealth, 108–27
  police, 74
  publication, 7, 20, 171

  scholarship, 172–4, 176, 178
  scope, 1, 21
  Scottish examples, 11
  self-interest, 156
  social rank, 81
  structure, 108, 128
  success, 8, 160–1
  taxation, 150–4
  trade, 111–13, 128–54
  translations, 161
  wages, 116–20
  warfare, 98–100
Wedderburn, Alexander, 161
Whigs, 2, 33, 90–1, 107, 174
Wilson, James, 162
Winch, Donald, 173
wine, 133, 134
Witherspoon, John, 162
Witzum, Amos, 175
Wollstonecraft, Mary, 159–60
women's rights, 160

yeomanry, 106